HORSEFEATHERS

and Other Curious Words

HORSE

With Illustrations by TOM FUNK

FEATHERS

and Other Curious Words

By CHARLES EARLE FUNK, Litt.D.

And CHARLES EARLE FUNK, Jr.

PERENNIAL LIBRARY

Harper & Row, Publishers, New York
Cambridge, Philadelphia, San Francisco, Washington
London, Mexico City, São Paulo, Singapore, Sydney

A hardcover edition of this book was published in 1958 by Harper & Row, Publishers, Inc.

First PERENNIAL LIBRARY edition published 1986.

Library of Congress Cataloging-in-Publication Data

Funk, Charles Earle, 1881–1957.
   Horsefeathers and other curious words.

   Reprint. Originally published: New York : Harper & Row, 1958.
   Includes index.
   1. English language—Etymology.   2. English language—Semantics.   I. Funk, Charles Earle.   II. Title.
PE1574.F76   1986   422   86-45100
ISBN 0-06-091352-5 (pbk.)

86 87 88 89 90 MPC 10 9 8 7 6 5 4 3 2 1

To B. M. F. and A. G. F.

FOREWORD

No, this book does not pertain to slang terminology, though, undoubtedly, some of the words discussed herein did originate as  slang. The title arose from a bit of information I stumbled upon some ten years ago when the old Vermont farmhouse we occupy during the summer months was about to undergo a face-lifting operation. The clapboards, after many, many years of unpainted exposure to sun, rain, hail, sleet, snow, and wind, were adhering to the structure apparently only through force of habit. An aged master carpenter to whom I appealed for advice said, "Well, seems if 'bout the only thing ye kin do is to rip off all them clabbuds. If they wa'n't so old an' curled up, ye moight put horsefeathers over 'em, and then cover yer hoose with asphalt shingles, but it's too late for that."

"Horsefeathers," I learned from him and other old-timers of New England and New York in the building trade, refers to rows of clapboards laid with the butt edges against the butt edges of shingles or clapboards so as to provide a flat surface over which asphalt or other shingles or siding may be laid. Subsequently I sought verification from the National Board of Fire Underwriters. This is the answer, in part, from its Chief Engineer, Mr. J. A. Neale:

We cannot document the following but some of our men who have been interested in building construction and building codes over the years remember its past use.

It refers, as indicated in your letter, to the tapered boards laid on wood shingle roofs to provide a flat surface for asphalt shingles to be laid on in re-roofing. The term "feathering strips," meaning the same thing, is found in some roofing manuals.

The term "horsefeathers" is used colloquially in New England and New York. Its use other than in the slang sense is disappearing and it is only the old-timers who now understand it.

Regrettably, neither the age of this legitimate, though trade, usage nor that of the slang usage can be determined. No printed record of the trade usage has been found, but the old-timers with whom I have talked, men in their seventies at least, say they knew its use forty or fifty years ago. And it may be older. Printed record of the slang usage—in senses equivalent to "bosh," "stuff and nonsense," "hogwash," "tommyrot," "applesauce," or, in ejaculation, "Heavens to Betsy!"—is also undated as to birth, but, to the best of my recollection, did not occur before 1925 or thereabouts. It is my belief, therefore, that some bright chap heard the term used by an upstate builder, cleverly told the tale in a New York speakeasy of the period, and that "Horsefeathers!" was then picked up by doubting Thomases and used thereafter to greet any incredible statement.

Why apply the term to ordinary feathering strips? That can't be determined. Perhaps the successive layers of new wood reminded one at a distance of the feathers on the wings of a chicken, except as to size. Relatively, then, they were feathers fit for a horse.

The parentage of the great bulk of all the words that we use in our speech or see upon the printed page is, in general, adequately explained in any dictionary that carries word derivations. One need know no more about the word "include," for instance, than that its source was the Latin preposition *in* and verb *claudere*, "to close," hence "to enclose," or about "liberty" than that it derives from Latin *liber*, "free," or about "speak" than that it comes from an Old English (Anglo-Saxon) word, *specan*. Such brief explanations, giving the Greek, Latin, French, Germanic, or like sources, suffice for thousands of words. It would be, to use a sesquipedalian erudite term of my youth, a work of supererogation, a superfluous act, to carry those explanations further.

The words discussed in this book are, accordingly, mainly those that piqued my own curiosity in younger days, terms usually left unexplained or but partly explained even in unabridged dictionaries. Why, for example, is a common tall roadside weed known in some parts of the country as a joe-pye weed? Why is butterscotch so named? Or belladonna? How did the nuthatch get its name? Or that insect, the earwig? Why is a certain Southern comestible called hush-puppy? How did it happen that, in a fireplace, the log supports became known as andirons or, sometimes, firedogs? There are hundreds of such peculiar terms, terms that appear to be compounds, though they are not always so.

And there are also other hundreds of words for which, for lack of space, the usual dictionary of household size can supply no more than the skeleton of the story accounting for them. We are told, for instance, that our word *arctic* is from a Greek word meaning "a bear," but the connection with the north polar region may be left to the imagination. We see by the morning's paper that So-and-so "has entered the arena of politics." The dictionary tells us that Latin *arena* meant "sand." How did the sense become transformed? *Grotesque,* we may learn, came from the same Italian source as "grotto," a cave or cavern. How did it then acquire so diverse a meaning as "incongruous, ridiculous, fantastic, monstrous"?

The serious purpose of this book is, then, to supplement the dictionary, to fill gaps where filling seems to be warranted and to supply explanations for many of the curious words the significance of which is not evident from the parts that compose them. But as I do not think that a reference work need be a dry-as-dust compilation; it has been my aim to provide a little fillip of entertainment here and there, to indulge in fancy—which I hope is always plainly labeled as such—when there is no clue to the original source of a word or term.

I am indebted, of course, to all recent dictionaries, abridged and unabridged; especially to the *Oxford English Dictionary* and its *Supplement,* to Wyld's *Universal Dictionary* for its excellent etymological treatment, and to Mathews' *Dictionary of Americanisms*. The works consulted in the preparation of material, however, are legion, embracing about every book on my shelves and including books of special nature, such as those on common plant names, borrowed from university libraries. Despite precaution, however, I have little doubt that I have gone astray from time to time in statement or in surmise. I shall welcome correction.

CHARLES EARLE FUNK

ADDENDUM TO FOREWORD

After having lived a full and, on the whole, happy life, my father died suddenly, as he would have wished, on April 16, 1957. He had just passed his seventy-sixth birthday less than two weeks previously.

At the time of his death, he had been working on the manuscript of this, his final work on the study of the origins and histories of English words and phrases, for upwards of a year, and had completed approximately 70 per cent of the task he had set himself. *Task,* though, is not the word to use, for he loved the study of words and took keen pleasure in successfully tracing an obscure use or etymology to its ultimate source. He also immensely enjoyed passing on to others the knowledge of those things that his research turned up. I can distinctly recall his surprise when he found that I, a chemical librarian, knew what horsefeathers were, without having to consult any reference, for my knowing the term took the edge off the story he was about to relate and which he has told here in his foreword. (The reason for my foreknowledge of this lies in the fact that I am among the legion of do-it-yourselfers. I had just recently re-roofed my house by laying asphalt shingles over the original wooden shingles and, on consulting *my* expert before the job was started, had been told that the practice of using horsefeathers, once common, had been pretty well abandoned in my locality. An explanation of what constituted horsefeathers had, of course, followed.)

(Incidentally, lest it occur to some reader that the original name for these feathering strips might have been *house*feathers, later corrupted through mispronunciation to *horse*feathers, let me point out to him in advance that this possibility has been explored. No substantiation for such a theory has been found.)

The interest that my father's stories aroused, as demonstrated by the success of his earlier books, led me to undertake to complete the present work along the lines he had begun. He had prepared a list of the words he planned to choose from in compiling the present group of tales, and I have generally based my selections on this list, as he had done. For the record, that part of the book covering the alphabet through *P* is, for the most part, my father's work. My contribution to this first part consists only of minor editing of his rough draft plus the addition of a few entries on which his research had been incomplete at the time of his death (*cuspidor, kangaroo court, Paris green*). That part of the book covering the alphabet from *Q* on is, for the most part, my work based on his list. My father had not conducted his search strictly in alphabetical order, though, and a few of the entries in the latter part of the alphabet are his (*starboard, sub rosa, tadpole, thank-ye-ma'am, thimblerig, thoroughfare*).

Like him, I have leaned heavily on the *Oxford English Dictionary* and on the *Dictionary of Americanisms* as primary reference tools, but to enumerate and acknowledge separately all of the works consulted would, in effect, constitute a catalogue of both his and my own libraries, and even so would be incomplete. Blanket acknowledgment is hereby tendered to all my sources of information, with grateful thanks.

CHARLES EARLE FUNK, JR.

HORSEFEATHERS

and Other Curious Words

stirrup cup

The Anglo-Saxon word which has become *stirrup* was *stigrap,* and if this were to be literally translated into modern English, it would become *"sty-rope"* or "climbing-rope." The Anglo-Saxon word is composed of the root *stig-,* from *stigan,* "to climb" (see under **steward** for *sty,* "to climb"), plus *rap,* "rope." This leads us to the conclusion that the first stirrups were merely short lengths of ropes thrown over the back of the steed, and having loops tied in either end. But the *stirrup cup* had nothing to do, either then or later, with any resemblance of these loops to cups. Instead, it could be translated today as "one for the road," for it was the cup of wine or other refreshment offered to the traveler who, having mounted, was in the stirrups and ready to take off upon a journey.

hoity-toity

Nowadays one rarely hears this except as an expression of surprise coupled with annoyance or indignation, usually uttered by a precise elderly person in condemnation of the behavior of a niece or granddaughter. And that reflects its source, for *hoity* at one time—some three centuries ago—described a person who indulged in *hoiting,* an obsolete word, but meaning "acting like a *hoyden."* The *toity* was added just for rhyme, as *scurry* to rhyme with *hurry* in *hurry-scurry.* The variant exclamation *highty-tighty* arose through mispronunciation, from the same change in vowel sound that, in the seventeenth century, caused *oil* to be pronounced "ile"; *boil,* "bile"; *join,* "jine," etc.

1

cucking stool

Often confused with the later and much less immodest *ducking stool*. The earlier device dates back, in England, at least to the eleventh century and was sometimes disguised under the Latin *cathedra stercoris* of the same meaning. When used, as it generally was, for the punishment of viragoes, and perhaps then modified in form, it was often merely called a *scolding stool*. Actually the *cucking stool* was a crudely constructed commode, upon which the culprit was securely fastened and exposed to the jeers of the townspeople for such length of time as the magistrate might determine. The punishment might be meted out also to dishonest bakers or other tradesmen. (See also **ducking stool.**)

mushroom

Another beautiful example of what will happen to an Englishman's attempt to pronounce a foreign word. Nothing whatsoever of *mush* in it, nor of *room*. It was, in the fifteenth century, a poor English rendition of the Old French *moisseron,* modern *mousseron.* Some then spelled it, and probably pronounced it, *muscheron,* and in following years at least a score of other forms appeared. But before the French name was introduced, the fungus had the far more descriptive name, *toad's hat.* If only that name were still in use we might now use that for the edible fungus and *toadstool* for the inedible.

steward

Authorities are in general agreement that *steward* is a descendant of the Anglo-Saxon *stigweard,* a combination of *stig,* "sty," and *weard,* "ward, keeper." However, they are quick to point out that it should not be inferred that this proves that the exalted position of steward, as major-domo, arose from such humble beginnings as the keeper of the pigsty. *Sty* is an old, old word, and its relatives are to be found in many, if not all, of the Teutonic family of languages, with a number of meanings, quite dissimilar. Even in English there have been such different meanings as "a path," "a ladder, or stair," and a verb sense, "to climb," as well as the common meaning today, "a pigpen." Skeat, in his *Etymological Dictionary of the English Language,* seems to have resolved the matter very prettily in saying, for steward, "The original sense was one who looked after the domestic animals, and gave them their food; hence, one who provides for his master's table, and generally, one who superintends household affairs for another." The key phrase is "one who provides for his master's table." This, far from being a menial task, has assuredly always been an important one, and it would be only natural that such a trusted servant would be given the greater responsibility of looking after the household in all other respects, too.

proud flesh

It is *proud* only by virtue of being swollen, as if by pride. In the same sense, we speak of grain which, by luxurious growth, is unseasonably *proud,* swollen beyond the normal stage of advancement.

stevedore

The Spanish, at one time the rulers of the seas, have left their contributions to seafaring terms, and one of these is *stevedore.* It is derived from the Spanish noun of agency *estivador,* "one who stows cargo," of which the corresponding verb form is *estivar,* "to stow cargo." From the same source is the English verb, now little used, *to steeve,* "to pack tightly." A further derivation takes us to the Latin *stipare,* "to press closely together."

cubbyhole

One might suppose that this had developed from the hole or den in which the young of the bear or fox may be found, but no. In rural parts of England one may still find places where *cub* means the shed or pen or stall for cattle, or the coop for chickens, or the hutch for rabbits, or even a monk's cell. It is a term, that is, for any small shelter. The diminutive, used chiefly by children referring to any small retreat of their own, is *cubby,* frequently extended to *cubbyhole.*

3

Amazon

To speak of a woman as an Amazon is to imply that she is physically well proportioned, but large—above average in height and figure. The term was first applied by the ancient Greeks to a tribe of warlike women who dwelt along the shores of the Black Sea and in the Caucasus mountains. Men were barred from the state, the ladies devoting themselves to fighting the Greeks, according to anecdotes related by professional storytellers of old. They also said that the name meant "without a breast," from a belief that each Amazon had had her right breast removed that it might not interfere with the use of javelin and bow. That derivation is regarded as doubtful nowadays. The Amazon river in South America was so named by the early Spanish explorer Orellana, who, in descending the river in 1541, battled with a tribe of Tapuya Indians whose women fought alongside the men.

hornswoggle

Nothing much can be said about this peculiarly American substitute for bamboozle, cheat, defraud, hoax, swindle. It was, apparently, a Kentucky coinage of the early nineteenth century, a period in which frontiersmen, especially, attempted to outvie one another in the creation of extravagant, highfalutin speech. Not much of it survived, so it is to the credit of the unknown hero who coined *hornswoggle,* based on heaven knows what, that it not only lived, but ultimately found its way into our dictionaries.

stereoscope

Over the space of many years, inventors and would-be inventors have been trying various means of making pictures more and more true to life. One avenue has been in portraying action, another has been in portraying solidity, that is, the reproduction or viewing of pictures in such a way that the pictures seem to be three-dimensional. The first to achieve some measure of success in this latter undertaking was Sir Charles Wheatstone, a nineteenth-century English physicist. Although it remained for a later scientist to perfect the device, yet it was Sir Charles himself who coined its name in 1838. *Stereoscope* is a compound from two Greek roots, the first, *stereos,* meaning "solid," the second, *scopein,* meaning "to look at." Adding these together, we get "solid to look at," or, more truthfully, "when looked at, seems to be solid."

crowbar

As said of various other words, some of our remote ancestors must have possessed wonderful gifts of imagination. Someone, about six hundred years ago, discovered that if the end of the ordinary iron prize or prise were sharpened to a point or beak, its use as a lever would be more effective. Someone then likened that beak to the neb or beak of a crow—and *crow* then became the name of such a tool, especially of one curved or bent toward its wedge-shaped end. The addition of the *bar* was notice to steel-makers, several centuries later, that the desired *crow* must be a straight rod.

tyro

To the Romans, an ordinary soldier was *miles* (pronounced *mee-less*), from *mille,* which literally means "a thousand" but in the figurative sense means "a great many, a horde." The new recruit, to distinguish him from the seasoned campaigner, was a *tiro* (plural, *tirones*). In Medieval Latin, the words were often spelled *tyro, tyrones,* and it is with this spelling that the word is most often used in English, although the spelling *tiro,* which may be preferable on an etymological basis, is sometimes used. The English plural, incidentally, is *tyros* or *tiros,* and the word has come to have the extended meaning of "a novice in any field, a greenhorn."

grubstreet

It refers nowadays to a literary hack who, for needed money, will turn out an article or even a speech on whatever subject he

5

may have a call. But the designation actually alludes to a street in London formerly bearing that name, since 1830 called "Milton Street," which from the early seventeenth century was, as Dr. Johnson said, "much inhabited by writers of small histories, dictionaries, and temporary poems." The description might apply to Johnson himself, forced into literary drudgery for many years after reaching London merely to obtain "grub."

stenography

By no means the invention of John Robert Gregg, nor even of his predecessor, Sir Isaac Pitman, stenography was an art known many centuries before either of these men walked the earth. As an English word, *stenography* has been recorded as early as 1602. It is derived from two Greek words, *stenos,* "narrow," and *graphein,* "to write," thus, literally, it is "narrow writing" as opposed to the "broad writing" that is the more ordinary script. Even *shorthand* is only slightly younger as a synonym for stenography—it has been in use since at least 1636 as a substitute for the now obsolete older word *short-writing* of the same meaning. This latter is an Anglicization of the still older word *brachygraphy,* the first part of which is from the Greek *brachus,* "short." *Brachygraphy* has been found in English as early as 1590 and is not yet wholly obsolete, although, I'm sure to the satisfaction of today's secretaries, it is only rarely encountered. Actually, of course, stenography, call it what you will, is of much greater age than even these word histories would indicate. It is known to have been practiced in the Roman Senate and there is some evidence that it was practiced by the ancient Greeks before the time of Christ. However, it is known that modern shorthand systems originated in England about the close of the sixteenth century.

aroint

"Aroynt thee, Witch, the rumpe-fed Ronyon cryes," is the way Shakespeare wrote it in *Macbeth* (Act I, Scene iii), and here, as well as in *King Lear* (Act III, Scene iv), his obvious meaning was "Begone! Get out! Scram!" but the source of his term may never

6

be known. No earlier instance of use has been turned up. Nor do we know positively what he meant by a *ronyon,* which, in *Merry Wives of Windsor* (Act IV, Scene ii), he spelled *runnion.* Dr. Samuel Johnson, in his dictionary of 1755, defined the latter spelling as "a mangy creature," but defined *ronion* as "a fat bulky woman." You may take your pick. *Rump,* of course, pertains to the posterior of an animal.

pot-walloper

A term gradually falling from repute. In its original form, *pot-waller,* in the early eighteenth century, it designated an Englishman who, by virtue of having his own pot to boil (to *wall,* in the speech still current then), was entitled to vote in a parliamentary election. An early alteration of *potwaller* was *pot-walloper.* For a hundred years it carried the same meaning. But then one who boiled a pot was thought, by some, to be in a demeaning occupation and, accordingly *pot-walloper* became a term of contempt, indicating one with the mind or ability of a scullion.

crosspatch

Back in the fifteenth century the jester or fool attached to the retinue of prominent persons was sometimes referred to as a *patch,* probably because his costume was often "a thing of shreds and patches." And whether or not this term was applied to him only when he was ill tempered is not now known, but such was the case by the end of the sixteenth century, and so it remained for another hundred years, though other than court fools were included. It was then, for additional force, that some genius made assurance doubly sure and labeled a person of ill-nature a *cross-patch.*

hopscotch

Back in the seventeenth century this children's game was called *scotch-hoppers,* which appears to be the earliest English name, although one writer says that the game itself probably "dates back to the beginning of the Christian era." But the "scotch" part of the name is in nowise related to the country of Scotland nor to its people. A giveaway to its real meaning is that in some English shires the game is called *hop-score,* for the lines marking the squares to be hopped are scored or *scotched* in the ground. Compare **butterscotch.**

Annie Oakley

She was born in Ohio in 1860; her full name, Phoebe Anne Oakley Mozee. At the age of sixteen she married Frank Butler, a vaudeville actor, and became a superb marksman; her skill, it was said, was such that by 1,000 shots with a rifle on one occasion she broke 942 glass balls tossed in the air. Touring with Buffalo Bill's Wild West Show in the 1880's and 1890's, she would demonstrate her marksmanship by successively centering shots through the pips of a playing card, usually the five of hearts. Through this feat her name became synonymous with a complimentary pass to a show, which, formerly, was a ticket punched by the manager when issued, not unlike the card perforated by Annie's shots. She died in 1926.

quagmire

He who ventures into a new undertaking, seemingly sound, only to find himself inextricably entangled in a hopeless mess, has become quagmired, bogged down, on shaky ground. The last term here is a nearly literal equivalent of the first, as *quag* seems certainly to be a variant of *quake,* "to shake," and *mire* is "muddy or swampy ground." Thus a quagmire is a piece of ground that looks firm, but shakes when walked upon, only to engulf the traveler. An obsolete form is *quickmire,* and the relation to *quicksand,* which has much the same treacherous properties, immediately comes to mind.

8

ducking stool

More modest than the *cucking stool* (which see), though still an unpleasant device for the punishment of scolds, prostitutes, or women judged guilty of witchcraft. It replaced the older device during the sixteenth century, though the older term was then sometimes used for it, and was still in use until the early nineteenth century. The device consisted of a chair, in which the culprit was secured, mounted at one end of a seesaw at the edge of a pond or stream. Those operating the other end of this seesaw could determine the number of times the culprit was ducked or dipped and the length of each immersion. The victim sometimes died, either from shock or drowning. In a similar device, a *ducking tumbrel*, the chair could be rolled into the water.

steadfast

"Guarding the town." Not exactly what most of us think of today in connection with *steadfast*, but etymologically speaking, this comes close to the original meaning. For *stead*, from the Anglo-Saxon *stede*, is closely related to the Dutch *stad*, "town," and *stede*, "place"; and to the German *Stadt*, "town," and *Statt*, "place." Words with similar spelling and meaning exist in most languages of Teutonic origin, and all stem back to a common ancestor, the Sanskrit *sthiti*, "standing, position." The Greek *stasis*, "standing, stoppage," and the Latin *statio*, "station," are from the same origin. *Fast*, in the meaning of "firm," comes from the Anglo-Saxon *fæst*, and it, too, has close relatives in many languages of Teutonic origin such as the German *fest*, "firm." The common origin of these seems to be the Old Teutonic root *fastu-*, "to keep, guard, observe." The Anglo-Saxon combination of these, *stedefæst*, "fixed in position," dates to the tenth century, and is the direct precursor of our modern *steadfast*, "steady, unchanging."

tympany

Used, today, as a collective noun to designate the aggregation of kettledrums in an orchestra, this word is actually the Anglicized form of the Latin *tympanum*, "a drum," from the Greek *tympanon*, "a drum," from *typtein,* "to strike, beat." The Latin word has also been taken directly into English with the original spelling preserved, in the same meaning, and there also exists a much older Anglicized form, *tympan,* which may have come through the Old French *tympan* rather than directly from the Latin. It seems probable that the modern use of *tympany* may have arisen from the mistaken belief that this spelling, or at least the pronunciation thereof, represented the plural of *tympanum* (i.e, as though the Latin plural were *tympani*), whereas its true plural is *tympana.*

Prince Albert

The prince himself was English, eldest son of Queen Victoria, ultimately reigning as King Edward VII. As prince, he traveled extensively, first visiting the United States in 1860. Social leaders were then greatly impressed by the long double-breasted frock coat worn by the prince at afternoon occasions and promptly adopted it, calling it a *Prince Albert* or *Prince Albert coat.*

arena

Thanks to the fact that the citizens of ancient Rome liked to see gory contests—gladiators fighting one another to the death,

 starved wild animals turned loose upon human victims—the ground of the amphitheaters was always liberally covered with sand to soak up spilled blood. And the Latin word for sand is *arena.* Nowadays an "arena" may never know blood, it may never see sand; it merely denotes a scene of contest—physical, mental, or even figurative.

starling

The Latin word for starling, and still the scientific name for the genus of which starlings are members, was *Sturnus.* This word, with the usual changes in spelling and pronunciation, became adopted into one after another of most of the European languages, finally reaching the Anglo-Saxon as *stær*, from which it became, in Middle English, *stare*. This name for the starling, although rare for many years, has still been in limited use as late as the early part of this century. However, it was over nine hundred years ago that someone applied to the stare the affectionate diminutive suffix that has become, in modern form, *-ling*, the original combination having had the form *stærlinc*. And it was this combination that has become our familiar *starling*.

hogwash

This is not slang, nor is it a recent coinage. Five hundred years ago it was the common term for the swill fed to swine. And, curiously enough, the earliest instance of its use traced by the *Oxford English Dictionary*, dated about 1440, reads "They in the kechyn, for iape, pouryd on here hefd hoggyswasch" (They in the kitchen, for jest, poured hogwash on her head). Some joke! In figurative contemptuous usage the term dates to the early eighteenth century.

star-chamber

Somewhat over five hundred years ago, the royal palace at Westminster contained an apartment which, it is presumed, was decorated with gilt stars upon the ceiling. By virtue of its decoration, the room became known as the *Starred* or *Star Chamber*. It was the practice of the reigning monarchs to hold special high courts of jurisdiction in this room—courts on which the king's council sat as judges, and from which there was no appeal. It is good politics, of course, for the king's counselors to play along with the wishes of their sovereign, and the natural result was that this special court came to be used by the king for the exercise of tyranny. The flagrant misuse of the power of the court became so great during the rule of James I and that of Charles I that, in 1641, the court was abolished by Act of Parliament. But the notoriety of the court had become such that the phrase *star-chamber court*, or just *star-chamber*, was applied to any trial proceedings in which the defendant could expect nothing better than arbitrary

11

and oppressive treatment, and in this sense the term continues to live today.

hoosegow

We changed the spelling most decidedly, but that was done only to preserve the American idea of a phonetic pronunciation—spelled as sounded to an American ear. That is, the Mexican term is *juzgao*, derived from Spanish *juzgado*, a tribunal. But to the ordinary Mexican the term means a jail, and that is the meaning given also to the American term. Literary use did not appear, or has not been traced, before 1920, but I am certain it was in collcquial Western speech a dozen or more years earlier.

dragonfly

So called because if a Walt Disney were to magnify this insect to airplane size it would be as fearsome a creature as any dragon slain by St. George: huge eyes; long, slender, glittering body of variegated hues; two pairs of large wings; and extremely strong jaws. And there's little doubt but that to the insect world upon which it feeds voraciously it is as dread as any dragon that walked the earth or flew above it. Another common name for this insect is *devil's-darning-needle* (which see). The scientific name of the genus is *Libellula*, "little book," fancifully conceived because the wings at rest remain partly open, resembling the leaves of a book-let.

twilight

The prefix *twi-* almost invariably has the meaning of *two*, in the sense of twice, or double, the nature of the suffix. This is certainly not the meaning here, yet it is a little difficult to trace the reason for the origin of the use of the prefix in this combination. One possibility is that the *two* meaning is that of *in two*, that is, half, rather than double. A second is that *twilight* may be a corruption of *'tweenlight*, in the sense of "between light and dark." This last may have occurred not in English, but first in German, for there was a Middle High German word *zwischenliecht*, from *zwischen*, "be-

tween," and *liecht,* "light," whereas modern German has *Zwielicht.*
Zwie, here, could be a contraction of *zwischen,* and, since it usually
has the value of *two* in a compound term, could have been translated literally into English as *twilight* rather than as *'tweenlight,*
which would have been more accurate.

starboard

It has no reference to stars at all, but probably few sailors, even,
know why this designates the right side of a vessel. Its origin
takes us back to the early ships of the Norse and other Teutonic
people. Though, with favoring winds, those vessels were driven
by sails, they were steered, not by rudders from the rear, but by
a paddle (*bord,* "board, paddle") over the right side. It was the
"steering paddle, or board." In Old English, *steorbord;* whence,
"starboard."

crawfish, crayfish

Either way you say it, American with *w* or British with *y,* the
name is derived from Old French *crevice* or *crevisse,* meaning
"crab," a term that then covered almost any of the larger crusta-
ceans. And because of the propensity of the critter to navigate
rearward, we have made a verb of the term, using it figuratively
to indicate an attempt, usually conspicuous, to withdraw oneself
from a stand or a commitment that has become undesirable.

oyez

Although pronounced "oh yes," it has no further tie with those
two words. It was an Old French addition to the law courts of
England after the Norman conquest. In the French of the period
it was written *oiez,* from the verb *oir,* "to hear." Used by the court
crier at the opening of the court, or by an officer calling for attention to a proclamation, it meant, "Hear ye! Hear! Hear!"

preface

"*P*eter *R*ice *e*ats *f*ish *a*nd *c*atches *e*els," was the favorite acrostic
carefully lettered above PREFACE in all schoolbooks in my gen-

eration. This, of course, had then to be reversed by some bright spirit and, on the lower edge, we read, "*E*els *c*atch *a*lligators; *f*ish *e*at *r*aw *p*otatoes." But the term itself is merely from the Latin *praefatio,* "a saying beforehand."

Argyll socks (sox)

Perhaps originally, ten or fifteen years ago, the American woman who first knitted a pair of these socks for husband, son,  or sweetheart did follow the traditional plaid pattern of the clan of Campbell of Argyll—light green crossed with dark green, and narrow independent cross lines of white. If so, though the name was retained by followers who adopted the idea, the plaid speedily lost all resemblance to that claimed by the Scottish clan. The Argyll sock of today's American, whether home knitted or machine produced, has become a variegated plaid affair of bright colors.

standpatter

The voluminous and authoritative *Oxford English Dictionary* offers 104 meanings of the verb *to stand,* alone and in combinations. Of these, the thirteenth reads:

> *Card-playing.* To be willing, or announce one's willingness, to play with one's hand as dealt. Opposed to *pass.*

The same source gives three meanings of the adverb-adjective *pat.* The third, in part:

> Exactly suitable or to the purpose.

Combination of these led to the verbal phrase *to stand pat,* which, incidentally, is the fourteenth meaning given for *to stand.* The phrase was coined by a poker player, and it meant, "to *stand* (that is, to play without drawing) with a hand that is *pat* (one not apt to be improved by drawing)." But then followed the almost inevitable extension of meaning into a nonspecialized sense, and

14

to stand pat came to be used, especially in politics, to denote the inactivity of a man who accepted the existing situation, not trying to improve it but at the same time doing nothing that would worsen it. Such a person, eventually, came to be known as a *standpatter,* a conservative.

hoodlum

The country is indebted to some unknown and unheralded genius in San Francisco for this underworld character. Time: about 1870. Attempts to trace the source of the word have persisted almost ever since, but without success. The first theory, advanced by Bartlett in 1877 on the strength of hearsay evidence, described it as an accidental coinage of a reporter assisted by his paper's compositor. A gang of ruffians, the story was, was under the leadership of one Muldoon. Fearing reprisals, the reporter spelled the name backward—*Noodlum.* Poor writing led the compositor to mistake the initial *N* for *H;* hence, *Hoodlum.* This account is still often circulated, though there is nothing factual to back it. Barère and Leland, in their *Dictionary of Slang* (1889), though admitting uncertainty, thought the word may have been derived from Pidgin English *hood lahnt,* "very lazy mandarin," because of the many Chinese in San Francisco, but they exited gracefully from that poor guess through the preface that the word was "probably of Spanish origin." The latest theory, and the most tenable in my opinion, was advanced by Dr. J. T. Krumpelmann in 1935 in *Modern Language Notes.* On the basis of the large percentage of Germans, many of them Bavarians, in San Francisco in the sixties and seventies, he thought it probable that *hoodlum* was nothing more than a slight mispronunciation of the dialectal Bavarian *hodalump* of identical meaning.

turtledove

The Romans listened to them coo, then named them in imitation of the sound they made, *turtur.* And this is the name that was taken directly into Anglo-Saxon before the time of the Norman Conquest. But in Old High German, the final *r*-sound was converted to an *l*-sound, giving *turtulo* for the male, *turtula* for the

15

female, and these forms were separately adopted into Anglo-Saxon as *turtla* and *turtle,* respectively. The two were later combined into *turtle,* regardless of sex, and this name eventually superseded the former *turtur* entirely. It was several hundred years later that the second element of the name was added, and the addition was really redundant, for a *turtle* was a dove and nothing else. Several hundred years more passed by (bringing us to the mid-seventeenth century) before the word *turtle* was applied, from an entirely different derivation, to the marine tortoise.

grotesque

Paintings discovered on the walls of the Baths of Titus, excavated by archaeologists in the sixteenth century, gave us our word "antic" through the Italian *antica,* "antique." But, though the learned world thus attributed the paintings to the ancients, the general public was more impressed by the finding of them in the excavated chambers, or *grotte,* of ancient buildings, and, therefore, called them *grotesca.* Any kind of comic distortion or unnatural exaggeration at all akin to the figures in these old Roman murals then became *grotesca,* a term that, through French influence, evolved into English *grotesque.*

stalemate

Originally, the term was just *stale*—the *mate* part was added, possibly originally in jest, because a stalemate, like a checkmate, serves to end the game. Unlike *checkmate,* and *chess* itself, both of which come from Arabic, *stale* seems to have originated in the French *estaler* (*étaler*), one of the meanings of which is "to fix," in the sense of "to set in place." The latter is related to the German *stellen,* "to place," which, in turn, has been traced to the Teutonic *stal,* "a fixed place."

craps

The book *Sucker's Progress* (1938), by Herbert Asbury, tells the entire story in half a dozen pages or so, but in brief the original game was a simplified form of the old game of hazard. In that game, *crabs* was the lowest throw. When hazard moved into France its name became *crabs* or *craps,* and it was the latter name by which the game became known in New Orleans, where it was introduced about 1840. Needless to add, the game did not remain confined to New Orleans. Within fifty years it became highly popular and has remained so, especially among Negroes, among whom it is often called "African golf" or "African dominoes."

potter's field

The original was a piece of ground outside Jerusalem bought by the chief priests with the thirty pieces of silver which, according to Matthew 27: 7, had been given to Judas for the betrayal of Jesus and which he later returned. The field was then set aside for the burial of strangers and the poor. The supposition is that the clay used by potters had formerly been obtained in this field.

attic

Yes, odd as it may appear, that portion of our homes that lies between the roof and the ceiling of the uppermost rooms which

we call "the attic" is derived from *Attica,* the country of ancient Greece of which Athens was the chief city. The architecture of the country was outstanding, the name, thus, being applied to various characteristic structural types. One such, conspicuous chiefly in structures of large design, included a low story above the main cornice, originally set off, on the façade, by short pilasters above the main pillars. Though the decorative effect was later omitted, the name *attic* was still applied to the low space, eventually also to any garret.

artesian

Centuries ago—some authorities place the date definitely as the year 1126, and others merely vaguely as recent as "about

1750"—an unknown genius bored a well in the region of France now known as Artois. By accident or design he hit upon a geological formation where a tilted porous stratum lay between two tilted impervious strata, and, in consequence, water was forced by natural pressure above the surface of the boring. But anything or anyone native to the province of Artois is, from its ancient name, *Artesien,* in French; transformed in English to *artesian.*

cockroach

Captain John Smith described this unattractive insect in 1624: "A certaine India Bug, called by the Spaniards a Cacarootch, the which creeping into Chests they eat and defile with their ill-sented dung." The Spanish name, however, is *cucaracha,* which the English, with usual disregard for foreign languages, converted to *cockroach.*

German measles

Though the existing amenities between nations may cause a German to name something unpleasant as *französisch,* a Frenchman to name the same thing as *anglais,* and an Englishman to call it *German,* the name of this ailment honors, rather than derogates, its specification. The disease was identified, that is, by the German physician Friedrich Hoffmann in 1740. Hence called, by some, *German measles.* Another name, sometimes used for the same disease, is *French measles.* This, it has been said, is in commemoration of the French physician De Bergen, who has been credited with making additional discoveries concerning the disease in 1752, but I have not been able to verify this, nor even to discover De Bergen's full name.

slowpoke

Of the many different meanings for the word *poke,* one, an Americanism dating to about 1860, is "a lazy person, a dawdler." The origin of this meaning is easily traced to the British use of the verb *to poke,* "to potter." But there is no indication of the reason for Jane Austen's use of the verb with this sense, for it was she, in *Sense and Sensibility,* who is the earliest on record with this meaning. But it must have been an American who first became discouraged with the extreme laziness of some poke of his acquaintance, and who coined the term to describe one who was the epitome of dawdlers—a *slowpoke.*

tomahawk

First rendered by Captain John Smith as *tomahack,* this word first came into English through him from the Renape Indian dialect of Virginia, whose word for this all-purpose ax was *tämähak,* a shortened form of *tämähakan,* "cutting tool," related to *tämäham,* "he cuts." Closely similar words are found in a number of other Indian dialects, for example in Pamptico (of the Carolinas), *tommahick;* in Mohegan, *tummahegan;* in Delaware, *tamoihecan;* in Abenaki, *tamahigan;* in Micmac, *tumeegun;* in Passamaquoddy, *tumhigen.* Captain Smith also reported the existence of a tool used as a pick-ax, which he named a *tockahack,* but there is no evidence that this was taken into English in general use.

dog Latin

Properly, this is just very bad Latin, a mongrel Latin—whence the name—composed of a mixture of Latin and English. But in my own childhood (in Ohio), what we called *dog Latin* was a gibberish of decapitated English words, the initial letters transposed to the rear, plus "ay"; as, "Ohnny-jay ust-may o-gay ome-hay." In other areas this form of lopped English was called "hog Latin," or "pig Latin," possibly because the sound resembled the grunting of hogs.

pipe dream

A dream full of illusions such as results from the smoking of an opium pipe, which was the source of the term. As American slang heard just about at the beginning of the present century, and apparently first appeared in print in Wallace Irwin's *Love Sonnets of a Hoodlum* (1901):

> *To just one girl I've tuned my sad bazoo,*
> *Stringing my pipe-dream off as it occurred.*

cockhorse

This plaything first attained notice early in the sixteenth century, but it is not certain why it was so named. The best guess is that the make-believe horse was one upon which its young rider was "a-cock," that is, was jauntily set upon the wooden horse or Father's knee.

auburn

The modern auburn-haired beauty has tresses of golden or reddish brown, but that was far from the color the Normans had  in mind when, after the Conquest of 1066, they invaded England. They used it to describe the prevailing hue of the Saxon hair—flaxen or yellowish white, that which we now ascribe to a towhead. Careless speech and faulty writing of the sixteenth and seventeenth centuries contributed to the shifted meaning. Old French *auborne* often appeared as *abrun* and *abroun* and even *abrown,* from which, by inference, "a brownish tint" was the natural conclusion.

blindman's buff

Probably Will Shakespeare played this when he was boy. At least he could have; the children of his day did play it, and were, perhaps, no more gentle in the sport than are some of today. One youngster would consent to be blindfolded and attempt, then, to grab one of the other players, each of whom would push or jostle him or, especially, give him a buffet, a slap upon the rump with

20

open hand. And that, in the language of the period, was a *buff;* whence the name of the sport.

flophouse

Although labeled slang in some dictionaries, this early-twentieth-century substitute is certainly convenient and expressive. It will undoubtedly gain prestige and, as long as need exists, remain in our language. We in America are barely acquainted with the Englishman's equivalent, *doss house,* and don't particularly like it; it sounds Chinese, though actually derived from Latin *dorsum,* "the back." But here in America we "flop" down on a bed, when tired, and a *flophouse* is a house or lodging for the weary who need a bed at a very, very low rate and must be content with other inmates, whether human or vermin.

slogan

It is very unlikely that advertising copywriters, who must spend many sleepless nights trying to devise catchy phrases to describe their wares, realize that the resulting *slogans* are direct descendants of ancient Gaelic battle cries. But the original was just that, for the origin of *slogan* is *sluagh-ghairm,* literally, "the cry of the host," from the Gaelic words *sluagh,* "host," and *gairm,* "a cry or shout." For the most part, these battle cries consisted chiefly or solely of the name of the clan or of the leader of the host, repeated over and over by the body of soldiers, in unison, as they moved into battle. This part of the technique, at least, is retained by today's slogan writers, who try, if it all possible, to work the name of their product into their phrases.

toilet

This word has had a rather curious development in the little more than four hundred years it has been in the language. Its origin was the French *toilette,* the diminutive of *toile,* "cloth." Its first use in English was as the name for the fragment of cloth used for wrapping clothes. Then it was applied to the cloth cover for a dressing table, such a cloth often being of rich fabric and workmanship. From here it was used for the collection of articles found on or associated with the dressing table, and then for the table itself. Next the term was transferred to the process of dressing, and some time later to the manner or style of dress as well as to the dressing room. It is almost exclusively in the United States that the use of the word has been extended to apply to the bathroom and particularly to the water closet, these being sometime adjuncts to the dressing room itself.

cobweb

Though this was, in fact, a web made by a cop, I don't mean a trap set by a policeman. No, six hundred years ago an ordinary spider, though more commonly called a spider, was also known as a *cop,* and when that term was combined with *web* its pronunciation was softened to *cob.*

doggone

Popular notion nowadays is that this is an affected or prim American version of "God damned." The fact is, however, that British writers, long before any record of American usage is found, were using "dog on it," as a form of mild oath, much as earlier writers had been using "a pox on it." I think it most likely, therefore, that *doggone* is nothing more than a misspelling of *dog on.*

claptrap

This definition which appeared in Nathan Bailey's dictionary of 1720 tells the full story: "*A Clap Trap,* a name given to the rant and rhimes that dramatick poets, to please the actors, let them go off with: as much as to say, a trap to catch a clap, by way of applause from the spectators at a play."

flapdoodle

Here's another coinage of the same nature as "flabbergast," but of later vintage. Its anonymous creator left no blueprint, but

22

probably drew it from the seventeenth-century slang *fadoodle,* which was used in like sense. The first use in print of the surviving term was apparently in Frederick Marryat's *Peter Simple,* published in 1834, and of course this writer may have been the one who modernized the older term. Its meaning? Twaddle; sheer nonsense.

ballyhoo

Several suggestions have appeared as the source of this term for the glib patter of the showman: (a) the village of *Ballyhooly,*  Ireland; (b) a circus blend of *ballet* and *whoop;* (c) the cry of dervishes, *b'allah hoo,* "Through God it is," at the 1893 World's Fair in Chicago. Dr. Atcheson L. Hench (*American Speech,* Oct., 1945) suggests that it may have come from the seaman's term, the *ballahou,* for a fast-sailing, two-masted vessel, with foremast raked forward, mainmast aft, rigged with high fore-and-aft sails, much used in the West Indies. The contemptuous term *ballyhoo of blazes,* used in 1847 by Melville in *Omar,* in derision of a slovenly vessel, may have been picked up by landlubbers, he thinks.

tocsin

Back in the days before systems of mass communication had been developed to anything like the extent they are today, it was necessary that some means be used to call the inhabitants of a community together in case of a general alarm or for the dissemination of important news. This was frequently done by means of an alarm bell, which was struck only on such special occasions. And a *tocsin* is literally "a striking of the bell." The word was taken into English directly from the French, where it had slowly developed in form from the Old French *toquassen,* and to which, in turn, it had come from the Provençal *tocasenh,* "strike the bell." This is made up of *tocar* (from which came the French

23

toucher), "to touch, to strike," together with *senh,* "sign, bell," the latter part from the Latin *signum,* "sign," which, in Late Latin, also had the meaning of "bell."

skin game

It was as early as 1812 when the verb *to skin,* meaning "to strip a person of his money," was first entered into an English dictionary of slang, so the meaning undoubtedly existed in speech long before that. But it was not until 1862 that the first recorded use of the compound word *skin game* made its appearance. The meaning was, at first, a game, such as a card game, in which the player had no chance to win, the house "skinning" him of his purse. Later the sense was expanded to its present status, when any person subjected to a set of circumstances wherein he has no choice but to emerge the worse for the experience is said to have been the object of a *skin game.*

germane

If you will cross-check the entry **cousin-german** it will be seen that *german* means "having the same parentage; closely related." And *germane* may be substituted, and frequently is. Nowadays, however, there's a growing tendency to apply the latter term to matters that may bear close relationship, that may be relevant or pertinent, rather than to persons having close relationship.

skiagraph

(Also spelled *skiograph, sciagraph.*) Long, long ago—reputedly in ancient Corinth—the art of making shadow pictures was born. That is, the practice of casting a shadow of the person or object upon a wall or other surface, then filling in the shadow with pencil or charcoal. Today we know such a picture as a *silhouette,* but they were earlier known by the name of *skiagraph,* from the two Greek words, *skia,* "shadow," and *graphon,* "picture." Later, when the art of taking pictures of people and objects by means of Roentgen rays was developed, it was realized that these pictures,

24

too, were really a sort of shadow picture. By that time the word *skiagraph* had been pretty well superseded by *silhouette* for the original meaning, so it was adopted by Roentgenologists to describe what many of us know better as an X-ray picture.

pin money

I suppose that the very earliest notion of *pin money* was literal —just enough money with which a wife could buy pins. This would have been an exceedingly small sum, indicated by the expression "not worth a pin," one of the earliest in our language. But in the early sixteenth century and onward the amount was considerably larger. "Money to buy her pins" was enough, not only for the purchase of pins, but for all other personal expenses. It was usually a fixed annual allowance in the olden days, and, in England, is still often provided for by the annual rentals of certain properties settled upon the wife.

highfalutin

It has been in the written language of America since 1839, so it was undoubtedly in wide use in much earlier common speech. But, regrettably, not until we reach a lexicographer's idea of heaven can the source of the term or the name of its coiner be ascertained. Bartlett (*Dictionary of Americanisms,* 1877) quotes a speech delivered in 1848 by Leslie Coombs, thus:

"I was at the Barnburner's convention in Utica, and the first person I heard was a good-looking, fat, rosy-looking man, who got up and ground out what we term at the West a regular built fourth-of-July— star-spangled-banner—times-that-tried-men's-souls—Jefferson speech, making gestures to suit the *highfalutens.*"

Black Maria

A police van for the conveyance of prisoners. Tradition says that the original, in Boston, Massachusetts, in the early 1800's, was named after a huge Negress, Maria Lee, but known as "Black Maria," who ran a lodging house for sailors, but who co-operated with the police in the arrest of any lodger who became unruly or violated the law. It is not known when the first van acquired the name, but a Boston paper of 1847 tells of "a new Black Maria" being put into service.

flibbertigibbet

Strangely enough, this does not appear ever to have been considered as slang. As evidence thereof the first printed appearance of which we have record was in a sermon, and at that, a sermon before His Majesty the King—King Edward the Sixth in the year 1549, sermon by Bishop Hugh Latimer. The word he used, however, was *flibbergib,* which he spelled *flybbergybe.* His meaning was that of today, a garrulous or flighty person. But Shakespeare, who wrote *flibbertigibbet* in *King Lear,* used it as other writers had done, as the name of a devil. And Scott, in *Kenilworth,* had it mean an impish youngster.

bandy-legged

Bowlegged; having the legs shaped for greater comfort in riding a horse, parenthesis-fashion. The term probably arose, back in the seventeenth century, through a comparison of legs so shaped with the curved stick, then called a "bandy," in the game of hockey as then played.

clapboard

Our English forebears just partly anglicized a German term back in the sixteenth century. The word that came to them was *klappholt,* in which *holt* (modern *Holz*) meant "wood, board," and *klapp* apparently referred to the clacking sound from boards smacking together. This *klappholt* and the early *clapboard* was used by coopers in making casks and was later used for wainscots. The American pilgrim, however, took the term and applied it to lengths of wood that he split much thinner. These later evolved into boards

26

thinner at one edge, so they would underlie the board above, affording greater protection against inclement weather.

skewbald

A *skewbald* horse (or other animal) is one that is basically white, but whose coat also has patches of some other color. It is thus similar to *piebald* (which see, especially for the derivation of *-bald*), and is sometimes used synonymously therewith, but when a distinction is made, *piebald* is used when the patches are black, *skewbald* when they are other than black. As a compound word, *skewbald* dates to the seventeenth century, but its predecessor, *skewed,* of the same meaning, is some two hundred years older. The derivation seems to be from the Anglo-Saxon *scuwa,* "shadow," which may be related to the Latin *obscurus,* "dark, shadowed," in the sense that the animal's otherwise white coat is shadowed by the other color.

guttersnipe

He, or quite often she, frequently a child or street Arab, gathers a living from the gutter, or less literally, from discarded rags, trash, or other refuse, including food. His mode of living, that is, resembles that of the snipe which pokes its bill into the mud lining a body of water for its food. The term, originating as slang, is not quite a hundred years old.

shenanigan

Many sources have been suggested for this Americanism, which seems to have been originated in California during or soon after the Gold Rush. The first recorded use was in that state in 1855. As the word has the sense of "trickery, deceit," most possible sources suggested have had similar meanings, such as the Spanish *chanada,* "a trick," and the Irish *sionnachuighim,* "I play tricks." However, despite the fact that, as Mencken remarks, the word has "an Irish smack," a very strong case is made by Spitzer (*American Speech,* Vol. 23, 1948 p. 210) for a derivation from the German *schinnagel,* "the nail holding the rim to the wheel," through the cant word *schinageln,* "to work," and *Schenigelei,* "a trick."

hubbub

The best I can do is to say "probably." That is, this term for a confused din, an uproar of sound from a multitude of voices, was probably taken from an ancient Irish war cry. The cry itself appears to have been *abu! abu!,* repeated over and over from the throats of yelling hordes. Edmund Spenser, in *The Present State of Ireland* (1596), describes it: "They come running with a terrible yell and *hubbabowe,* as yf heaven and earth would have gone together, which is the very image of the Irish *hubbabowe,* which theyr kerne [foot soldiers] use at theyr first encounter."

madcap

In its earliest sense, as in Shakespeare's day, this meant simply one who was crazy, a maniac. *Cap,* just because it covered the head, was sometimes used for "head," and *mad,* used literally, meant "crazy." Of course it was also used, and still is, somewhat playfully, in describing one who acted impulsively or recklessly, in much the same manner as we now say, "He's got bees in his bonnet."

billingsgate

Just why the gate, once an entrance to the old city of London, was known as *Billings,* even back in the thirteenth century, cannot be determined. Presumably that was the name of its builder, but Newcourt's map of the city in 1658 says the gate was "Founded by Belen ye 23th Brittishe Kinge." At any rate, a fish market became established near it in the sixteenth century which soon acquired an unenviable reputation for the coarse vituperative language of the fishwives. Hence, to this day *billingsgate* denotes vulgar and violent abuse, though the market itself passed out of existence long ago. (P.S. The theory seems not to have been advanced before, but it seems to me quite probable that "Belen's gate," with careless pronunciation, could easily have been corrupted to "Billin's gate" and then to "Billingsgate."—C.E.F., Jr.).

highbinder

One's immediate interpretation of the sense of this word is largely sectional. In eastern America it is associated with a ruffian, a gangster, and that was its earliest application—a member of a gang of rowdies in New York City who, in 1806, called themselves *Highbinders*. But, especially in California and later in New York City, the term was applied, in the 1870's, to any member of a Chinese secret society organized for blackmail or assassination.

banjo

In Thomas Jefferson's *Notes on Virginia* (1788) he says that this instrument is "proper to the blacks, which they brought  hither from Africa, and which is the original of the guitar, the chords being precisely the four lower chords of the guitar." But your dictionaries tell that *banjo* is probably a Negro corruption of the far older *bandore,* known to the ancient Greeks as *pandoura,* a musical instrument of three strings. It seems not to have occurred to anyone that both may be right. The Greeks had contact with Ethiopia, as well as Egypt, from the days of Homer, and might well have introduced the *pandoura* into such regions of Africa.

flittermouse

It isn't a mouse, for it has wings, and mice don't. But it does fly rather swiftly and dartingly, so it can be said to flitter, and being a mammal with a body not unlike that of a mouse in size, and sometimes in color, it is not surprising that this creature was known to our ancestors as a *flittermouse,* after the German *Fledermaus* or the Dutch *vledermuis.* But the older and better-known English name was *back,* a name now lost in English dialects, though remaining

29

as *bawkie-bird* in Scotland. Today we know this flying mammal as a *bat*.

skedaddle

There has been a great deal of controversy, which has still not been resolved, over the origin of this word, and even some difference of opinion as to whether it was born in England or in America. The earliest recorded use for the American *skedaddle,* "to flee precipitously," that has been found is 1861—that for the English, "to spill (as milk)," is 1862, but since spilt milk has, in effect, fled abruptly, this sense may actually derive from the former. Bartlett, in his *Dictionary of Americanisms* (4th ed., 1877), reviewed the controversy thoroughly as of that date, and little new has been turned up since. Thus various writers claim to have traced it to the Greek *skedannumi,* "rout"; the Welsh *ysgudaw,* "to scud about"; and the Irish *sgedadol,* "scattered." Others have claimed Swedish and Danish origins, but no one really knows, for sure.

high-muck-a-muck

We take into our speech words from all manners of strange sources. Thus when Canadian and American reached the Chinook tribes dwelling north of the Columbia River in the far West, they adopted many terms known to all the tribes, combining them sometimes with French and English words. Among the Indian phrases, according to Charles J. Lovell (*American Speech,* April, 1947), was *hiu muckamuck,* meaning "plenty to eat." It was catchy, and it is Lovell's conjecture that, as we do with numerous slang expressions, the traders began to use it without regard to its original meaning, but in the sense "big bug; chief man." And, naturally, because they "could not frame to pronounce" *hiu* aright, they made it *high*.

pink-stern

Pinkeye designates an inflamed eye, but *pink-stern* has nothing to do with color. It names a type of small boat, one with its stern shaped like that of a sailing vessel known as a *pink* or *pinky*. Both names are corrupted from the Middle Dutch *pincke*, first applied to a flat-bottom sailing vessel which was subsequently built with a narrow stern, the so-called *pink-stern*.

tintinnabulation

Chiefly known to us because of its use by Edgar Allan Poe in "The Bells," this word is based on the Latin *tintinnabulum*, "a bell," from *tintinnare*, "to ring." It seems probable that *tintinnare* and its relatives were coined in imitation of the sound of bells, quite as our *ding-dong, ting-a-ling*, etc., were coined for the same purpose.

chucklehead

Has the same meaning as *chowderhead*, but the first element is from the dialectal word *chuck*, meaning "a chunk," such as "a chunk of coal; a chunk of bread," any lump, that is, which is of irregular size.

runabout

My son, now in his teens, drives a convertible. When I was in my teens, I drove a roadster. In my father's youth, the automobile body style of equivalent popularity to these was the *runabout*, but in his father's youth, the *runabout* was a light, horse-drawn vehicle. All of these are, or were, handy means of transportation for the driver with, perhaps, one or two passengers. But here, again, we have an example of changing meaning for a long-established word, for ever since the fourteenth century a *runabout* has also meant a footloose wanderer, a vagabond, or tramp, having been used in *Piers Plowman* in this sense.

arrowroot

A tropical American plant now cultivated commercially for the nutritious starch obtained from the root. The name, however, according to Sir Hans Sloane, a British naturalist who wrote of this plant in 1696 in his catalogue of Jamaican plants, arose from its use by Indians to counteract the effect of poisoned arrows. "But," says the *New International Encyclopedia*, "it is not improbable that the name is really another form of *ara,* an Indian word." No one now living can be certain. I'd love to be able to assert confidently that the Indians used the root to tip their arrows with poison, thus opposing Sir Hans.

barrel house

Now it's a form of music, crude jazz, or a type of blues performed originally in low-class night clubs. The name itself came from any  rough or low booze joint in which drinks were drawn from the barrels in which the liquor was delivered or where such barrels were prominently displayed. It is at least seventy-five years old. *Peck's Bad Boy* (1883) has the "Boy" tell that his "Pa . . . thought he had a snap with me in the drug store . . . ; but after I had put a few things in his brandy he concluded it was cheaper to buy it, and he is now patronizing a barrel house down by the river."

flimflam

"She maketh earnest matter of euery flymflam," was listed as one of the *Prouerbes in the Englishe tongue,* compiled by John Heywood in 1546. So the word must be considerably older than that date, the earliest in recorded print. It had no known source, except that it seems to have been a reduplication, for added effect, on *flam,* "a whim," "a falsehood," or just "nonsense."

shyster

This Americanism was probably coined early in the nineteenth century, since its first recorded use, as cited in the *Dictionary of American English,* was in 1846. Partridge, in his *Dictionary of Slang and Unconventional English,* suggests that *shyster* is a variant of *shicer,* "a person or thing of no account, worthless," although the latter may actually be the newer word. In any event, there is some reason to believe that both are derived from the German (possibly through Yiddish) *Scheisse,* "excrement."

doch-an-doris

Any Scot can tell you that this has the same meaning as "stirrup cup," and is literally "a drink at the door," that is, a parting drink. Sometimes it is written *doch-an-dorach,* but in any case it represents the Gaelic *deoch,* "drink," *an,* "the," and *doruis,* "door."

gazebo

If the eighteenth-century inventor of this term had known, he might have had many a chuckle over the labors he invoked upon later scholars. From what source did he obtain it? Some think it from some unknown Oriental source, but the general consensus now is that he just made it up. As he wanted a term for a structural lookout, he may have taken the ordinary word *gaze* and, under the pretense that it was from a hypothetical Latin verb of the second conjugation, *gazeo,* produced the future form, *gazebo,* "I shall see." Incidentally, the term is wholly unrelated to the American slang *gazabo,* which is also sometimes spelled and pronounced *gazebo,* but which is from Spanish *gazapo,* "one who is shrewd."

Stygian

Derived from the Latin adjective *Stygius,* from the Greek *Stygios,* all are related to the River *Styx,* that river in Greek mythology which separated the land of the living from Hades, the land of the dead. The name of the river is closely related to the Greek adjective *stygnos,* "hateful, gloomy," and this, too, is the meaning most often associated with our adjectival use of the river's name.

horse chestnut

Our English name is nothing more than a translation of the sixteenth-century Latin botanical name, *Castanea equina.* The name, according to a late-sixteenth-century writer, was "for that the people of the East countries do with the fruit thereof cure their horses of the cough." It is much more probable, however, that *horse* merely indicated "large," as is the case with a number of other materials—the horse bean, horse mackerel, horse-radish, for example.

choler

The ancient Greek physicians believed that there were four *humors,* or primary fluids, which governed the body—the blood, or *sanguis;* the yellow bile, or *chole;* the black bile, or *melas chole* (giving our word *melancholy*); and the phlegm, or *phlegma.* A superabundance of *chole* in one's system was supposed to cause that individual to become hot tempered, highly irascible, ready to fly off the handle; *choleric,* in fact.

shinplaster

In early colonial days there were both poverty and hard work, the work being of such a nature that cuts, bruises, and blows could well have been the daily fare of our forebears. When the injury was to the shin, it was usual to apply a poultice of sorts, and, among the poorer classes, this often took the form of a small square of paper previously soaked in vinegar, tobacco juice, or some other decoction of soothing, if not medicinal, value. These, of course, were *shinplasters.* With the advent of paper currency of dubious value, the size thereof being reminiscent of the makeshift poultice and the value often also of the same magnitude, the term was transferred to the scrip, and even yet paper scrip of low real or imagined value is known by the same term.

pinafore

That's what it was; "pinned afore," pinned at the front (of a dress). The item pinned was some sort of wash material which served as an apron or bib to protect the front of a child's dress— a dress then worn by either girl or boy child. That was back in the latter part of the eighteenth century. Many years ago, however, though the name was retained, the garment underwent a face-lifting. As now worn, by women or girls, it requires no pins and covers most of the dress.

blunderbuss

Though it's a loud blusterer to whom we give the name now, it was formerly, from the mid-seventeenth century, a short gun of  large bore and short range which scattered many slugs or balls. The Dutch, who invented it, called it, accurately enough, *dunderbus,* "thunder tube," because of its noisy firing. The English in adopting it, quick to see how blindly the shots were carried, just substituted *blunder* for *dunder.*

knickerbockers

We are so accustomed to this term that we can scarcely realize it is barely a hundred years old. It seems that it must date back to the days of Peter Stuyvesant, when the Dutchmen on Manhattan Island all wore flaring breeches now called *knickerbockers.* But, though the name of this garment is often credited to Washington Irving, and some credit is certainly due him, we really owe it to the British caricaturist George Cruikshank, who, in the 1850's, illustrated an English edition of the satire *A History of New York,* written by Irving in 1809 under the pseudonym "Diedrich Knicker-bocker." The garments of the alleged author, in these illustrations, and of his fellow Dutch burghers led to the adoption of *knicker-bockers* for knee breeches of any kind.

hurly-burly

We're all familiar with Shakespeare's "When the Hurley-bur-ley's done, When thè Battaile's lost, and wonne." But the earlier form was *hurling and burling*—or, as written in 1530, *hurlynge and burlynge. Hurling* had long then meant "strife" or "commotion"; *hurling-time* referred specifically to the Wat Tyler rebellion in the reign of Richard II. But, despite the fact that *burl, burling,* and *burly* have each been long in the language, none has been used in a sense that would normally associate it with *hurling* or its contracted form, *hurly.* We are forced to conclude that *burling* and *burly* were added merely to duplicate an effect by sound.

piebald

Thank fortune, one may be *bald* without being *piebald.* The element *pie,* in this case, relates to the *magpie,* a bird with feathers splotched with two colors, a bird called *pica* by the Romans, whence the English *pie.* Originally one of the two colors was, as with the bird, always a white spot, having thus the appearance of a *bald* spot. Actually, therefore, *piebald* originally related to the white-spotted *pie.* (See also **skewbald.**)

three-tailed bashaw

In Turkey the title of *bashaw* or *pasha* is applied to military officers and civil servants of high rank, being comparable to general, admiral, or governor. There are three grades of bashaw, and it was formerly the practice, especially during military maneuvers, to designate the grade by tying an appropriate number of horse tails to the standard of the officer, that with three tails denoting the highest rank. Thus a *three-tailed bashaw* was in fact a commanding general or admiral. The term came into English slang to describe a man of great importance, or, more often, a man who disported himself in such a way as to imply that he thought himself of great importance.

shilly-shally

When first recorded (1674), the air of indecision expressed by this term was rendered in much more recognizable form. The picture we have is of some Caspar Milquetoast of the day standing irresolutely and murmuring, *"Shall I? Shall I?"* In the course of literary evolution, the question became reduced to *shally-shally,* but was accompanied by a parallel change of vowel, retaining the form of the question, to "*Shill I? Shall I?*" Ultimately both paths of alteration converged, yielding the present *shilly-shally.*

chop suey

The *chop* is English, in the sense of "chipped" or "cut," but the *suey* is Chinese *sui,* "bits." Like the term itself, the concoction or comestible is of mixed origin. As explained to me, forty years ago, it was first devised by a Chinese operating a restaurant in Brooklyn, who composed it of bits of fried or stewed chicken or pork, rice, noodles, and sesame seeds or oil, and served the steamy mess in its own juice. But I'll accept as more authentic the statement by Herbert Asbury in *Gangs of New York* (1928) that it was the invention of a dishwasher in San Francisco about 1860. Yes, you're right; I've never asked for it a second time.

shindig

Although one authority cites a purported Southern United States meaning of "A sharp blow on the shins," this may only be a transferred meaning, from the appearance of the word, to an accidental kick received during a spirited dance or party. It seems much more likely that a *shindig* is a U.S. alteration of the much older British word *shindy,* which is preceded by *shinty* and *shinny.* This last is a ball game of considerable antiquity (seventeenth century or older) somewhat resembling field hockey. Its name may have been derived from a call used in the game, "*Shin ye! Shin you!*" or from the Gaelic *sinteag,* "a skip, jump."

dingbat

Mr. Bartlett, in the fourth edition (1877) of his *Dictionary of Americanisms,* decided that this owed its origin to a *bat,* or piece of wood or metal, that could be *dinged,* or thrown. Well, maybe so. That's probably as good as any explanation, though the source of any bit of slang is, usually, highly dubious. At any rate, we Americans use it, as we do its derivative, *dingus,* as a momentary name of anything of which the proper name is out of mind or unknown. (See also **thingum.**)

unkempt

The verb of which *kempt* is the past participle is *kemb,* "to comb," and it derives from the Anglo-Saxon *cembam* and ultimately

(Apologies to H Hoffman)

from the Old Teutonic *kembjan.* The only modern survivor of the verb is this form as it appears in the combinations *unkempt* and *well-kempt,* but the meanings most often implied in modern usage are, respectively, "ill-groomed, slovenly" and "well-groomed, neat," rather than the literal meanings of "uncombed" and "neatly combed." In all other uses, *kemb* has been replaced by its descendant, *comb.*

bluenose

Nowadays it is (a) a person of puritanic habits, such as, allegedly, those of the Back Bay area of Boston, or (b) a Nova Scotian to whom this term is applied. But in the first quarter of the nineteenth century it was applied generally to one from northern New England or adjacent provinces of Canada. The indicated color of the nose was not due to overindulgence in strong drink, one may assume, but to long-continued exposure to cold and inclement weather, such as experienced by lumberjacks, mariners, and fishermen. The term is also given to a variety of blue potato grown in Nova Scotia.

garrote

They did it first with cords twisted tighter and tighter by a stick, a method copied from carriers who thus secured loads upon their mules. The stick itself was the *garrote.* "They" were the Spanish Inquisitors of the fourteenth century and later, who sought and employed all sorts of methods of torture to extract confessions. In this, the muleteer's cord, passed around a stake, was tied about the arms, legs, and thighs of the victim and slowly tightened by the *garrote,* even perhaps cutting its way to the bone. At a later time the term was applied to an instrument of capital punishment in Spain and Portugal whereby death was accomplished by strangulation.

shilling

Shilling is a purely Teutonic word, found in all languages of the Germanic group with appropriate spelling in each. In English, it dates back to the Anglo-Saxon *scilling*—from there to the Gothic *skilligs*. It has been adopted into most of the Romance languages, again with appropriate changes in spelling. The root is uncertain, but seems probably to be *skel-,* "to divide." It seems always to have been a unit of currency, and a subdivision of the major piece of currency of the country, e.g., in England, of the pound. As for the *pound* itself, it was originally so-called because, in fact, it was a pound (Troy) of silver, though this has not now been true for many years. But despite the purely Teutonic background of the *shilling,* but not of the pound, the abbreviations of both come from their Latin equivalents. Thus the £, denoting the pound of money and the *lb.* indicating the pound of weight are both from the Latin *libra,* "pound," while the *s.* for shilling is the abbreviation for the Latin *solidus,* a monetary unit equal to 25 *denarii* (from which comes the *d.* for pence). The English abbreviation for shilling is *sh.* rather than *s.* In former times the abbreviation actually used for shilling was the long *s* (ʃ). Written quickly, this soon degenerated into nothing more than a slant line (/), and it is from this degeneration that the slant line has received the name, *solidus,* that it is now known by.

bigwig

Although humorously employed nowadays to designate a person of real or self-fancied importance, the start of the allusion was in fact indicated by the size of the wig a man wore. That was back in the times of Queen Anne of England and Louis XIV of France. Wigs had been courtly fashion for a half century or more, but by the beginning of the eighteenth century they attained exaggerated proportions, some covering the back and shoulders and floating down the chest. The status of a man was marked by the style of wig he wore, and the more important in state or occupation, the more imposing his wig. Eventually the fashion passed, though the wig or peruke is still retained in British courts of law.

pickaback

If we count only three generations to a century, our ancestors were carrying their children or others *pick-a-back* twelve generations ago and calling the manner by that name, or one very like it. That is, in the original dialect the term may have been *pick pack,* which may have referred to a *pack picked* (pitched) on one's shoulders. In the past hundred and fifty years the term has often been corrupted to *piggy-back* or the like, but great honored men have, on occasion, been carried *pickaback;* none has yet been carried *piggy-back.*

thoroughfare

Strange that New York thought it had to create a new word for its cross-state toll road—the Throughway. Beyond the temporary distinction of application to that one highway, there is nothing in the word that does not already exist in the long-established—six hundred years—word *thoroughfare*. *Thorough* is the ancient spelling of *through; fare,* now used chiefly for "passage money," formerly meant "passage, way." And *thoroughfare* has long indicated a "through way between places."

love apple

Just the ordinary common tomato, but my mother was averse to eating it. In rural Ohio, the home of her girlhood, it was known only as *love apple* and, believed to possess aphrodisiac properties, was therefore feared by virtuous maidens. The reason for the name, with the properties suggested by it, was entirely due to a mistake in translation. From South America, where the plant was discovered, it was introduced into Spain in the sixteenth century and from there into Morocco. Italian traders then brought it to Italy, where it was called *pomo dei Moro,* "apple of the Moors." From Italy it went to France, and there is where the mistake was made. Whoever the grower, his knowledge of Italian was faulty. Guided by the sound, he obviously thought *pomo dei Moro* meant, in French, *pomme d'amour,* "apple of love." And it was by the latter name or its English translation that the tomato was introduced into England in the early seventeenth century and thence to North America. And in Germany the common name is still *Liebesapfel,* "love apple," although *Tomate* is gaining ascendency. Needless to add, perhaps, any notion that the tomato arouses sexual desire or is even faintly poisonous has now completely died out.

daisy

One wonders whether coming generations will think that we, in this day of countless new inventions, have shown like imagination

and poetry in the coining of names as that given to our early forebears. It does not so appear. Certainly not in such words as telephone, automobile, airplane, radio, television, electric refrigerator. But consider the common field plant, the *daisy.* Even a thousand years ago it was observed that the white rays of its flower opened with the rising sun, exposing its golden disk through the day, and folded again in the evening. They called it *daeges eage,* "day's eye."

gantry

You may spell this *gauntry* if you like, or even *gauntree,* but the present preference is *gantry.* Nowadays the chief application of the name is to a traveling crane, a wonderfully ingenious device mounted on overhead rails in machine shops or the like by which the operator is able to hoist and transport heavy pieces to any portion of the shop. Our word, greatly altered through transition in French, came from Latin *cantherius,* "trellis" or "framework," probably of the nature of the "horse" used by modern carpenters.

Big Ben

This is the great deep-toned bell which strikes the hours of the clock in the clock tower of the Houses of Parliament, London. The tower carries five bells in all, the other four striking the quarter hours in the famed Westminster chimes. The great bell, weighing thirteen and a half tons, was cast in 1858, and was named Big Ben after Sir Benjamin Hall, who was First Commissioner of Works at the time when the clock was erected.

flea-bitten

Maybe the dog or horse with coat of the color that we call *flea-bitten* has been at some time infested with fleas, but, whether so or not, that is unessential. The color term originated back in the latter half of the sixteenth century. Some discerning groom or dog fancier saw that the reddish flecks on the coat of his lighter-colored animal were very similar in appearance to the reddish marks left on his own hairy arms by the bites of fleas. So what more natural than to describe the coat of his animal as *flea-bitten?* It saved time searching for a more definite color; easier to think of than, say, mottled gray or speckled sorrel.

sherry

The Romans of Caesar's day are remembered for, among other things, their fondness for good wines, so it may be fitting that Caesar's title has been perpetuated, even though indirectly, in this common table wine. For the name *Caesaris* was given to a town in Spain in his honor, but the name soon became modified to the more native-sounding *Xeres,* and still later to *Jerez.* And it was in this town that the wine was made, and from which it found its way to England. Unable to cope with Spanish pronunciation, the English gave the wine the name of *sherris* as a close approximation, and later, since this sounded like a plural, the name was changed to the synthetic singular, *sherry.*

gangplank

In England it's a *gangboard,* though both here and there the same thing is also called a *gangway.* In any case, whether plank, board, or way, it's a means of "going" aboard or off a ship. And that, in Old English, is what a *gang* was—a "going." In later times *gang* began to mean also a set or group of things that "go" together, thus giving us the sense of a band of persons who go or act co-operatively.

sub rosa

Under the rose; i.e., confidentially, in secrecy. Legend attributes the origin to a rose handed by Eros to Harpocrates, god of silence, accompanied with an injunction not to reveal the love affairs of Venus. Accordingly, in the customs of ancient councils, said to date back to the fifth century B.C., a rose hanging from the ceiling enjoined all present to observe secrecy on matters discussed. In later times, and until quite recently, the ceilings of dining rooms, decorated with roses or rosettes, were indication that private conversation would be confidential. Because the German *unter der Rose* is also of great antiquity and has identical significance, the custom of a rose on the ceiling was probably a Teutonic observance.

dillydally

Who first used it, or when, is not known; probably some harassed mother back in the sixteenth century, annoyed with the dalliance of a loitering son—or husband—made *dally* more emphatic by duplicating it with *dilly.* At least, the *dilly* prefix has no separate meaning of its own, any more than *shilly* has in the analogous term, *shilly-shally.*

loophole

The kind of *loop* now attached to this *hole* is seldom used or heard of any more. In the late Middle Ages, however, a *loop* was a narrow window, in a castle or other fortification, through which an archer could direct his missiles, but so narrow as to be a baffling target for an opposing bowman. The masonry of the window widened inwardly to permit a wider range for the defending archer. Possibly to avoid confusion between *loop,* "window," and *loop,* "a fold," the first became identified as *loophole.*

daystar

It is usually Venus, though it may at times be Jupiter, Mars, Saturn, or Mercury. At any rate it is the planet that appears in the eastern sky shortly before the sun rises, accordingly also called the morning star.

dormouse

This creature is certainly not a *dor,* or beetle, nor related to anything that flies, nor is it exactly a *mouse,* though small and a

 member of the rodent family. In fact, the source of its name has long been a matter of speculation and is still obscure, though in use for some five hundred years. But because the animal is noted for sleepiness, the consensus is that the first element, *dor,* is from the same source as *dormant,* or,

that is, from the Latin *dormire* "to sleep," to which *mouse* was then added because of general appearance.

highball

There's no doubt that this term has long been used by American railwaymen as that of a signal to the locomotive engineer to proceed. The signal itself was a ball large enough to be plainly visible which, when hoisted to the top of a mast at the approach to a small station, indicated that a train could proceed without stopping, that neither passenger, freight, nor express was awaiting it. Presumably this sense was somehow transferred to an iced alcoholic beverage about sixty years ago, but if so, the connection has not yet been determined. Possibly some passenger who had over-indulged in the beverage vaguely saw a resemblance between the floating ice at the top of the glass to the ball of the signal, and the tall glass to the mast.

chopfallen

"To lick one's chops," usually interpreted as indicating supreme pleasure, such as that from lapping the last taste of gravy or the last crumb of cake from one's jaws, not only shows us the meaning of *chop* in this term, but also pictures the exact opposite, the antonym, of the whole term. One who is *chopfallen* has been made supremely unhappy; he has had the ground knocked out from beneath him; he is crestfallen; he has a hangdog appearance, or, in brief, he has been so taken aback, so discomfited, that his chop, or jaw, has fallen open.

sheet anchor

The derivation is somewhat obscure, although some authorities believe that the name for this emergency anchor comes from *shot-anchor,* or *shoot-anchor,* since, if an emergency actually came about, it would have been "shot" (dropped quickly) from its supports. To bolster this theory, attention is called to the derivation of *shoot,* which came into the language through the Anglo-Saxon *sceotan.* which then passed through the Middle English form, *scheten.* It may also be worth noting that Scottish dialect *sheet* for "shoot" may have had something to do with our present form, as many capable British shipmasters were drawn from Scotland. Be that as it may, the modern meaning, "something which may be relied upon," is a direct descent from the emergency nature of the *sheet anchor.*

belladonna

"Beautiful lady," but why this name for the deadly nightshade? Two highly contradictory accounts have been given. The English naturalist John Ray (1627–1705) said that a cosmetic made from the juice of this plant was used by, especially, Venetian ladies to enhance their beauty. This is probably the true origin of the name. But a botanist of the mid-nineteenth century asserts that its name arose from the use of the deadly juice by an Italian criminal, one Leucota, who poisoned beautiful women with it.

hurry-scurry

Oddly enough, in the earliest use of *hurry,* in the last years of the sixteenth century, it was nothing more than a variant of *hurly,* meaning "disturbance, tumult." That is the sense in Shakespeare's *Coriolanus* (Act IV, Scene vi): "His remedies are tame, the present peace, And quietnesse of the people, which before Were in wilde hurry." And, in fact, through the next century or two we had *hurry-burry, hurry-durry,* and *hurry-curry,* all imitating *hurly-burly,* before finally settling upon *hurry-scurry* in the middle of the eighteenth century. But not only was *hurry* coined in this manner; so was *scurry,* though it did not find separate place in the language until another hundred years had passed.

pettifogger

One could be pardoned for thinking this was a person who "fogged" an issue by quibbling over petty matters, which is exactly what he does. Such was not the origin of the word, however, as *fog* was not used in such a sense in the mid-sixteenth century when *pettifogger* made its appearance. Nevertheless the true source is uncertain. Some think that *fogger* came from the name of a prominent family of German merchants, *Fugger,* of that period, and indicated a trickish lawyer. Others connect it with *pettifactor,* an agent or factor who handles small matters. The safest course is to throw up one's hands and say, "I don't know."

thingum, thingumajig, thingumbob, thingummy

All of these are meaningless extensions of the word *thing* in its special use as a term to denote an object or person which the speaker cannot or will not name specifically. *Thingum* was first recorded in the late seventeenth century, the other forms followed (not in order) in the eighteenth and nineteenth centuries.

chestnut

An old joke or oft-repeated story. The reason for this designation has never been proved, but George Stimpson, in *A Book about a Thousand Things* (1946), says: "The generally accepted story is that [it] originated in a play entitled 'The Broken Sword,' in which the chief characters are Captain Zavier, a Baron Munchausen type of storyteller, and Pablo, a comic person. This play contains the following colloquy:

CAPTAIN ZAVIER: I entered the woods of Collaway, when suddenly from the thick boughs of a cork tree—
PABLO: A chestnut, Captain, a chestnut.
CAPTAIN ZAVIER: Bah, I tell you it was a cork tree.
PABLO: A chestnut; I guess I ought to know, for haven't I heard you tell this story twenty-seven times?"

Mr. Stimpson attributes the perpetuation of *chestnut* in this sense to the English-born American actor William Warren, who had played the part of Pablo, at a stage dinner where he repeated Pablo's concluding line after hearing an old joke. But as this William Warren died in 1832, whereas *chestnut* only came into popular use about fifty years later, it is more likely to have been his son, William Warren, Jr., also a player of comedies, who died in 1888, who repeated Pablo's line.

arras

In English this is the name of a kind of tapestry richly woven with scenes and figures, and also of the hangings of this material which, in olden days, were hung around the walls of large rooms, often so spaced as to furnish concealment for an eavesdropper, a lover, or a knave The French call such material *tapisserie;* the English name is that of a town, Arras, in Artois, France, which was

47

famed for the excellence of tapestry of this nature produced there. (See also **tapestry.**)

earwig

As none of these insects has any interest whatever in wigs, why this curious name? The clue, nevertheless, lies in that second part.

For many, many centuries, popular superstition had it that the insect's chief aim in life was to enter the ear of any warm-blooded animal, chiefly man, and then by the aid of the pincerlike appendage at the end of its abdomen, bore its way into the brain—to *wiggle,* that is, through the inner ear into the brain. It doesn't do any such thing, of course, yet if we called it an "ear wiggler" the old popular notion would be self-explanatory. The scientific name is *Forficula auricularia*, Latin for "ear forceps" or "ear pincers."

upholstery

To uphold means, among other things, "to maintain, to preserve intact," and it was but a slight extension of this to arrive at "to keep in repair." It was in this latter sense that the word *upholder* was coined, to apply to one who dealt in the sale, manufacture, or repair of clothing and furniture. Such a person was also called an *upholdster* (which has the equal meaning of "one who upholds"), and, by elision of the hardly pronounceable *d,* this became an *upholster*. Hence the materials with which an upholster dealt were named *upholstery,* but by now with complete loss of any reference to clothing except occasionally in a figurative sense. Also, in the course of time, the noun *upholster* became obsolete, to be replaced by the longer *upholsterer*.

shambles

Suppose your wife (or mother) came home after two weeks of vacation in which you were left to shift for yourself, took one look

48

at the house, threw up her hands and exclaimed in dismay, "This place! It's a shambles!" Would you interpret her remark to mean: (1) "I don't know how, but you've turned everything into a footstool"; (2) "I see you've opened up a butchershop"; (3) "Have the stockyards expanded? How come our home is now a slaughterhouse?"; or (4) "You're a rotten housekeeper—the whole place is a mess!" Today, of course, meaning (4) would be the one she intended, but, strangely enough, at different times in history, any of the other interpretations would have been accurate, for this is the curious path that the word *shamble* (now usually in the plural form but with singular case) has taken. It all started with the Latin *scamellum,* "a footstool," the dimunitive form of *scamnum,* "a bench." Going through the Teutonic *scamel* and the Scandinavian *skamel,* it became the Anglo-Saxon *sceamel* (remember that the Scandinavian *sk* and the Anglo-Saxon *sc* had the value of *sh* in modern English), while retaining the meaning of "a low bench, footstool." This happened over a thousand years ago. Even before the Norman Conquest, the meaning began to change, having, by then, the sense of "a merchant's display counter," and by the fourteenth century it was specifically "a counter or shop for the sale of meat." Various spellings were used during this period, of course, and the *b* had been introduced probably during the fifteenth century. Before 1600 the meaning had been expanded to include "a slaughterhouse," or, figuratively, "a place of carnage," and the modern spelling had been evolved. The modern, milder meaning, of "a place in general disorder," is so recent that none but, perhaps, the most up-to-date dictionaries will be found to give this sense, although some fairly recent ones do give the sense just preceding this, i.e., "a place laid waste as by bombing."

petcock

None of the various word tracers has attempted to explain why the small shut-off valve was so named. Though a *cock,* it is distinctly no one's *pet.* Until someone turns up with a better explanation, I suggest that *pet* was merely a contraction of *petty* or *petit,* meaning "small, minor, inferior." An objection to this theory is that we have no record that the valve was ever known as a "petty cock"; it was *petcock* (or *pet-cock*) from the earliest printed use, around the mid-nineteenth century.

galosh

Seldom encountered but in the plural, *galoshes*. Nowadays it is rarely other than a rubber or rubberized-fabric overshoe, but in former days, extending back to ancient Greek times—yes, it's a very old term, though its antique form was then *kalopous*—it may have been of wood, like the French *sabot,* or a sandal with a wooden sole and leather upper, or even like the Mexican *huarache,* all of leather. Whatever the material, with us it's *galosh;* in France, *galoche;* in Spain and Portugal, *galocha;* and in Italy, *galoscia*.

shako

This time our modern word shows evidence of Hungarian influence, even though the ultimate derivation seems to be from the Germans. Starting with the German *Zacke,* "a peak," the trail leads next to the Hungarian *csákós suveg,* "a peaked cap." This became abbreviated to *csákó,* which was then taken into French as *schako,* and back into German as *Tschako,* still with the meaning of "a pointed cap." From the French, we took our word, dropping the *c,* but retaining the meaning. This was applied to a form of military headgear, which did, then, come to a point. Proving to be rather impractical as an item of battle dress, the point was flattened off, until now the military *shako* is a flat-topped hat best described as a truncated cone. The one-time peak is retained only symbolically by affixing a pompon or a plume at the front of the hat.

beachcomber

Lives there a man who hasn't at some time envied the *beachcomber,* that wastrel who, without a care in the world, strolled some beneficent Pacific isle, taking shelter from sun or storm under a broad tree, and deriving sustenance from plentiful vegetation and marine life, free for the taking? Such, at least, was the *beachcomber* of a century back; literally, one who combed the beach in carefree manner. More recently the term has taken on a sinister bent and denotes, perhaps, a person of low character who, on alien shores, makes his living through disreputable means.

fanfare

Nothing at all to do either with a fan or a fare, but, as still happens when we try to take a foreign word into our language, a

syllable or two got lopped off the original word, some three centuries ago, and the meaning was altered. That is, the original was the Spanish word *fanfarria,* meaning "bluster, presumption, haughtiness." And, because persons of that sort demand that notice be taken of them, their approach had to be announced by the blast of a trumpet or the like. So, in the progress of the Spanish term through French and into English, it came to mean the flourish of a trumpet or the call of a bugle or a noisy demonstration.

ultramontane

As the Church of Rome grew stronger, it acquired converts in many of the lands both near to and distant from Italy, including those in Europe to the north. And, of course, to retain these converts, it was necessary to appoint representatives in these countries who would represent the Church to the natives. Now, the north of Italy is bounded by mountains (the Alps), and it became the practice to refer to one of these representatives as *ultramontanus,* "one who is beyond the mountains," which is made up of the Latin *ultra,* "beyond," plus *mont-,* the combining form of *mons,* "mountain," together with a masculine personal suffix. The word (with suitable variations appropriate to the language) was taken into French as early as the fourteenth century, and also into Spanish, Portuguese, Italian, German, and Dutch. It entered English in the late sixteenth century, since which time there have been a number of minor variations in meaning. That now most commonly in use is "one who supports papal policy."

pernickety

We have not much to say about this; no one knows its ancestry. It is alleged to have been born in Scotland, chiefly, I'd say, because the earliest appearance in print so far noted was in the works of Scottish writers. But the date of such appearance was 1808, and that would scarcely account for the use of the term—or its variant, *persnickety,* as we used it in Ohio seventy years ago—in all parts of the United States. If of Scottish origin it must have been early enough to have been carried to America by emigrants in the first half of the eighteenth century.

xerography

A word of very recent coinage, dating only to about 1940, this, like most words in English having the initial *x,* is based on Greek roots. It is made up of the combining forms of *xeros,* "dry," and *graphein,* "to write," hence has the literal meaning of "dry writing." Although on an etymological basis it could be applied, therefore, to writing with a pencil rather than with ink, actually it is used exclusively in connection with a photographic process in which the latent image is formed as an electrostatic charge and is developed through the adhesion of a dry powder to the charged areas. This is in contrast to other photographic processes where the latent image is developed by processing with solutions of chemicals.

cheesecake

Though originally—fifteenth century and later—this denoted a cake or pie of light pastry containing cheese, the custardlike preparation used as filling by today's good cooks may or may not include cheese in the composition. But the modern product is delicious. And because it also delights the eye, users of American slang have applied the term, in recent years, to photographs featuring attractive feminine legs.

flabbergast

Someone whose identity will never be known dreamed this up about the year 1770. At least it was reported as a new word in 1772—"Now we are *flabbergasted* and *bored* [another new word] from morning to night." Possibly the inventor coined it by joining forcibly the two words *flabby* and *aghast,* but he left no notes to furnish a definite clue.

Jolly Roger

The earliest of pirates' flags was, when displayed, no more, likely, than a plain black sheet. Later some of the pirates began to embellish them with designs in white of grinning skull and crossbones, and by the mid-nineteenth century such was the general ensign. To the English, about the middle of the eighteenth century, the black flag of pirates became known as a *Roger* or, eventually, a *Jolly Roger.* No writer of the period gives a reason for such designation, so a guess may be in order. *Roger,* perhaps then pronounced with a hard *g,* among members of the underworld —the "canting crew," as they were called—had long been a term applied to a beggar or "rogue." *Jolly,* of course, meant "carefree." It would follow, therefore, that the *Jolly Roger* would represent the flag of carefree rogues. Please, however, this surmise has nothing to do with the reply "Roger!" used in radio communication to signify "Right! Received!" That is an arbitrary term for the letter *r,* derived from military signaling.

cuspidor

The "spit-box" and the "spittoon" were known early in the past century, the former usually containing sand or sawdust and more or less immovable, and the latter of earthenware or metal, small enough to be cleaned from time to time. They were reasonably necessary adjuncts to a saloon or club frequented by men who chewed tobacco. The euphemistic *cuspidor* (variantly spelled *cuspidore, cuspadore*) has had a vague and largely unrecorded history. The mighty *Oxford English Dictionary* has been able to trace its use to 1779, but the manner in which it was then used implies that it was already a well-known term. No further printed use has been recorded until 1871, when one Eugene A. Heath patented an "Improvement in Cuspadores (Cuspidores)" in both the United States and England. No dictionary printed in the interim includes the word, but Bartlett's *Dictionary of Americanisms,* 4th ed., published in 1877, does so. Since six years is usually much too short a time for a term not already in common use to become entered in a dictionary, there is a strong implication that it existed in the intervening century in the spoken, if not in the written, language. The derivation is commonly ascribed to the Portuguese *cuspir,* "to spit" (*cuspidor,* "one who spits"), from the Latin *conspuere,* "to spit into," but Mencken also notes a Dutch word, *kwispedoor,* or *kwispeldoor,* "a cuspidor," which he suggests may be the source of our English form. Only in Spanish do we find a close cognate which is probably also of the same common origin, *escupidera.*

stopgap

One of the many meanings of *to stop* is "to dam, to plug up," as in "to stop a leak," or "to stop a drain." And a *stopgap,* even in its modern sense of some temporary measure to fill a need, is, both literally and figuratively, something to "stop" a "gap."

shakedown

Shake, which comes ultimately from the Teutonic *skakan,* at one time during its life in our language had the meaning "move away from, travel, wander." From this sense it acquired the meaning of "take away without permission, steal." This, in turn, led to the coining of *shakedown* in the sense of extracting unwilling tribute, as may be practiced by those who exact "protection" payments from their inferiors. A *shakedown* cruise of a new ship, on the other hand, comes from the more modern sense of *shake,* "tremble, quiver." When grain, for instance, is measured out, rather than weighed, full measure is not obtained until the grain is literally *shaken down* in the container, in order that all the voids are filled as tightly as possible. In the case of the ship, the agitation due to the voyage fills the analogous function of bringing any faults to light.

hidebound

The literal sense related first to cattle which, under conditions of extreme emaciation resulting from disease, lost the fatty tissue normally lying under the skin. After death, then, the hide of any such animal cannot be loosened from the ribs or backbone. The condition, using this term, was first described in 1559. The figurative sense, however, is actually derived from the costive condition sometimes affecting some of us mortals, during which the skin seems to be rigidly constricted. From this condition those persons whose minds are firmly fixed, inelastic, cramped, of set and rigid opinion, are said to be *hidebound*.

Ferris wheel

It was first seen at the Columbian Exposition held in Chicago in 1893, the "World's Fair," and was the greatest attraction of all the  amusements then offered. No doubt larger ones have since been built, but this first one, rotating between two pyramids, was a framework of steel, 250 feet in diameter, and carried 36 cars, each capable of holding 40 passengers. It was designed by and named for George Washington Gale Ferris (1859–96), an engineer of Galesburg, Illinois.

battledore

This was originally a paddle-shaped wooden bat used by women as a mangle, or "beetle," for linens, back in the fifteenth century. There is no certainty as to the origin of the name, but it might then have been a play upon words—*battle* instead of *beetle,* and because *beetle* was also the name for a hard-sheathed insect for which another name was *dor* or *dore,* the two might have been combined humorously into *battledore.* Our ancestors enjoyed their jokes, too. The name also denoted a paddle for removing loaves from an oven or for propelling a canoe. And, when the game of rackets, subsequently called "battledore and shuttlecock," reached England in the sixteenth century, the name was applied to the racket, because of its shape.

flagstone

Among the four or five words spelled f-l-a-g recorded in your dictionary may be: (1) a banner; (2) a plant; (3) a wing feather of a bird; (4) a coin; (5) a flat slab of stone. And, though there are some differences of opinion, your dictionary may indicate that these *flags* are independent of one another, separate words from separate sources. It is the fifth that gives us *flagstone*. But this *flag,* possibly left by Norse invaders, originally referred to a slice of turf, a piece of sod. It is only through resemblance to such a slice of turf that a pavement stone is a *flagstone*.

hiccup

We say, somewhat fatuously, that this name is an echo of the sound, yet, strangely, the French idea of the same sound, written *hoquet,* is pronounced "aw'keh," and the Spanish idea, written *hipo,* is pronounced "ee'po." We also spell our term *hiccough,* though without affecting the pronunciation. Prior to the seventeenth century our English ancestors said *hicket,* more nearly representative of the actual sound, to my ears. And it is close to the Dutch *hikke,* Danish *hicke,* and Swedish *hicka.*

thimblerig

The trick may have been practiced in the time of the Pharaohs; if not, probably some variant of it was. Certainly someone then knew that the hand is quicker than the eye. In England it was known as "the thimble trick" two and a half centuries ago, and then, as now, the trickster at horserace or fair would exhibit a pea and three thimbles or small cups, then, at first with modest wager, challenge a bystander to guess under which thimble he had hidden the pea. A hundred years later, when *rig* became a slang term for "to cheat or trick," our present word came into use, and it was, of course, a simple step to transfer the application to any form of trickery or jugglery.

sesquipedalian

It was the Roman poet Horace who coined this very long adjective that is used to define a word that is very long. It appears in line 97 of one of the last of his works, published shortly before his death in 8 B.C., the *Epistle to the Pisos,* better known as *Ars Poetica* (The Poetic Art):

> *Et tragicus plerumque dolex sermone pedestri*
> *Telephus et Peleus, cum pauper et excul, uterque*
> *Projicit ampullas, et sesquipedalia verba,*
> *Si curat cor spectantis tetigisse querela*

I am indebted to Miss Dorothy Gardner for assistance with the translation, of which the following is a free rendition into verse:

> *By use of ponderous speech to tell each tragic part*
> *Did Telephus, the pauper, and Peleus, outcast,*
> *Attempt to touch with grief the watcher's kindred heart,*
> *Emitting yard-long words and spouting forth bombast.*

Literally, *sesquipedalian* means "a-foot-and-a-half long," from *sesqui-,* "one-and-one-half," and *pedalis,* "foot-long," from *pes,* "a foot." Figuratively, and it is in this sense that Horace coined it, the word is entirely equivalent to our *yard-long, block-long, mile-long,* etc., which we use to express an indeterminate length that is substantially more than is necessary, or than is expected. Miss Gardner also points out to me that the Greeks anticipated us here, too, with terms such as *amaxiaia remata,* "words large enough for a wagon."

pennyroyal

Somewhere along the line someone with a cleft palate or a mouthful of mush must have been responsible for this word. Its Latin name, in the thirteenth century was *pulegium,* corrupted along with French usage to *puliol.* To distinguish it from wild thyme, *rial,* "royal," was added. But then, along in the sixteenth century, Mr. Mushmouth came along, and through means that have not yet been figured out, managed to induce people to alter *puliol* to *penny,* thus educing *pennyroyal,* as the alteration of *rial* to *royal* followed natural steps. In France it's still *pouliot.*

thespian

Some two and a half millenniums ago—specifically, in the sixth century B.C.—there lived a Greek playwright whose name was Thespis. None of his plays or poems have lived to the present, and his name is remembered almost entirely because of the generally accepted view that it was he who invented the Greek tragedy. From his name the adjective *thespian* was coined to describe, first, a tragic play, then, a tragic actor. By now the word is used as a name for any actor, tragic or otherwise.

fiddler crab

It is also known just by the simpler name, *fiddler.* The reason? Merely because it brandishes its outsize larger claw in a manner suggestive of the action of a violinist handling his bow.

Argus-eyed

Extraordinarily vigilant. This, too, comes from Greek mythology. The goddess Hera, wife of the supreme god Zeus, jealous of his affection for the nymph Io, turned her into a cow and then appointed Argus, possessed of a hundred eyes and able to see in all directions, as guardian and caretaker. Notwithstanding this precaution, Zeus had his messenger, Hermes, kill the hundred-eyed Argus, whose eyes were thereupon transferred to the tail of the peacock.

fizgig

Chaucer and other early writers called a frivolous or giddy girl a *gig,* and such was indeed slang usage even to the eighteenth

58

century. So, presumably because she seemed to fizz or sputter as she ran gadding about, such a girl or woman became a *fysgygge,* as it appeared in sixteenth-century spelling. Since then varied meanings have been applied, all associated in one way or another with *fizz.*

barnstormer

He did not take barns by storm, as a soldier might; he merely did his storming in barns—his furious dramatic declamations. He was an actor, that is, or one who would be. He was one of the large number of second-rate itinerant players who roamed the countryside in bands, giving a play wherever they could attract an audience. Dickens describes such a troupe in *Nicholas Nickleby.* Whenever a proper theater was not available, they made shift in a barn. It was not until about the mid-nineteenth century, however, that *barnstormer* was applied to such an actor. Late in the century the term was also applied to any American political speaker making a rapid campaign tour to arouse the electorate in his behalf.

jolly boat

Chances are that the members of the crew handling one of these rarely were, if ever, rollicking or gayhearted. It is, or was, a workboat, one used formerly around sailing vessels, chiefly in harbors, in carrying out errands in small duties about the ship. It was, in fact, a yawl of small size, the source of the name being the Danish *jolle,* "yawl." Another of the numerous instances of English mispronunciation of alien words.

dewclaw, dewlap

Though the names of different parts of animal anatomy, the terms may have, in part, a common explanation. That is, the *dew-claw* is that rudimentary inner claw, sometimes present in dogs, which hangs loosely in the skin above the other toes and which brushes, not the soil, but only against the "dew" on the grass. Similarly, the *dewlap* of cattle, dogs, or turkeys is the *lap* or fold of skin hanging loosely under the throat, and which, some say, brushes against the "dew" on the grass. In this latter term, however, others think that the element *dew* is a corruption of some word that can no longer be traced.

serendipity

Perhaps the best definition that I've heard for this is that "Serendipity is the art of finding what you're not looking for." This agrees pretty well with the explanation of Horace Walpole, who coined the word in 1754 after reading the old fairytale *The Three Princes of Serendip*. Walpole wrote that these princes "were always making discoveries, by accidents and sagacity, of things they were not in quest of." Even though Walpole, in coining the word, made quite clear the meaning he intended it to have, Bernard E. Schaar has conducted research into the matter that convinces him the princes were being maligned (New York *World Telegram & Sun*, Sept. 10, 1957). He is convinced, after close study of the fairytale, that the princes of Serendip (now known as Ceylon) were highly educated, and that their seemingly fortuitous discoveries were no more accidental than are the wondrous results achieved by today's highly trained scientific investigators, whose very training leads them to recognize the worth of an experimental result even when the experiment does not proceed according to plan.

wormwood

Nothing to do either with worms or with wood, the word is an alteration, adopted beginning in the fifteenth century, of the earlier *wermod*, which is found in eighth-century Anglo-Saxon. It is known that the Teutonic *wer*, in other applications, means "man," and that *mod* is an ancestor of *mood* with the meaning of "courage." On this basis, it has been suggested that the herb was named "man's courage" in reference to its medicinal or aphrodisiac qualities. The word, incidentally, has been traced to the Old High German *wermota*, which has come down to modern German as *Wermut* (pronounced *vehr-moot*) and which, in turn, became the French *vermouth*.

banister (baluster)

"Over the banister leans a face," sang the poet, little knowing perhaps, the true poetry of his song. *Banister,* you see, is a careless mispronunciation of *baluster,* introduced about three hundred years ago. And *baluster,* the proper word, was formed from Greek *balaustion,* which was originally the term for a specific flower. Our poet thus sang, in effect, "Over the flower of the wild pomegranate leans a face, Tenderly soft and beguiling." Greek architects used the outlines of these flowers—doubly curved, slender above and bulging below—for series of short pillars supporting handrails or copings, thus giving us the modern sense.

figurehead

It was ornamental only, usually carved (from wood) into the figure or bust of a person, sometimes quite imposing, and it was  placed beneath the bowsprit at the very bow of a ship, directly above the cutwater. Thus, most grandly, it led the vessel. Whatever the country, wherever the port, it was in the fore. But it had no function. However beautiful the carving, however emblematic the design, the vessel could have been handled just as well without it. And so it is with him or her who accepts an appointment or position that carries neither duties nor responsibilities. The imposing name of such a figurative *figurehead* lends prestige to the enterprise or organization.

johnnycake

I wish it were possible to tell with certainty why this New England corn pone is so named, but all accounts are tinged with speculation. The present name was in use early in the eighteenth century, and, though some folks did speak of the same rather durable ration as *journey-cake,* it is much more probable that *johnny* preceded *journey* than the reverse. However, some fifty or sixty years earlier than our first record of *johnnycake,* New England housewives were serving what was then called *Jonakin* or *Jonikin* to their households. Susan F. Cooper, many years later, described these as "thin, wafer-like sheets, toasted on a board . . . eaten at breakfast, with butter." Dr. M. M. Mathews, in *Dictionary of Americanisms,* suggests the possibility of a relationship between *Jonakin* and *johnnycake.*

chowderheaded

Here's a curious bit of slang traceable back more than four hundred years, though, like much current slang, the earliest term cannot be explained. *Chowder* here does not denote a stew; it's just a mispronunciation of *cholter,* for *cholter-headed* was the form that began to appear in the early nineteenth century. But that, which made no sense either, was a corruption of *jolter-headed,* used through the previous century, and, in turn, it was derived from the earliest form, *jolthead.* Heaven knows the source of that, but it, too, meant a blockhead, a stupid or clumsy person.

seneschal

The final syllable rhymes with the second syllable of *marshal.* *Seneschal* has had an odd history. It comes into English in its present form from the French word of the same spelling, but it originated with the Old Teutonic *seniscalc,* "senior servant," from the roots *seni-,* "old," and *skalk,* "servant" (the pronunciation of the *sk* in *skalk* was probably similar to that of the *sk* in the modern Scandinavian languages, or roughly similar to *sh* in modern English). The word was taken into the Romance languages generally, with suitable modifications of spelling, and was even Latinized (*siniscalcus*), being finally adopted back into modern German in the form *Seneschall.* The functions of a seneschal are quite similar to those of the major-domo—both are in charge of the retinue of house servants. *Marshal* has had a very closely similar history. The second part of the word has the same derivation as the above, and the first part is from the Teutonic *marah,* "mare." The antecedent of a mare was, originally, any horse, or even, specifically, a stallion, our word having been derived from the feminine form of the original. So a *marshal,* at least by the origin of the word, was literally a horse servant, a groom, or stable boy.

joe-pye weed

Legend hath it that this common tall weed of New England, blossoming with purple flowers in late summer, was so named "from an Indian of that name, who cured typhus fever with it, by copious perspiration," in the phrasing of the botanist Constantine S. Rafinesque in 1828. Though that legend has been repeated over and over again by subsequent botanists, its veracity has been questioned in recent years by hard-headed fact finders. Since typhus has been known by that name only since 1785, when and where was this cure effected? To what New England tribe did this Indian of curious name belong?

Probably the entire story will now never be uncovered, but, writing in *The Scientific American* (vol. 61, 1945), "On the Fable of Joe Pye," anthropologist F. G. Speck and librarian Ernest S. Dodge tell of learning through old diaries of the existence of a Joseph Pye, alias Shauqueathquat, in 1787, and, from other evidence, advance the possibility that he was a descendent of the original Joe Pye, a medicine man probably living near Salem, Massachusetts, in colonial times.

wishbone

The little innocent game was probably known to Shakespeare—that where two people break the fork-shaped breastbone of a fowl while making a wish. And, of course, it was the act of *wishing* upon a *bone* that resulted in this name for, in technical language, the bone known as the *furcula.* But the name *wishbone* seems to be an Americanism, and it dates only about to the middle of the nineteenth century. The much older British name is *merrythought,* undoubtedly because of the merry thoughts that take place during the wishing game, especially if the two people playing are of opposite sexes. Incidentally, the technical name, *furcula,* is the dimunitive of the Latin *furca,* "a two-pronged fork."

John Barleycorn

This legendary gentleman, sometimes styled Sir John Barleycorn, was apparently conceived about the year 1620. That we gather from the use of the name as a title to "A pleasant new ballad . . . of the bloody murther of Sir John Barleycorn," of that period. And the gentleman, if so he was, was even then a personification of malt liquor, or the grain of which it was made. But it is not likely that his name would still be known were it not for Robert Burns. "Inspiring bold John Barleycorn," he wrote in "Tam o' Shanter," "What dangers thou canst make us scorn!" See also his poem "John Barleycorn."

barefaced

Bottom, in *Midsummer Night's Dream,* has suggested that he play the part of Pyramus in a "French-crowne colour'd beard, your perfect yellow," and Quince replies, "Some of your French Crownes haue no haire at all, and then you will play bare-fac'd." The meaning is thus clear, "having no hair upon the face, beardless." Because it is the stripling or boy who is beardless, and because the stripling or boy is usually bold, impudent, shameless, or audacious, the latter is now the usual use. For example, Dickens has the beadle, Mr. Bumble, say to Oliver Twist, who pleads not to be apprenticed into the "chimbley-sweepin' bisness," "Well, of all the artful and designing orphans that ever I see, Oliver, you are one of the most bare-facedest."

sedan

This is a curious example of a word for which the true etymology is not known with certainty, yet for which many authorities have proposed almost as many possible derivations. The only item upon which there is relative unanimity is that the sedan, an enclosed chair seating one person and carried by bearers, was introduced into England in 1634 by Sir Sanders Duncombe, it having been brought from Italy. Dr. Samuel Johnson began the guessing by suggesting that the name was taken from the town of Sedan in northern France, but modern authorities find nothing to support this, even though the 1864 edition of Webster's dictionary cites this as an alleged derivation. The *Oxford English Dictionary* hazards the guess that the word may be derived from the Latin *sedes,* "seat," through the Italian *sedere,* "to sit," but admits the etymology is obscure. The 1941 printing of *Webster's New International Dictionary,* 2nd. ed., offers the observation that the word comes from the Latin *sella,* "chair, saddle," through the Spanish *sillón,* "armchair, side-saddle." The 1946 revision of the *New Standard Dictionary* takes an entirely different slant, proposing that the word is a play upon the first five letters of Sir Sanders' given name, with transposition of the *de,* reversed, ahead of the *an.* About equally plausible would be the suggestion which, so far as I know, has not been advanced before: that Sir Sanders was one of those given to spelling names backward, did so with his name (*srednas*), and, to get a pronounceable word, eliminated the *r* and reversed the *na,* finally dropping the last *s* to avoid the appearance of a plural.

forecastle

Now it is merely the forward and, usually, raised part of a ship; the part, below the deck, where the sailors live. That still explains

fore, but the *castle* section has become so completely obsolete that, indeed, anyone pronouncing the entire word other than "fo'ksl" labels himself immediately as a landlubber. But in the fourteenth and later centuries that forward part of a vessel used in naval warfare served as a floating fortress or *castle.* By its eminence the captain could command the decks of an enemy, and through embrasures in its parapet, shot could be directed.

hellgrammite

This must have started as an Indian name, though if so no one as yet has succeeded in figuring it out. Undoubtedly the name was in wide use long before his time, but present records indicate its first appearance in print in a July, 1866, issue of the publication *Wilkes' Spirit of the Times,* by the American explorer Admiral Charles Wilkes, who wrote thus: "There is another bait for bass called *kill devil*—a sort of indescribable Barnum-what-is-it thing, about three inches in length. An old friend of mine denominated them hell gramites." Other names are *dobson* and *grampus.* They are the larvae of the large four-winged insect, the dobson fly or *Corydalis cornutis.*

tête-à-tête

This adverbial phrase, implying an intimate conversation, is a direct lift from the French, and has the literal meaning "head-to-head." The phrase has been given both adjectival and noun uses in English as applied to chairs so designed as to permit the exchange of confidences, meals served for two persons, and the like. It is interesting to note that the French *tête,* "head," has no relation whatever to the Latin *caput,* "head," as would be expected, but instead is derived (through the Old French *teste*) from the Latin *testa,* "a pot," a slang term for "head."

devil's-darning-needle

The common name in the United States of the dragonfly (which see). We abridge it sometimes to *darning-needle,* and, a hundred years ago, Thoreau and others spoke of the insect as *devil's-needle.* The name is fairly obvious: large staring eyes which remind one of Satan himself, and an extremely slender and long body, not unlike a needle.

windjammer

The earliest use of this term in English is reported to have been in the 1870's, with the meaning of "a horn player." It seems probable that the nickname was coined from the German word for *wind,* which has the same spelling, and from the German verb *jammer* (pronounced *yahmmer,* and from which we get the English *yammer*), which means "to moan, cry, wail." Hence the horn player, who might seem to an unappreciative hearer to be making moaning or wailing sounds with his wind, was given the slang name of *windjammer*. The next oldest use in English is the meaning "a talkative person, blowhard, windbag," and since such a one, too, is making noises with his wind, this meaning seems to be a logical extension of the first. But the most common meaning in English today, which dates from the very last of the nineteenth century, is "a sailing vessel or one of its crew." Here we can only suppose that, in the great rivalry between steam and sail, the men of the sailing ships bragged so loudly of the merits of sail that the supporters of steamships tacked onto them this term, from where it was transferred to the ships as well.

bandoline

Could be that under another name this hair dressing is in use today. It was a sticky aromatic ointment used by dandies of a century back for keeping hair smooth and mustache waxed and pointed and it was made from the boiled pips of the quince. Later it was also used in the making of jellies and soups. The name was probably coined from the French *bandeau*, "band" or "fillet," and Latin *linere*, "to anoint."

subtle

Light as a feather—or better, thin as gossamer. Either of these expressions describes fairly accurately the gentleness which is characteristic of true subtlety, but "gossamer" is a close translation of the Latin word from which *subtle* originates. *Subtle* was brought into English from the Old French *soutil* (alternately spelled *sotil* or *sutil*) with the meaning of "thin (rarefied), fine, delicate." But the French word came from the Latin *subtilis,* a contraction of *subtexilis,* "finely woven" (literally, "underwoven"), from *sub,* "under," and *texare,* "to weave." For many years an alternate spelling of the English word, *subtile,* existed in parallel with the presently accepted spelling, this being based directly on the Latin ancestor.

jimjams

Maybe you think *jimjams* is a new word. Well, in the plural form, it is—relatively so, though it dates back about sixty years. But as a singular it goes back four hundred years. A rhymester of that period wrote:

> *These be as knappishe knackes* [*knick-knacks*]
>   *As ever man made,*
> *For iavells* [*rascals*] *and for iackes* [*jacks*],
>   *A iymiam for a iade* [*jimjam for a jade*].

But from some fantastic trifle, as the slang term then meant, when resurrected sixty years ago it was in the sense of fantastic manners, peculiarities of behavior. And, pray tell, what manner of behavior is more peculiar than that of one overcome by continued overindulgence in spirituous liquor? So *jimjams* became synonymous with delirium tremens. Always seeking novelty of expression, generally ephemeral, we Americans often substitute such variations as *jimwillies,* or just *jimmies,* or even *willies.*

dead horse

Undoubtedly there was once a pathetic story about a poor man who, painfully, saved enough money to make a down payment on a horse that he greatly desired to help him till his land; the sad part being that the horse died long before the buyer had made enough to pay the remainder of his debt, demanded by the seller. Hence the expression, known for two hundred years, "paying for a dead horse." But alas, the story is now entirely hypothetical. No one knows what the original tale may have been.

scalawag

The word, which seems to be a true Americanism, has had several other spellings, the most common of which is *scallywag,* but *scalawag* seems to be the original and, today, is the one most favored. It was first recorded by John Russell Bartlett in the first edition (1848) of his *Dictionary of Americanisms,* in which he defined it as "a favorite epithet in western New York for a mean fellow; a scape-grace." In his fourth edition (1877) he says, "A *scalawag* has been defined to be, 'like many other wags, a compound of loafer, blackguard, and scamp.'" Although many authorities have speculated on the probable origin of this term, with little agreement, I find what seems to be a significant entry in Elwyn's *Glossary of Supposed Americanisms* (1859), wherein he says, "*Scaly,* for a shabby, mean person, is our New England word." Thus, considering the contributions of Bartlett and Elwyn together, and bearing in mind the close proximity of New England and New York, there seems to be an excellent chance that a *scalawag* was. at first, a *scaly wag,* or, in modern parlance, a "crumb bum."

Frankenstein

In 1818, Mary Wollstonecraft Shelley, wife of the poet, Percy Bysshe Shelley, published her first novel. It dealt with the super-

natural, though bearing the noncommittal title *Frankenstein, or the Modern Prometheus.* It was a story telling about a young Swiss student, Victor Frankenstein, who found a way to create life artificially and who, eventually, constructed a body in human form and endowed it with life. But he had no way to imbue it with a soul. Without that controlling element the monster was abhorrent to all whom he would make his mate, and when Frankenstein, his creator, refused to create a mate, he took revenge by murdering, first, Frankenstein's friend, and then his brother, his bride, and finally Frankenstein himself. The book became very popular, but, unfortunately, Mrs. Shelley had not thought to give the creature a name. Hence, readers and others who wished to refer to it acquired the habit of using the title of the book instead. The consequence is that *Frankenstein* has been often applied to any agency of whatever nature that brings about harm or ruin to its proponent or its creator.

penny-a-liner

Always used contemptuously of writers who write to fill space, who use many words but say little. It was applied originally to journalists of the early nineteenth century who, paid at space rates, padded their copy with all the bombast it would bear. With all due respect to the lovers of Dickens there are many, many pages in some of his novels which lead one to suspect that he was, at times, an accomplished *penny-a-liner*.

terrier

Hunting dogs are used for different purposes, according to their several natures, and the peculiar property that distinguishes the class of *terriers* is their ability to dig out burrowing animals from their lairs. It is this earth-moving attribute that has given the class its name. An old name was *terrier dog,* which is a half-translation of the French *chien terrier*. If fully translated, we would have had *burrow dog,* for the French word *terrier* has the meaning "a burrow, a hole in the ground." It comes from their *terre,* "earth," which is from the Latin *terra,* "earth."

argosy

A merchant vessel, especially one richly laden. The term dates to the sixteenth century, to a period when such vessels plied a brisk trade with England from a certain port in Italy. That port was Ragusa (now in Yugoslavia and called Dubrovnik). A ship hailing therefrom was, of course, "a Ragusa," a term rapidly degenerating in dockside language into "a Ragusy," and hence to *argosy*. In *The Merchant of Venice* Shakespeare has:

> *There where your Argosies with portly saile*
> *Like Signiors and rich Burgers on the flood*
> *Or as it were the Pageants of the sea,*
> *Do ouer-peere the pettie Traffiquers*
> *That curtsie to them, do them reuerence*
> *As they flye by them with their wouen wings.*

bandog

Dictionaries for the collegiate trade, slavishly following one another, continue to carry this term, though, except in the works of Sir Walter Scott, a student might never run across it. It simply means a dog, usually a large one such as a mastiff, that is kept tied—*band* here being used in the sense of that which binds, a strap, chain or the like. The word used to be spelled, more properly, *band-dog*. Scott contracted it to *bandog* and so it remains.

saturnine

The planet Saturn was named after the Roman god of the same name, but any symbolic similarity ends there. For Saturn, the god, was feasted with unrestrained merrymaking, and we still recall these riotous feasts in our term *Saturnalia*. On the other hand, Saturn, the planet, was the seventh and most remote planet known to ancient astronomers, and this remoteness was presumed to confer a cold and gloomy attitude upon those under its influence. In sharp contrast to the gay Saturnalia, then, we have the adjective *saturnine*, "gloomy, dull."

haversack

Just think, as far as original meaning is concerned, this soldier's carryall might just as properly have been called a "gunny sack." That is, the original German term was *haber sack*, literally "sack for oats," and it referred especially to the bag, usually of canvas, in which a cavalryman carried oats for his mount. French and English cavalry adopted both bag and name, with slight alteration, and, naturally, found the bags convenient for holding personal items in moving from place to place. And so did other travelers, the flexible *haversack*, with strap over the shoulder, being easier to carry than is the modern suitcase, though perhaps less commodious.

charwoman

In the United States she would be called a Martha-by-the-day; a general houseworker; cleaning woman; mother's helper; or, perhaps, housemaid or maid. We're not familiar, that is, with *char* or *chare* as a synonym for *chore,* "a piece of work, an odd job," applied especially to any of the multitudinous small tasks involved in household labor. But such feminine laborers have been *charwomen* in England for some four hundred years.

galligaskin

Although Noah Webster tried hard to determine the sources of words included in his dictionary of the English language, a hundred-odd years ago, he went far astray  at times. And this term, rarely used in America but formerly common in England, was an instance. It is the name of the wide, very loose breeches worn in the sixteenth and seventeenth centuries. The intrepid Webster said that the name came about because "these trowsers were first worn by the *Gallic Gascons,* i.e., the inhabitants of Gascony." But it is really a greatly perverted form of Old French *garguesque,* which meant, "after the fashion of the Greeks," referring to a style of Greek nether garment.

tenterhooks

When cloth is fabricated, it is necessary or desirable to stretch the piece in order to even out the threads and to make the material straight. Before the development of modern machine methods, whereby this is accomplished in the mill as a part of the routine of manufacture, it was the practice to stretch the fabric on frames, usually out of doors, which frames were known as *tenters.* The frames were fitted with pins or hooks to hold the cloth, and these were, of course, *tenterhooks.* The precise derivation of *tenter* is not well established, but it is fairly certain that it comes, eventually, from the Latin *tendere,* "to stretch," through the French. *To be on tenterhooks* is, literally, "to be stretched torturously, to be on the rack," hence, figuratively, "to be subjected to agony approaching that of torture."

72

heirloom

Sad might you be if told that, as heir to your grandfather's estate, the only things you would receive after all taxes were paid would be "all my various *looms*," but it might be far better than you think. The old gentleman may have been testing your knowledge of Scottish or northern English dialect and used an old, old meaning that survives only in those areas. A *loom*, that is, might just possibly include the mechanical device used for weaving, but in its earliest meaning a thousand years ago it included all implements, tools, and household items of any kind, everything other than real estate. Such were the original *heirlooms*, but that sense has long since been lost and the term has degenerated into a coverall for any item of whatever nature that has been in a family for two or more generations.

quacksalver

Known in our language for some four hundred years, the term nevertheless was soon felt to be unmanageably long and was reduced to *quack*, with which we are more familiar today. The *quacksalver* was originally an unscrupulous or false physician, one who *quacked* (hawked, or bragged of) his *salves* (ointments). Today, the quack is any charlatan, though still often a make-believe or unethical medical doctor. The word is supposed to have come to us from the Dutch, but the ultimate origin is in considerable doubt, as the same term, with suitable modifications in spelling, is known widely throughout the Germanic languages.

lollipop, lollypop

Travelers in England must have, at least, known of this confection, for it has been familiar to English children, and perhaps their parents, for more than a hundred and fifty years. But to the best of my knowledge and belief it remained unknown to American children until the early twentieth century, perhaps about 1910. Be that as it may, however, the sad fact remains that the origin of the name is a deep dark mystery, though it may somehow have been related to the dialectal word *lolly,* sometimes used in northern England to mean "tongue."

satire

Not too long ago, an inept actor or group of actors might have been driven off the stage by being pelted with an assortment of fruits and vegetables thrown by the disgruntled audience. If the play were a satirical one, the object of the satire would, figuratively, also have been the recipient of the barrage, for *satire* is indirectly derived from the Latin *lanx satura,* "a full dish"—that is, a dish composed of several sorts of food, a potpourri. Dropping the dish (*lanx*), *satura* came to have the meaning of a medley, or more specifically, a short play with a great variety of subject material. Along the way, the spelling became *satira,* and the play developed into a critical commentary. Finally, with the same meaning, the word was adopted into English with its present spelling.

dauphin

As this is French for "dolphin," one may be excused for the thought that its use (from 1349–1830) as the title of the eldest son of the King of France was in playful jest. That was not so. It was originally the title of the lords of the province of Dauphiné, the last of whom, dying childless, bequeathed his possessions to Philip of Valois, with the proviso that his title should pass continuously to the heir to the throne.

hedgehog

This is one of the European members of the porcupine family. Or rather, it is the English name of that member, as its French name is *hérisson,* which might be translated "bristler," and its German name is *Igel*. But despite the *hog* part of the name, neither it nor the porcupine is remotely related to the porcine or swine species of the animal kingdom; *hog* refers merely to the swinelike appearance of the snout. And in England it makes its home chiefly among the hedgerows bordering the roadsides; hence the name. As for the *porcupine,* its name seems to be a highly corrupted form of the Latin *porcus spinosus,* "thorny pig."

gargoyle

Architects and masons of the thirteenth century certainly had an odd sense of humor. Obviously it was their duty to provide  means whereby rainwater should be diverted away from the walls immediately below the roof of cathedral or other imposing edifice. So expert workers in stone were set to carve spouts for this purpose. And these sculptors undoubtedly vied with one another to think up and effect fanciful concepts, thoroughly practical, but also agreeably ornamental, and, often, highly amusing. Many of these were grotesque animals in form; another might be in the shape of a demon; others, perhaps, angels; and another a monk or prelate. But whatever might be represented in stone, all spewed forth streams of water from throat and mouth during a fall of rain. French for "throat" at that period was *gargouille,* giving rise to our English *gargoyle,* by which we know these monstrous carvings.

unmentionables

Prudery is always with us, only the subjects about which we are prudish vary. Often it is difficult—even impossible—for a later generation to understand the reason for some particular prudery of its ancestors. Toward the end of the eighteenth century, for example, it became impolite to mention the words *trousers* or *breeches.* Since it was obviously necessary to refer at times to these ubiquitous garments, various euphemistic terms were coined for the purpose, and *trousers* became *inexpressibles, inexplicables, ineffables,* or *unmentionables.* Later, when *trousers* regained its standing in polite society, it became imprudent to talk about undergarments, especially women's undergarments, and these became *unmentionables.* Modern advertising practice has, by now, pretty well removed all traces of prudery, at least with respect to items of clothing, leaving *unmentionables* without definite standing at present.

sucker

Literally, "one who or that which sucks." In this sense, one application is to the not-yet-weaned young of any animal, and it is this application that has led to the figurative meaning of "dupe, simpleton." For the greenhorns, those "not yet dry behind the ears," are by this term endowed with the ingenuousness and naïveté that are presumably characteristic of a babe too young to be removed from his mother's breast.

Charterhouse

This is the name of one of the great public schools of London. But whether or not the institution has a charter, the fact has no bearing on its name. Its site was originally that of a Carthusian monastery, an order which derives its name from that of the French village where it first arose. That village was La Grande Chartreuse. Its early English spelling was *Chartrous*. Combined with the fact that the monastery then bore the French name, *maison Chartreuse,* "Carthusian house," the Londoners quite naturally amplified *Chartrouse* into *Charterhouse*.

fifty-fifty

In equal amounts: an Americanism which, since early in the twentieth century, has had the contracted meaning of 50 per cent for you (or one person) and 50 per cent for me (or another person).

Charles's Wain

The wain—four-wheeled wagon—of Charles the Great, and this is the name applied by some, even back around the year 1000, to the constellation, the Great Bear, *Ursa Major,* the Big Dipper.

To some eyes, that is, the bowl of the Dipper had the appearance of the huge wagons of old, the stars in the handle being the long shaft. And, of course, no greater man ever lived worthy of such a wain than Charlemagne, Charles the Great. Tennyson, in "New Year's Eve," has the line, "Till Charles's Wain came out above the tall white chimney-tops."

sarcastic

True sarcasm wounds the one against whom it is directed as deeply as though it were the flesh rather than the spirit receiving the attack. The Greeks recognized this, and invented an appropriate metaphor. From the word *sarx,* "flesh," they had already coined *sarkazein,* "to tear the flesh in the manner of a dog." And from this they invented *sarkastikos,* "bitterly cutting, caustic," or, exactly, *sarcastic.*

willy-nilly

Many years ago there existed, in Old English, a verb that was the negative of *will,* "to desire, to be in an acceptable or purposeful frame of mind." This verb of negation was *nill,* "to be unwilling, not to will." It is known to have existed as early as the ninth century in Anglo-Saxon, and its use continued in good standing until about the first of the seventeenth century. Since then it has become obsolete or archaic except as it has been used specifically in conjunction with *will* in one of several expressions signifying known futility. These expressions have included such combinations as *willing . . . nilling; will I, nill I; will ye, nill ye; will he, nill he* (sometimes in the reverse order), all of which imply that "such a thing will be, or will happen, regardless of the desires of the person affected." All these forms have now been contracted into the single expression of futility which is our *willy-nilly.*

bandbox

This box had nothing to do with a company of musicians, as I thought when a very young child. But, back in the seventeenth century, it was a box of thin wood—chip, it was called—in which lords and ladies kept the very wide collars or "bands" of lace or plain linen that were then in vogue. When starched to stand up, they were simply "bands," but when extending flat across the shoulders and down the chest, they were called "falling bands." Our Puritan forebears are depicted with small plain falling bands, and the clerical collar of today owes its origin to that band.

gremlin

He was born during the early stages of World War II, sired by British aviators, but otherwise of uncertain parentage, though  possibly from the womb of the Irish term *gruaimin,* "an ill-natured runt." He was very small, though wholly invisible. And it was his delight to ride in anyone's airplane and perform mischievous tricks upon engine, wings, gun, propeller, flaps, or other part, unaccountable but most annoying or disastrous to the flyer. He was just some sort of goblin who resented man's use of the air for the waging of warfare.

strait-laced

Often, because of the similar pronunciation, misspelled "straightlaced." The first element was *streit* in Middle English, having been introduced in about the fourteenth century. It came from the Old French *estreit,* "tight, close, narrow," and similar words (Spanish *estrecho,* Portuguese *estreito,* Italian *stretto*) are to be found in the other Romance languages. All are derived from the Latin *strictus,* the past participle of *stringere,* "to tighten, bind tightly." *Lace* came in to the languge at about the same time, also from the French (*lacier*) from the Latin *laciare,* "to ensnare." Here, too, there are closely related words in the other Romance languages. The two words have been found together as early as 1430 in their literal significance of "tightly laced," but the compound term is not found until the sixteenth century. It was about at the same time that the figurative use of the term became established, for the strictures laid upon the body through the tight lacing of the bodice were quickly seen to be closely similar to those laid upon one's conduct through what seemed to be excessive prudishness.

cutpurse

The pocket as an ordinary adjunct of man's outer attire is not very old, dating back only a few centuries. Before that time anything that a man carried with him had to be in his hands or hung about his person. And money was just as necessary an evil then as it is now. And, being gold or silver, it was heavy and difficult to conceal. Such coins were customarily carried in leather pouches or purses hanging from one's girdle. What could be simpler than for three or four ruffians to jostle the wearer while one of the number cut the purse and released the coins, or for a deft hand to cut the cord by which it hung? The penalty for detection, however, was severe. Thereafter a *cutpurse* was marked by the absence of one or both ears.

harlot

An old dictionary in my possession, Thomas Blount's *Glossographia* (1656), has this to say of the origin of this word: "Metonymically"—a word used as a substitute for another—"from *Arlotta* and *Harlotha,* Concubine to *Robert* Duke of Normandy, on whom he begat *William* the Bastard, Conqueror, and King of *England;* in spight to whom, and disgrace to his Mother, the English called all Whores Harlots." But, though an interesting story, it was taken by Blount from a piece of vague guesswork made by another writer a hundred years earlier, William Lambarde. The word is actually a modification of Old French *harlot,* used in such a manner as we use "fellow."

tenderfoot

First appeared in the literal sense of "having tender feet," as applied to horses, and recorded in this sense in the late seventeenth century, in England, as the adjective *tenderfooted.* The use of the word as applied to a person is conceded to be an Americanism, and probably arose also in the literal sense, referring to one who, unused to traveling, became footsore. However, the earliest recorded use of the word is not in this literal meaning, but in the figurative one of "a greenhorn, a novice." This meaning has been dated to as early as 1849, and was popularized by the emigrants to California in the gold rush of that time. A slightly earlier use (1842) of the adjective in the sense of "timid" has also been found in American usage, but this sense has not survived.

pell-mell

Authorities disagree here. Some have it that, of Old French origin, this was a combination of *pesle,* a "shovel," and *mesle,* "to mix." Hence, "mixed as with a shovel." But others, though agreeing with the source of the second element, take it that *pell* was never more than a reduplication. The French coiners, back in the twelfth century, are not telling. It was widely borrowed by English writers of the sixteenth century, used by Shakespeare in *Henry IV,* Part I (Act V, Scene i): "Nor moody Beggars, staruing for a time Of pell-mell hauocke, and confusion."

jew's-harp

As far as has yet been ascertained, no Jew had anything to do with the introduction of this so-called musical instrument into England, with its naming, or with its previous invention, or with the slightly earlier name, *jew's-trump*. Both names date from the sixteenth century, and both are peculiar to the English language, the latter still used in Scotland. The French name, formerly *trompe,* is now generally replaced by *guimbarde*. All sorts of theories have been advanced to account for the name, but none stands up in the cold light of day.

logrolling

Now political slang expressing exchange of support upon favored legislation, this found its birth in an honorable custom among neighboring American frontiersmen establishing a new settlement. A house of some sort was, of necessity, the first consideration. It might be temporary and of rude construction. But as soon as opportunity permitted, a site was selected for a permanent home. For warmth, as well as protection against marauding Indians, such homes were erected from the trunks of trees cleared from land to be used in later planting—log cabins or log houses. And for mutual assistance, neighbor would assist neighbor in bringing logs to the site and erecting the walls. This mutual assistance constituted *logrolling*.

wigwam

The 1864 edition of Webster's *Dictionary of the English Language* (G. & C. Merriam) offers the following etymology, and most other authorities are in general agreement:

From Algonquin or Massachusetts *wēk,* "his house," or "dwelling place"; with possessive and locative affixes, *wēkou-om-ut,* "in his (or their) house"; contracted by the English to *weekwam,* and *wigwam.*

char-à-banc

Even if you know your French, but have never actually seen this vehicle, the name, "car with bench," will not give you much of a picture of it. Actually this "benched carriage" strongly resembled the motor bus that has replaced it. It was long and narrow, and the transverse "benches" or seats faced forward.

telltale

Tell and *tale* are closely related in an etymological sense, one being the verb form and the other the noun form of the same word. The original sense was in the concept of counting, and related parallel terms are found in the Anglo-Saxon *tellan, talu;* Dutch *tellen, taal;* German *zählen, Zahl* (number); Old Norse *telja, tala.* *Tell,* in the sense of "to count," exists today as *teller,* "one who counts money or votes"; *tale* in the counting sense has pretty well vanished (*tally,* which would seem to be related, is of different origin). So it would seem likely that a *telltale* might have been a scorekeeper or reckoner, but there is no evidence that the word was ever applied in this sense. Instead, a *telltale* is simply a bearer of tales, a tattler.

G string, gee string

Let me say at the outset that the reason one or the other of these terms was given to the type of breechclout worn by some  American Indians has never been definitely determined. The early plainsmen who, apparently, were first to use it did not leave explanatory notes. But I shall offer a conjecture: That which the American Indian used for a cord was, of course, a length of sinew or a strand of gut, and, naturally, such a strand tied around one's waist to carry the single strip of cloth or flexible hide running between the limbs from front to back was of such thickness as not to cut the flesh. Now, among any group of plainsmen in frontier days there was likely to be one, at least one, who toted and played a fiddle. Necessarily having to replace its string from time to time, it would occur to him that the cord of the Indian breechclout might serve as the heaviest of its strings. That would be the *G string.*

roundabout

One of the earlier descriptive names of that form of a hoop-skirted dress known as a *farthingale* (which see), *roundabout* was obviously coined with particular reference to the encircling lower part of that garment. Later, in extension of the same sense, it became applied to garments which encircled the body completely, such as a greatcoat, as well as a woman's dressing gown. Finally, early in the nineteenth century (and the use has persisted into the twentieth), American clothiers effected a major shift of emphasis with respect to the area surrounded by adopting the same word, *roundabout,* as the name of a short jacket reaching no lower than the waist, such as is worn by small boys.

harebell

Dictionaries hazard merely the guess that these wild hyacinths, so common in England and Scotland, were "perhaps" so named because they grow in places frequented by hares, but I prefer to think the ancient Saxons had a more poetic notion. "Yes," they may have said, "they are plentiful where hares abide, and the hares love to tinkle them as they pass, so we shall call them the *harebell.*"

telegraph

An old pun has it that there are three ways to spread news rapidly: telegraph, telephone, or tell a woman. But the French inventor Chappe had no pun in mind when he gave this name to the instrument which he had devised in 1793, for transmitting messages by means of a sort of semaphore. It comes from two Greek words, *tele,* "far off," and *graphein,* "to write." There have, since Chappe's day, been other devices known as telegraphs, but the word has now become restricted almost entirely to the electromagnetic instrument invented by Morse in the 1830's. *Telephone,* too, was coined much earlier than the invention of the instrument with which it is now associated. The first element is the same as above—the second is the Greek *phone,* "sound, voice."

banana oil

Actually an aromatic liquid having the odor of a ripe banana, chiefly employed as a solvent for lacquers. Chemically it is isoamyl acetate, if you know what that is. But when your young son says, "Aw, that's just banana oil," in terms of derision or of praise, his slang usage is that he regards the "that" as either nonsense or as flattery.

daredevil

One so reckless as to be willing to dare the devil himself. Curiously enough, though we've had all sorts of foolhardy, devil-may-care, harebrained madcaps throughout history, it was less than two hundred years ago that the term *daredevil* was pinned upon such an individual. And, as is so disheartening to the researcher, there is now no clue as to the identity of the person so described. The earliest literary usage is insipid: "I deemed myself a dare-devil in rhime," said John Wolcott in *Odes to Mr. Paine* (1794).

roughrider

It may surprise many of the younger generation—those who grew up in this age of mechanization—to learn that the term *rough-rider* was not coined specifically as a name for Teddy Roosevelt's cavalry regiment of the Spanish-American War. Instead, the word originally was used to describe a man who specialized in breaking horses to harness, that is, a bronco buster. The word has been known in print at least since the early eighteenth century, and probably existed in speech long before that time. As for the Rough Riders of Roosevelt, a major reason for their acquiring the sobriquet was that many of the members of the regiment were just that—bronco busters and cowboys recruited from the "Wild West" by Roosevelt himself.

lodestar, lodestone

Obviously, *lodestar* indicates the star or other force or attraction that points the "lode." But if that isn't clear, perhaps it should be explained that, early in our language, *lode* carried the meaning "way" or "course." Similarly, a *lodestone,* now more frequently spelled *loadstone,* was originally a piece of stone containing strongly magnetized iron which was used by mariners to point out the way, to direct them on their course.

Sanhedrin

Historically, this is the correct spelling for this ancient Jewish council, but the spelling *Sanhedrim* is often seen. The word comes from the Greek *synhedrion,* "council," which is made up of *syn,* "together," and *hedra,* "seat," hence, literally, "seat together."

halibut

For the past six or seven hundred years, the common name in England for any of the flatfish—skate, flounder, plaice, turbot, or whatever—has been *butt.* The most highly  prized of all, the one formerly reserved for eating upon holy days, was the largest of the flatfish, so large that some run up to three or four hundred pounds and to seven or eight feet in length. These, some five centuries ago, were termed *haly* (holy) *butts,* whence cometh our present spelling. But the eating of this "holy flounder" is no longer confined to feast days of the church.

chapbook

This item still circulated when I was small, though it was begun in the early nineteenth century. It and its kind were, in a way, the forerunners of the modern "comic" books, though the reading matter in any that came my way, at least, could never be called lurid. The contents—short stories, poems, tales by explorers—of those presented to me at Christmas were highly moral, as I recall, and the illustrations most demure. But the name of these board-covered cheap volumes was in no wise connected with the young "chaps" who read them; originally they were "chapmen's books," some of the various items sold by retailers or peddlers—*chapmen* —especially in England.

bamboozle

My third edition (1737) of Nathan Bailey's *Universal Etymological English Dictionary,* first published in 1721, contains "A Collection of the Canting Words . . . used by Beggars, Gypsies, Cheats, House-Breakers, Shop-Lifters, Foot-Pads, Highway-men, etc.," and carries this entry: "A BAM, a Sham or Cheat; a knavish Contrivance to amuse or deceive." *Bamboozle,* a verb of like sense, is not shown but is the same age, late seventeenth century, and is among the terms listed by Jonathan Swift in 1710 as among the slang terms of "Continual Corruption of our English Tongue." Others were *banter, put, sham, mob, bubble, bully.* The word is not related to *bamboo.* In fact, clues to its origin are lacking.

linsey-woolsey

One rarely knows through what influence a word has been created. Possibly some little Ælfrida of the fifteenth century at her mother's knee could not rightly say "linen," and the mother and father, thereafter humoring the child, also said *linsey.* No one knows. But, if we add to the fanciful story, we may then also assume that the father, weaving a textile of flax and wool, went a step further in childish speech and called his weave *linsey-woolsey.*

teetotum

This ancient gambling game was played by spinning a toplike device having four sides or segments which were marked, respectively, with the letters A, T, N, D. The players spun the device one after another, and their fate was established by that face of the toy that lay upward at the end of the spin. Each letter was the initial of a Latin word having, in the game, some special significance, as follows: T, *totum,* player wins the pot; A, *aufer,* player takes one stake from the pot; D, *depone,* player puts one stake into the pot; N, *nihil,* player takes or puts nothing. Later the letters were changed to correspond to English words, but it is from the winning face of the older form that the device and the game took their name—T for totum, shortened to *teetotum.*

Argonaut

An adventurer, especially one who sails the seas in search of fortune or adventure. This present-day interpretation arose from those so called who, in 1849, lured by reports of vast gold fields in

86

California, endured great hardship to reach that land of promise, especially those who went by sea first to Central America, thence by land through jungle and mountain to the Pacific, and by ship again to San Francisco. The name actually derives from the Greek legend of the search by Jason, in the ship *Argo,* for the golden fleece. He and his fifty companions were *Argonautes,* from *Argo,* the ship, and *nautes,* "sailor."

lich gate

Our remote forebears went all out at a burial, and this is just one of the reminders. The *lich* (rhymes with *rich*) was the corpse, borne from house to churchyard. It was carried over a *lich way* or path to the solemn sound of a *lich bell,* and at the *lich gate,* or roofed entrance to the churchyard, the coffin was placed upon a *lich stone* to await the arrival of the clergyman, and was then finally carried to the *lich rest* or grave. Previous to death, perhaps, a *lich owl* may have shrieked its ominous prophecy.

whippersnapper

The word itself is merely a balanced extension of *whip-snapper,* "one who cracks a whip." Its use is most often in the sense of "one who cracks a whip loudly to make a fearsome noise because he himself would have no attention paid to him otherwise." In other words, "an insignificant, impudent nobody."

chaparajos

We picked this up from our Mexican neighbors and have abbreviated it to *chaps.* Rightly, we should say *chaparreras,* a term used by Mexicans for a kind of leather breeches worn over the trousers to protect the legs when riding through *chaparral,* a dense tangle of dwarf oak and thorny shrub common in the Southwest.

jerrybuilt

Jerry, whoever he was, was a bad egg, or at least one held in contempt. He first appeared on the literary scene in the early eighteenth century as *jerrymumble* or *jerrycummumble* in some such sense as a tumbler or one who is knocked about. Scott, gruesomely, has a *jerry-come-tumble* dancing at the end of a hangman's rope. And we had a *Jerry-Sneak,* an unkind appellation for a browbeaten husband. Latest to appear was the *jerrybuilt* cottage of about a hundred years ago, certainly too unsubstantial to be still standing, but being replaced daily through the efforts of modern *jerrybuilders.* No record exists of the identity of the first Jerry deserving such continued reproach.

hangdog

There's no evidence that I have found of the actual hanging of any dog nor of the actual appearance of any person who had com-mitted such an act. So the only inference that can be drawn is that someone gifted with high imaginative powers, about three centuries ago, figured that a dog, if hung, would have a cringing abject demeanor, or that the person capable of hanging it would have a contemptible sneaky aspect, and thus applied the term to one of such character or appearance.

leghorn

Whether it be straw hat or chicken is all the same. The original of either was produced at Legorno, Italy, or, as the English had previously misnamed it, *Leghorn.* Even yet, though the Italians have renamed it Livorno, it remains *Leghorn* on British and American maps.

roulette

See entry under **roué.** As shown there, the French word *roue* (no accent) means "a wheel." A *roulette,* of course, is "a little wheel." And all those who have played the game of chance of the same name are well aware that it is a little wheel that governs the destinies of the players.

bambino

Italian for "infant, baby," and applied specifically to images of the infant Jesus in swaddling clothes now exhibited generally at Christmas. The term has the same root as Greek *bambaino,* "to stutter," and was probably suggested by the prattle of an infant.

sanguine, sanguinary

So similar in appearance, so similar in etymology (both are derived from the Latin *sanguis,* "blood"), these words are quite different in meaning, and care must be exercised not to use one when the occasion requires the use of the other. *Sanguine,* literally "bloody," has been used to describe something that was actually bloody or was blood-colored (and is still correctly, though rarely, used in this sense). From this, it was used to describe a person of ruddy complexion, that is, one of good blood, healthy. Then it was but a slight change of meaning to apply it, in its present sense, to one who is of hopeful disposition, or confident of success, for these are attributes supposedly borne by one who is healthy. *Sanguinary,* also with the literal meaning of "bloody," is used more with respect to bloodshed, and is properly applied to a person who is bloodthirsty, delighting in carnage, of cruel disposition.

Darby and Joan

Typification of marital contentment. Names and allusion are assumed to be from a set of verses appearing in *The Gentleman's Magazine* in 1735 under the title, "The Joys of Love Never Forgot: a song." The author was presumably Henry Woodfall, though that is not certain. The third stanza reads:

> *Old Darby, with Joan by his side,*
> *You've often regarded with wonder:*
> *He's dropsical, she is sore-eyed,*
> *Yet they're never happy asunder.*

soft sawder

To treat a man with soft sawder is to flatter him—to "butter him up." But why? Well, *sawder* is an obsolete spelling of *solder,* and is still a phonetic spelling of a dialectal pronunciation of the word. And *solder,* a low-melting alloy used for uniting certain metals, is derived from the Latin *solidus,* "solid." The transition from *solidus* to *solder* took place through a now obsolete verb form, *sold* (approximate pronunciation is *sawd*), meaning "to unite by soldering or welding." Now, one of the objects of flattery is to get the flatterer "in solid" with the person being flattered. And soft solder is easier to apply than is the hard variety, even though it may be less durable. The final link in this particular chain of evidence is obvious.

hillbilly

Probably the best and, according to the *Dictionary of Americanisms,* the first printed description appeared in the New York  Journal, April 23, 1900: "A Hill-Billie is a free and untrammelled white citizen of Alabama, who lives in the hills, has no means to speak of, dresses as he can, talks as he pleases, drinks whiskey when he gets it, and fires off his revolver as the fancy takes him." In more recent years the territory has been vastly increased and the habits enlarged to include addiction to stringed musical instruments, often as accompaniments to group or individual nasal singing of so-called "hillbilly songs." *Billy,* tracing back through some four centuries of usage, just means "fellow."

teetotal

There are various accounts of the origin of this word, all more or less well documented, and the evidence indicates that it probably came into being both in America and in England, independently, within the space of a few years, early in the nineteenth century. The earliest use, though, seems to have been American, in the form *tetotally,* the extra *e* being added later. In any event, the word was coined in connection with the temperance movement to signify absolute abstinence from alcohol by emphasizing, through repetition, the initial sound of *total—T-total.*

chanticleer

In the old, old tales of the exploits of *Reynard the Fox,* fragments of which have been traced to the tenth century, this was the proper name of the cock—"So sawe they comen doun the hylle to hem chauntecler the cock," in the first printed edition by William Caxton in 1481. The name, taken from some old French version, was in recognition of the far-reaching early-morning summons of the cock, "the clear singer," from *chanter,* "to sing," and *cler,* "clear."

jerkwater

Strongly divergent views appeared in 1945 in relating the origin of this. James L. Marshall in *Santa Fe, the Railroad That Built an Empire* says that that railroad was so named because the crews "jerked water" by bucket from wayside streams to fill the locomotive tender. But the *Engineman's Magazine* in September of the same year gives the laurels to the New York Central, which, in June, 1870, made the first installation, at Montrose, New York, of water pans between the tracks whereby locomotives could scoop up water.

Both of these explanations strike me as lame and inadequate, however. Marshall may have been partly right, though certainly not in applying "Jerkwater Line" to the whole Sante Fe Railroad. A branch line, yes—one feeding one or more towns too small and insignificant to have regular main-line service. Train crews on such lines had plenty of time to fill tenders by bucket brigades, and, naturally enough, the one-horse towns on such branch lines were scornfully "jerkwater towns."

Arctic

It relates, of course, to the region around the North Pole, but the ancient Greek astrologers and mariners called it by this name from the constellation that circumscribes the area of the heavens above it, the Bear, which in Greek is *arktos*. That about the South

Pole then became *antarktos,* from *anti,* "opposite," and *arktos,* "Bear"; hence, "opposite the north." Through Latin adaptation, the names have been further modified to *arctic* and *antarctic.*

mumble-peg

It was *mumbly-peg* in my boyhood, probably contracted from *mumblety-peg* from an earlier *mumble-the-peg.* But the game seems to have disappeared from the American scene entirely. I don't know why, unless it may be that mothers are more fearful lest their young roughnecks cut themselves with a sharp knife. The name derives from the manner in which the game was played in England from the early seventeenth century and as brought by boys thence to America. From various positions, toe, knee, elbow, fingers, each player in turn flipped his opened knife with sufficient force to stick in the ground. If unsuccessful, the other players had the privilege of driving a peg into the ground with an agreed number of blows struck with the handles of their knives, a peg which the loser was then supposed to withdraw with his teeth. My memory may be faulty, Mummy, but I doubt that after one game of *mumbly-peg* any knife was then sharp enough to produce serious injury.

fifth wheel

Nowadays used contemptuously or at least disrespectfully of a person or thing as useless or needless as an extra wheel for the support of a vehicle ordinarily running on four. But in original use the term was applied to a metal wheel or circular plate (sometimes a segment of one) having an important service and never touching the ground. It lay horizontally beneath the forward part of the body of a wagon or carriage and was attached to the upper side of the front axle, thus supporting the body while the vehicle turned a corner or the like.

wardrobe

There are a few words native to the Teutonic languages which, in these, are spelled with *w,* but which, on having been adopted into the Romance group, were spelled with a *g,* or, perhaps, with *gu.* One of the latter is represented by our word *guard.* This started in Old Teutonic as *warda* and was taken into most Romance languages as *guarda,* but became modified, in Old French, to *guarde* or *garde.* It seems to have been in France that a room, generally adjoining a bedchamber, was set aside in which to keep clothing, and this room was named *garderobe*—or it may have been in Italy that it began, where the room was called *guarda-robba.* But in northeastern France, where the language was under the influence of the neighboring Teutonic tongues, the first element underwent a reversion to the Teutonic form, and the word became *warderobe,* in which form it was taken into English, elision of the first *e* following later.

hobbyhorse

The term itself is merely repetition, as, six centuries ago, a *hobby* was a horse, a small horse, probably a nickname for *Robin.* But

hobbyhorse comes to us from the sixteenth-century morris dance, commonly held throughout England at Whitsuntide —mid-May. Although the characters in these festivals chiefly represented Robin Hood and others of his company—Friar Tuck and Maid Marian invariably—there was also always a horseman ostensibly astride a small horse, dancing fantastically among the group. In reality the horse was a gaily caparisoned framework of wicker or the like, surmounted by an imitation of a horse's head, all carried by the rider. The morris dance has long since departed; the *hobbyhorse,* considerably modified for the sport of young children, is the sole survivor.

chameleon

Ancient Greeks had some of the most peculiar and original notions. Heaven knows wherein anything in the nocturnal skies to warrant the names they gave to many of the constellations, and here again they seem to have let imagination run riot. This small lizardlike reptile, for reasons one can't even guess, rejoices in the Greek name *chamai,* "dwarfed," *leon,* "lion"—"the dwarfed lion." And the ancients also thought these creatures could go for interminable periods living only on air.

sang-froid (sahn·frwah)

We are all impressed by those, like the "private eyes" of television and whodunits, who remain calm, cool, and collected amid the greatest stress. This time it was the French who had a word for it—actually, two words telescoped by frequent use into one. *Sang-froid* is a direct lift into English from the French, dating back at least to the eighteenth century, and possibly introduced about the time of the Norman Conquest. The literal meaning is "cold blood," and the derivation is from the Latin *sanguis,* "blood," plus *frigidus,* "cold." We would say that a man who exhibits *sang-froid* is "cool as a cucumber."

hardtack

If this term were not already available it is possible that today's mariner would invent a term of similar import, such as "hard grub," as all that was intended by *tack,* a hundred years ago, was food of any sort. *Hard tack* was literally hard food, or, that is, biscuit of more than ordinary hardness to have on hand in rough weather. The modern slang equivalent is *dog biscuit.*

tattletale

This word is an American colloquialism, but its antecedents are well established in English. The first part, *tattle,* dates back to 1481 with the publication of Caxton's translation of *Reynard the Fox* from the Flemish. As then used, the word had the meaning "to speak hesitatingly, to stammer," being Caxton's rendering of *tatelen* ("tattling"), a variant of *tateren.* Low German has a related *tateln,* "to gabble, cackle." But *tattle* acquired other mean-

ings, such as "to chat," "to gossip," and eventually, "to tell tales."
It is presumably to indicate precisely which meaning was intended
that our Americanism was invented, for a *tattletale* is specifically a
tale bearer.

April fool

Since April is the first month of spring, when all things are green,
it stands to reason that people are green then too, and, no more
than half awake after a long winter hibernation, in prime condition
to be easily hoaxed. The custom was apparently brought across the
channel from France to England about the beginning of the eighteenth century, as Jonathan Swift, in his *Journal to Stella,* enters
under March 31, 1713, that he and others had been contriving "a
lie for tomorrow."

chafing dish

We are so accustomed to the use of *chafe* in the sense of "to
abrade; to fret," as to overlook that its earliest meaning (derived
from Latin *calefacio*) was "to make warm." And the *chafing dish,*
or *chafer,* as first called, was designed for that purpose. They were
used and so named five hundred years ago. In a will of the following century a man bequeathed to his sister "a chaffyndyche."

hotspur

This title, or designation of extreme impetuosity, was first bestowed upon Sir Henry Percy, eldest son of the first Earl of
Northumberland, born in 1364. He was only a lad of fourteen
when he saw active service, but it was not until six years later that
gained the title "Hotspur"—a name by which he was known the
rest of his life—in another of the continuing conflicts against the
bordering Scots. In later years, dissatisfied with the treatment he
received from Henry IV, by whom he had previously been greatly
honored, Hotspur took up arms against the king, but was killed in
battle, July, 1403.

mugwump

According to the King James Version of the Bible, Genesis 36:15 reads: "These were dukes of the sons of Esau . . ." But when John Eliot, in 1663, translated the Bible into the tongue of the native Indians of Massachusetts, he used *mugquomp,* meaning "chieftain," as the equivalent of "duke." As *Mug-Wump,* the word appeared in 1832 in the ironical sense of one who would like to be considered a chieftain or vastly important great man. But fifty years later, or, to be exact, in the presidential campaign of 1884, though at first applied in derision to members of the Republican party who, it was said, thought themselves too virtuous or too important to support the Republican nominee, James G. Blaine, it was taken over by those men themselves as a term for an independent Republican. Since then anyone, even in England, who fails to vote in accordance with the policies of his party is considered a *mugwump,* or, as waggishly said of one such independent, "His mug is where his wump should be."

hoodwink

To get the original significance we must go back to the old, old meaning of *wink*—to have one's eyes closed. Thus, in the sixteenth

century, when fashion decreed head coverings of cowls or hoods, often attached to the cloak, one became *hoodwinked* or blinded when the hood fell or was drawn over the eyes. Thieves and purse snatchers took advantage of the fashion to *hoodwink* victims. But the term and practice were also employed in the game of blindman's buff. Hawks and falcons were also *hoodwinked* when being carried.

fife rail

A mariner's term, now indicating a rail round the mainmast of a sailing vessel with holes into which belaying pins may be inserted. Originally, however, according to Admiral W. H. Smyth's *The*

96

Sailor's Word-Book (1867), it formed "the upper fence of the bulwarks on each side of the quarter-deck and poop in men-of-war." By repute, the fifer had his seat on this "upper fence" while the anchor was being hoisted.

dandelion

They used to call it *lion's-tooth* in England before the sixteenth century, but someone then got fancy notions and began to use the French name of this common European weed, *dent de lion,* though it has the same meaning. Of course, it didn't make sense to the average Englishman to spell something *dent de* and pronounce it *dan de,* so he soon changed the whole thing into *dandelion.* The name, incidentally, refers to the shape of the deeply indented leaf, not to that of the flower.

saltpeter

An alternative spelling, preferred in England, is *saltpetre.* Chemically, saltpeter is potassium nitrate, a compound essential to the making of gunpowder and also of important value as a fertilizer. The name comes from the Latin *sal petrae,* "salt of the rock," so-called because it is sometimes found in nature as an efflorescence on rocks or soil. However, saltpeter is definitely not to be confused with *rock salt,* even though it has a saline taste. Rock salt is merely sodium chloride (table salt) which has been induced to form large, rather than small, crystals.

viscount

In Latin, the word *vice* (two syllables) meant "alternate, in place of," and, although it had the standing of a noun, there arose the practice in later Latin, and particularly in medieval Latin, of using it chiefly as one element of a compound noun. A number of these compounds were taken into the various other Romance languages, and they are found in French chiefly with the spelling *vis-* or *vi-*. So the Old French word for that member of the lower nobility who was an alternate count became *visconte* or *viconte* (modern French, *vicomte*), from the medieval Latin *vicecomes.* On being taken into

English, the spelling of the first part retained the French form, whereas the spelling of the second part was altered to the English form, to give us the half-French, half-English term *viscount*.

peanut

So called only because the nut somewhat resembles a pea in size. In the early days of American colonization it was known as the *ground-nut* or *ground-pea,* because it developed under the surface of the ground, and those names still occur, especially in England. Another name is *earth-nut*. Discovered first in South America by Spaniards, it was introduced by them into equatorial Africa, from whence Negro slaves brought the name *nguba* with them to the plantations of the Southern United States, where it speedily became *goober*. The English, slow to accept the shelled and roasted nuts for human consumption, long knew peanuts as *monkey-nuts,* because the simians in the zoo avidly consumed all that were tossed to them.

St. Swithin's Day

Many of the saints' names have become associated in folklore with vagaries of the weather, some with actual occurrences (cf. **St. Martin's summer**) and some with respect to weather to be anticipated. Swithin (sometimes *Swithun*) was Bishop of Winchester in the ninth century A.D., and upon his death was buried in the churchyard. According to some reports, during the century after his death it was recalled that he had performed many miraculous cures, and it was decided that he should be canonized and his remains re-interred in the cathedral. The date selected was July 15, 971. On this date, rain fell so hard as to require postponing the ritual, and continued for forty days thereafter. Hence the saying that, "If it rains on St. Swithin's day [July 15], it will rain for forty days," which dates to at least the sixteenth century.

fiddle-faddle

There was no definite source; the word *fiddle* was in the language and, four hundred years ago, it had taken on the meaning "to act aimlessly," so, just like such duplications as flip-flop, jim-jams, helter-skelter, and the like, someone turned it into *fiddle-faddle*. Thus since the sixteenth century this nonsense word has implied aimless or idle action or conversation, or any thing or occupation that is of little consequence: "Pete's sudden interest in postage stamps is just so much fiddle-faddle."

larboard

The first element, *lar,* is often assumed to have been a corruption of *lade,* thus making *larboard* the side of a vessel for loading, the side opposite the "steering side" or *starboard*. The assumption is logical, but the sad fact is that it cannot be traced—as a lawyer would say, "not proven."

hushpuppy

Which of the Southern states is your preference? The invention of this comestible, or at least the name for it, has been claimed by most of those south of the Potomac, though never even approximately dated by any, so you may make your own choice. The account of the origin of the name, however, is always strikingly similar, the difference being chiefly in the personnel of the group assembled for the meal and the one distributing the largesse. The account now circulated by the Tallahassee (Florida) Chamber of Commerce is the most colorful of those I have seen, so, without prejudice, I shall follow it. It is taken from *The Southern Cook Book* (1939), compiled and edited by Lillie S. Lustig, S. Claire Sondheim and Sarah Rensel, and published by Culinary Arts Press, Reading, Pennsylvania. With the permission of the publishers to quote, this account, slightly abridged, reads:

"Years ago the Negroes of Tallahassee . . . would congregate on warm fall evenings for [sugar] cane grinding. . . . After their work was completed, they would gather around an open fire, over which was suspended an iron pot in which fish and corn pones were cooked in fat.

"The Negroes were said to have a certain way of making these corn pones which were unusually delicious and appetizing. While the food was sizzling in the pot, they would spell-bind each other with 'tall' stories of panther and bear hunts. On the outer edge of the circle of light reflected by the fire would sit their hounds, their noses raised to catch a whiff of the savory odor of the frying fish and pones. If the talking ceased for a moment, a low whine of hunger from the dogs would attract the attention of the men, and subconsciously a hand would reach for some of the corn pone which had been placed on a slab of bark to cool. The donor would break off a piece of the pone and toss it to a hungry dog, with the abstract murmur, 'Hush, puppy.'

"The effect of this gesture on the hounds was always instantaneous and the Negroes attributed the result to the remarkable flavor of what eventually became known as 'The Tallahassee Hush Puppy.' "

I take no responsibility for the accuracy of this account. In fact, a more recent cookbook says that the fried dainty and its naming were inventions of colonial days. And another, also recent, attributes the naming to Northern soldiers accompanying General Sherman on his famous march through Georgia. The "puppies" similarly "hushed," according to this account, were hungry dogs which followed the Northern army.

roué

Back in the days when criminals, real or fancied, were punished by being put to torture, the French word *roue* (no accent mark), meaning "wheel," and derived from the Latin *rota,* came to have the special meaning "torture wheel." From this, in turn, was coined the verb *rouer,* "to torture (break) on the wheel." Now the Duke of Orleans, about 250 years ago, was rather a disreputable rakehell, and surrounded himself with companions of the same ilk. Of these, it was said that they were *roués* (note accent mark), "men deserving to be broken on the wheel." And the term is still applied to one who is a dissolute wastrel.

100

causeway

Although now a dialectal word, *causey* is the basis for this, and no pun is intended. That is, a *causey* is a raised footway or embankment over marshy ground made firm by stamping or pounding. Probably it is derived from Latin *calx,* "heel." Such an original footway might later be widened for the accommodation of carriages. If so, it then was known as a *causey-way,* or, eventually, *causeway.*

sumpter horse

This story goes all the way back to the ancient Sanskrit, in which language was the word *sakta,* "attached," the past participle of *sanj,* "to adhere." This led to the Greek *sattein,* "to fasten," which later became, "to pack, to put a burden on a horse," from which was derived *sagma,* "a pack saddle." The latter was taken directly into Latin, where it was eventually corrupted to *salma* with the meaning of "a pack, a burden." The next path on the journey was Old French, into which the Latin word was adopted with the spelling *somme,* and the French modified their word to *sommetier* to describe the pack-horse driver. And this is the word that was taken into English, early in the fourteenth century, with the spelling *sumpter,* "a pack-horse driver." It was the horse he drove, of course, that was called the *sumpter horse,* this term having been recorded in the fifteenth century. In the following century, the name of the horse became shortened to *sumpter,* and these two terms have continued to exist to the present time as synonymous expressions describing a pack horse.

mud puppy

One wonders sometimes what sort of beverage our forebears may have been consuming when they bestowed names upon some of the odd-looking critters they found in America. These salamanders, either the hellbender or the Necturus, no more resemble a puppy than they do a cat. They have four legs, and the resemblance stops about there. They look more like undersized alligators than like anything canine. Undoubtedly the name was bestowed by an early traveler or settler, but it did not break into print much before seventy-five years ago. Another, and more fitting, name for the hellbender was *mud devil.*

padlock

The lock of this name dates from the fifteenth century, but the name poses a riddle. Our language contains *pads* of varying kinds and descriptions, but there was only one, totally obsolete now, which was in use before that date. The toad. So it may have been that the removable lock of five centuries ago had somewhat of a likeness to the shape of a toad, and was thus so called.

daffodil

It's a long way 'round, but the name of this plant and its flower were originally and properly still should be *asphodel,* though the later name denotes a kind of narcissus rather than a true asphodel. In the fifteenth century, perhaps at first in imitation of some king or prince who lisped, folks began to change *asphodel* to *affodill.* Then in the sixteenth century, perhaps to give the word a Frenchified aspect (such as in altering *Albert* to *D'Albert*), the name suddenly gained a new initial, and *daffodil* was born. The names *daffodilly* and *daffodowndilly* are merely poetic substitutions, used as early as the sixteenth century, even by so renowned a poet as Edmund Spenser.

vinegar

In times past, the only source of vinegar generally known was wine that, on turning, became sharp and acrid to the taste. And it is precisely this that is shown by the name, for it comes from the Old French *vyn egre* (which led to the modern French *vinaigre*). *Vyn,* or *vin,* comes from the Latin *vinum,* "wine," and *egre,* or *aigre,* is from the Latin *acer,* "sharp, pungent."

St. Martin's summer

The phenomenon of a spell of warm, bright, pleasant weather occurring well after the official start of autumn is known to people in many parts of the world, and the event, known to North Americans as *Indian summer,* is known by many names. Thus, St. Martin's Day is November 11, and when the summerlike weather occurs near that date, it is *St. Martin's summer* to the British (*été de la Saint-Martin* to the French). Similarly, St. Luke's Day is October 18, and All Saints' Day is November 1, and thus we may have, if the weather co-operates, *St. Luke's summer* or *All Saints'* (or *All Hallows') summer* at an earlier time of year. Incidentally, the reason for the name *Indian summer* has never been explained with full satisfaction to all concerned. It has been known and used at least since the late eighteenth century.

jackanapes

Now, any man or boy who apes his betters or pretends to be more than he is. Apparently, however, this was originally an ex-

tended meaning of the earliest application, perhaps when memory of the first use had faded. That is, the first historical use was derisive, applied to William, Duke of Suffolk, when that knight was baselessly arrested for treason against Henry VI in 1450 and ultimately beheaded. The satirical appellation arose from his heraldic emblem, a clog and chain such as were then characteristic of the fastening attached to a tame ape. But within a hundred years the significance of the satire was gone, and, though the name remained, it referred just to any ape, whether tame or not, or to a man or boy behaving as one.

tatterdemalion (-demallion)

It is generally conceded that the first part of this word (which dates to the early seventeenth century) is nothing more than *tatter,* or, more probably, *tattered,* "ragged." With respect to the second element, it has been suggested that it may have come from the French *maillot,* from Old French *maillon,* "swaddling clothes," also, "an acrobat's tights." However, most authorities agree that the second part of the word was coined from pure fancy, just as was the second part of *ragamuffin,* with which *tatterdemalion* is synonymous.

applejack

Sorry, but there was no Jack who had a hand in naming the American brandy derived from cider, nor any John either, unless it may have been John Barleycorn. Perhaps the tippler who first discovered that cider would ferment just happened to use the John-apple, so named because it ripened on or about St. John's Day, June 24. New Jersey, back in the early nineteenth century, was the great producer of applejack. Hence, because of its prompt action, the brandy was also known as "Jersey lightning." New England was slow to adopt either name, preferring to call the juice by the more sedate name, "apple-john."

knapsack

As an essential of a soldier's field equipment, both knapsack and haversack are now obsolete. Whereas the latter carried his field rations, the *knapsack* was for personal items, such as changes of clothing. However, such were not in accord with the original German military usage. The *haversack,* as stated elsewhere, carried grain for a cavalryman's horse; the *knapsack,* as its name implies —German *knappen,* "to eat"—was a sack or wallet of considerably lesser size which held the rations of the soldier.

daddy longlegs

A frequent name in America for this insect is *granddaddy long-legs,* as any reader of Mark Twain knows. In England it is sometimes called *father-long-legs* or *Harry-long-legs,* the latter possibly in allusion to a fancied resemblance to his Satanic majesty, the Lord Harry. But the paternal or patriarchal name, applied without any regard whatever to the sex of this member of the spider family, is due only to the fact that its slender legs are excessively long, perhaps because some men appear to have legs reaching from the neck down. The crane fly, a fly with very long slender legs, is also sometimes called *daddy longlegs*.

St. Elmo's fire

St. Elmo, even though described in some reference works as the patron of navigators, seems likely to be a figment of the imagination, although it has been suggested that his name may be a corruption of St. *Anselm,* St. *Erasmus* (the patron of Neapolitan sailors), or of *Helena,* the sister of Castor and Pollux. In *An Etymological Dictionary of Modern English,* Weekley agrees that the saint, whether Elmo or Helen, is probably apocryphal, and suggests, with much merit, that the phrase goes back to the Greek *elene,* "a torch." Certain it is that this play of electric luminosity about the mast tips of a ship would strongly resemble a torch of magnificent, though eerie, proportions.

handsome

The meaning has changed a bit. Five hundred years ago the idea behind it was "somewhat handy; easy to deal with," but that original sense has now disappeared. Or, rather, it has given place to a more miserly notion that that which is most handy, most easy to deal with, is that which is also most pleasing. And thus, for more than three hundred years, men have spoken of a *handsome* sum of money, a *handsome* cargo from Spain, *handsome* praise from Sir John, and, most commonly nowadays, a *handsome* man, implying one of admirable face or figure, one pleasing to the eye.

ant lion

Hundreds upon hundreds of these have their diminutive pitfalls amid orange groves of Florida or wherever ants are numerous and the soil is composed of dry and very fine sand. Properly the name should be confined to the larvae, known also as doodlebugs, rather than to the adult insect, which resembles a dragonfly. The louse-like larva buries itself in the sand and, by throwing descending sand away from the edge by violent motions of its head, digs a funnel-shaped pit with smooth sides that may be an inch to two inches in depth, so smooth and steep than an incautious ant may slip to the bottom, where it is immediately seized by the formidable projecting mandibles of the "lion" awaiting it. Rainfall must be most discouraging; all trace of the laborious construction is wiped out by the first few drops, and the infant must wait until the sand is again bone dry before it may begin to set the table for the next meal. (See also **doodlebug.**)

tapestry

The art of decorative weaving seems to have been well developed in many of the Oriental countries long before it was learned in Europe, and Persia, especially, has long been known for the craft of its weavers in turning out fine fabrics. Thus it is probably from the Persian that this word stems, though it has been traced with certainty only back to the Greek *tapes,* "cloth wrought with figures in various colors." The diminutive is *tapetion,* and this was taken into Latin as *tappetium* or *tapetium* from which it spread into the Romance languages as *tapiz,* finally settling in French as *tapis.* One who wove such figured cloth was then called, in French, a *tapissier,* and his products were known, collectively, as *tapisserie.* This is the form that was taken into English as the ancestor of our present word, with the spelling *tapissery,* which spelling was very soon corrupted to that still used.

recipe, receipt

Whether your wife cooks from a *receipt* or from a *recipe* makes no difference, for today the terms are equivalent in meaning. Both are derived from the Latin, *recipere,* "to receive," the former from the participial form, *recepta,* the latter from the imperative form, *recipe,* "take!" The *receipt* was originally any set of directions for making up a formulation, whether in cookery or medicine, but in the course of time has pretty well lost its medicinal meaning. *Recipe* was used in its literal sense by physicians as the first word in a set of directions for compounding a medicinal preparation (in this sense, now abbreviated ℞), but, because of similarity to the older term, also came to be used as the name for the set of directions, and thence also to a set of directions in cookery.

John Bull

The long-drawn-out War of the Spanish Succession, 1701–1714, in which the allied armies of England, Austria, the Netherlands, and Prussia were finally victorious  over the combined forces of France and Spain, was not altogether popular in England. It cost many lives; it disrupted commerce, and the expense was enormous. All this was seen by the eminent physician and witty author Dr. John Arbuthnot. To get others to share his views he resolved, in 1712, to satirize the struggle for power. The first of his satires bore the title, *"Law is a Bottomless Pit.* Exemplified in the case of the Lord Strutt, John Bull, Nicholas Frog, and Lewis Baboon, who spent all they had in a lawsuit."* These characters were intended to represent, respectively, Spain, England, Holland, and France—especially, as of the first and fourth, their rulers, Charles II of Spain and Louis XIV of France. The satires were later expanded into five parts, published under the title, *History of John Bull.* From Arbuthnot's generalized characterization of the English people in this series England has subsequently been personified as *John Bull.*

cat-o'-nine-tails

In this day it seems amazing that this instrument of punishment was actually authorized in the British Navy until as recently as 1881. It came into use in the late seventeenth century, and was probably greatly modified from time to time according to the nature of the person commanding the punishment and its dura-tion, but at best the bare back of its victim might be literally flayed. A description in 1788 says it "consists of a handle or stem, made of rope three inches and a half in circumference, and about eighteen inches in length, at one end of which are fastened nine branches, or tails, composed of log line, with three or more knots upon each branch."

feverfew

French is not the only language to suffer mutilation when lifted bodily into English. Latin has also súffered. In Roman times a plant, the centaury, was known to possess properties which could soothe a feverish person. For that reason the plant was also known as *febrifugia*, from *febris*, "fever," and *fugare*, "to drive away." Passing through French, the people of England took this at first to be *feferfuge*, later corrupted in common speech to *feather-few*, *fetter-foe*, and, eventually, *feverfew*.

jayhawker

Though natives and residents of Kansas now proudly proclaim themselves to be *Jayhawkers*, such publicity a hundred years ago was likely to be followed by a fight and bloodshed. Among the settlers of the territory they were abolitionists, men chiefly from nonslaveholding states who fought against pro-slavery settlers to keep Kansas free. Who coined the term and when are not now likely ever to be known. We know only that it was prior to 1858. Some folks maintain that there was once, and perhaps may yet be, an actual *jayhawk*, a bird which robbed the nests of other birds. The bird has never been seen, so, in order to supply a deficiency, Mr. Kirke Mechem, of the Kansas State Historical Society, gaily provided a description in 1944 in a brochure, "The Mystical *Jayhawk*." His account was from the writings, "now unfortunately apocryphal," of "a famous Spanish ornithologist" with Coronado's expedition. And the mythical bird described by this mythical Spaniard somewhat resembled a huge parrot, curved beak, iridescent blue and red feathers, and wings and talons so powerful as to enable the bird to fly off with a buffalo in each claw. Well, far be it from me to be unable to invent something less staggering. I think it at least possible that some early spinner of yarns, inspired by authentic, though incredible, tales of the curious habits of the pack or trade rat, would not be outdone and came up with a bird having the keen vision of a hawk and the garrulity of a jay. Or, if that doesn't suit, we could suppose that the original *jayhawker* was given the title by fellow plainsmen in complimentary recognition of his keenness of sight coupled with humorous recognition of his constant flow of chatter.

caterwaul

This is just the *waul* or alluring musical call (or howl)—musical, presumably, to the female, that is—of a courting tomcat. Chaucer has the Wife of Bath say, in the Prologue:

> *"Thow saist thus that I was lik a cat;*
> *For who so wolde senge the cattes skyn,*
> *Than wold the catte duellen in his in;*
> *And if the cattes skyn be slyk and gay,*
> *Sche wol not duelle in house half a day;*
> *But forth sche wil, er eny day be dawet,*
> *To schewe hir skyn, and goon a caterwrawet."*

And the cat with fine clothes, male or female, does the same to this day.

tantamount

Our present adjectival use, which dates to the mid-seventeenth century, was preceded by a noun use, of slightly greater age, and a verb use some 350 years older, both now obsolete. It is to the verb use that originated in the tongue known as Anglo-French that we must look for the beginning of the word, which was then rendered as *tant amunte,* "to amount to as much," made up of the French *tant,* "as much," plus the Anglicized French *amunter,* "to amount to." From these beginnings it was only a matter of time until first the noun, "that which amounts to as much," and then the adjective, "that amounts to as much, equivalent," senses were developed.

St. Anthony's fire

St. Anthony, "The Great" (A.D. 251?–356?), was an Egyptian ascetic, and one of the pillars of the early Christian Church. During his life he was reportedly tempted sorely by the devil, who took many forms, including that of a pig. It was through this temptation that St. Anthony became the patron of pigs, which, in turn, has given his name to *St. Anthony's nut* and *St. Anthony's turnip,* both of which are foods favored by swine. His bones, discovered in 561, were finally enshrined at Vienne, France, where they are said to have performed miracles of healing during an epidemic of erysipelas in the eleventh century. For this reason, erysipelas, a feverish disease accompanied by reddening and itching of the skin, has since been popularly named *St. Anthony's fire.*

rasher

In the United States, we refer to "a slice of bacon"; our British cousins more commonly would order "a rasher of bacon," and expect to receive the same portion implied by our term—a single thin slice. Some have suggested that the *rasher* is so-called because, being thin, it may be cooked *rashly* ("quickly"). Others prefer to believe that the word is derived from the long-obsolete verb, *to rash,* "to cut, slash." I find more plausible than either the suggestion made by Dr. James Mitchell in his book, *Significant Etymology,* where he offers the theory that *rasher* is a misspelling of *rasure,* "a thin slice, a shaving," from the Latin verb *rado, rasi, rasum, radere,* "to scrape, shave, scratch."

handkerchief

An incongruous word, when you come to analyze it. The *chief* is an early misspelling of Old French *chef,* "head," and *ker* is a corrupt contraction of Old French *covrir,* "cover." Thus *kerchief,* back in Chaucer's time, was a square of cloth used as a head covering, though, approaching the Norman French, he wrote it *coverchief.* But of course the idea of a *kerchief* being only a head covering was quickly lost, and in no time at all both men and women began to appear wearing a "brest-kerchief," a "shuldur-kerchief," or a "nekke-kerchief," furnishing protection of a sort for breast, shoulder, or neck. But it was not until the early sixteenth century, apparently, that our English ancestors adopted the refinement of wiping the nose with a square of cloth, though the "napkin" for wiping the mouth or face after a meal had been introduced in the previous century. So, as *kerchief* had long since lost any distinctive application, this new soft square, equally useful as a napkin or for wiping the nose, and, in the fashion of the day, carried negligently in the hand, became a *handkerchief,* a *kerchief* to be carried in the *hand.* Later still, when garments were designed with pockets, we had *pocket handkerchiefs,* literally (now follow this closely), coverings for the head to be held in the hand inserted in one's pocket. A literal accomplishment is somewhat more difficult as one recalls that the *pocket handkerchief* is now usually an adjunct of feminine attire and that it commonly reposes, not in a pocket, but in a handbag.

juke box

According to Lorenzo D. Turner, in the dialect of the Negroes living on the islands lying off the coast of South Carolina, Georgia,  and Florida—a dialect called Gullah— *juke* is associated with anything connected with a place of ill repute; a *juke house* (sometimes just a *juke*) is a disorderly house. From his researches he found evidence also that the term was derived from dialects in Senegal, French West Africa, whence came the ancestors of most of these Negroes. Thus we may ascribe to African tribes the common name of our electrically operated, nickel-in-the-slot music box.

rarebit

It may have been a deliberate attempt to "glamourize" the dish; it may have been suggested in humorous vein; or it may have been a failure to understand the country humor in the original name, but whatever the reason, the word *rarebit* is used only to designate the cheese dish, *Welsh rabbit,* normally also in combination, as *Welsh rarebit.* Similar terms originating in popular humor are *Adam's ale* (water), *Scotch coffee* (hot water flavored with burnt biscuit), *Missouri meerschaum* (corncob pipe), *Cape Cod turkey* (codfish), and so on.

annus mirabilis

A wonderful year. It now means any year which the speaker regards as especially outstanding, notable. But, in England particularly, the term refers to the year 1666, the year that marked two notable events: a victory over the Dutch fleet and, in September, the great London fire in which a large part of the city was destroyed. Both events were commemorated in a poem by John Dryden having the title "Annus Mirabilis."

paddywhack

In England, perhaps because all Irishmen (each known as "Paddy") have no love for the English, a *paddywhack* generally denotes a towering rage or, sometimes, the kind of thrashing that is most likely to accompany such a rage—a real, genuine, downright whacking. But in America, where "Pat" or "Paddy" may be less given to fits of temper, the *paddywhack* has become considerably gentler. It is still a punishment for a misdemeanor, usually one committed by a child, but it is rarely more than a spanking, often not very drastic.

Oh yes, for unfathomed reasons the ruddy duck is locally called *paddywhack,* often abridged to *paddy.*

catchpole

The original of this, back in the twelfth century, was the surname of mixed language, *cassa pullum,* "the fowl catcher," denoting a legitimate occupation, such as "cowboy" does today. But the fowls so caught were seized for the payment of taxes. Hence, in time the *catchpole* or *catchpoll* became a minor court officer, a bailiff.

112

exclamation point (or mark)

It is the American practice to add *point* or *mark;* the British are content with *"exclamation,"* or occasionally with the older terms, *ecphonesis* or *epiphonema.* The mark itself(*!*), however, came into English use about three hundred and fifty years ago, borrowed from earlier Italian usage.

dachshund

True, Harold, *Dach* does mean "roof" *auf Deutsch,* but what, then, will you do with *shund?* It's meaningless. No, the first element is not *Dach,* but *Dachs,* and the meaning of that is "badger." This low-built hound (*Hund*), in other words, was especially used in Germany for hunting badgers, during the years long gone by when the baiting of badgers was a popular sport. This breed of dogs is thought to be very old, as its counterpart appears in ancient Egyptian paintings.

hand-in-glove

Originally, about three hundred years ago, those using this metaphor worded it *hand and glove*—that is, being on terms of intimate relationship comparable to that of one's hand and the glove for it. But whether through elision—*hand 'n' glove*—or through deliberate intent to indicate even closer intimacy, a snuggling intimacy as it were, seventeenth-century *hand and glove* became nineteenth-century *hand-in-glove.*

sadism

It is too often true that men of infamy tend to live in history longer than do men of good will, and so it is with Comte Donatien Alphonse François de Sade, usually called the Marquis de Sade. The Comte was a French soldier who lived from 1740 to 1814, but he is better known as a sexual pervert and an author of obscene writings. Most of his adult life was spent either in prison or in asylums for the insane. A form of perversion described by him consists in the obtaining of gratification by practicing cruelty upon the loved one, and it is to this practice that his name has been given. By extension, *sadism* is now applied to a love of cruelty, and a *sadist* is one who receives pleasure through the practice of cruelty.

kangaroo court

In *A Hog on Ice,* my father stated that, "The source of the name [kangaroo court] is mysterious, for it is American, not Australian."  That he was not wholly convinced of this is indicated by his having entered into correspondence, shortly before his death, with Mrs. H. E. L. Patton, of Kew, Victoria, enlisting her assistance in trying to establish whether, in fact, the term may not have originated in Australia. Mrs. Patton's efforts were, at first, wholly fruitless, seeming to substantiate the belief expressed earlier. Ultimately, however, the query was published in the Melbourne *Age* (April 22, 1957), where it elicited the following letter to the editor from Mr. J. D. Seymour of Longwarry North, Victoria, published April 26:

"Many years ago when I was working on Hamilton Downs station, about 200 miles south of the present site of Alice Springs, I put the same question to an old hand. I had seen many 'sundowners' calling at homesteads and huts for a handout and wondered why the irresponsibles didn't take a chance and steal a horse for their long walkabouts.

"The oldtimer answered: 'If they did, maybe they'd soon find themselves in hoppers' court.' Asked what he meant, he said: 'That's what we call it.'

"The manager was more explicit. 'It comes,' he said, 'from the kangaroos in the back country where they seldom, or never, see a white man, and the only lethal weapon they know is a blackfellow's spear. They feed in small bunches. When they sight a man out of spear range they sit up and stare, sometimes for five minutes, and then turn and leap for the horizon. It is from that dumb sense of inter-communication common to all animals and the resemblance of the staring bunch to an inquiring council and quick decision that we got the term Kangaroo Court.'

114

"No doubt Australian 'forty-niners' took the term to California as the Americans brought their idioms to this country less than a decade later."

tam-o'-shanter

Robert Burns, the national poet of Scotland, wrote of the wild ride of Tam o'Shanter (Tom of Shanter), when Tam rode through a furious storm "whiles holding fast his gude blue bonnet." Tam's bonnet, presumably, was the wide floppy hat favored by the Scottish Lowlanders and faintly resembling a beret. Just why is not clear, but some time after Burns' poem was published, the name of its hero became applied to this type of headgear, and the association remains down to the present, although now often abbreviated to "tam," or at times "tammy."

huggermugger

Perhaps this term should be passed over in silence, for its source is certainly as concealed and secret as is meant by *huggermugger* itself. Undoubtedly the rhyming term in one or another of its several variations—*hoker-moker, hocker-mocker, hucker-mucker,* or even *hudder-mudder*—had long been in colloquial use before the sixteenth century, but it first appeared in print in Sir Thomas More's *Dyaloge on the Worshyp of Ymagys* (1529): "He wolde haue hys faythe dyuulged [divulged] and spredde abrode openly, not alwaye whyspered in *hukermoker*." And on another page of the same work he wrote, ". . . these heretyques [heretics] teche in *hucker mucker*."

andiron

The only excuse for the present formation of this word is that the object itself is usually, though not always, composed of iron. The name of this device for supporting wood in an open fireplace came into the language from Norman French and, properly, we should still be calling it *andier* or the equivalent Saxon word, *aundyre*. The latter, through misinterpretation, produced our present word. The ending *yre,* you see, was also an independent spelling of *yren* or *yron,* five hundred years ago, and consequently was thought also to mean "iron."

king's evil

The "evil," scrofula, was not possessed by a king, but, because the kings of France and those of England were all anointed with consecrated oil, it was formerly a popular belief that, merely by a touch—"the king's touch"—a person afflicted with scrofula would be cured. In France, the power of so healing *le mal de roi* was first ascribed to Clovis in the fifth century; in England, the claim was that Edward the Confessor of the eleventh century was the first ruler to possess such divine power. Actually, however, the practice of "touching" an afflicted subject for the *king's evil* can be traced only to Louis IX in France and Edward III in England, of the thirteenth and fourteenth centuries respectively. It was abolished in both countries during the nineteenth century.

Javelle water

Correctly, we should always spell it *Javel water,* and even more properly call it *eau de Javel,* as the encyclopedias generally record it and as it appears in French. The chlorinated bleaching agent known by the name was first produced by the Javel works near Paris in 1792.

ambergris

As any Frenchman knows, this is a misspelling of *ambre gris,* meaning "gray amber," and is used to distinguish the soft, animal secretion of the sperm whale, gray in color, from the hard, fossilized resin, *ambre jaune,* "yellow amber." But at one time, because both of these were found along coasts of the sea, the yellow amber, that which we now call "amber," was thought to be hardened ambergris of different color. Amber itself was known in ancient Greece, but was called *elektron.* Through this name and the properties exhibited by the material when rubbed were derived our terms "electric," "electricity," etc.

116

fetlock

Sorry, but maybe it would be best to slide over this. It is the tuft or *lock* of hair that grows at the back of the pastern joint of the leg of a horse, or the part of the leg where this lock grows, but the word experts of our language have been able to do little more than make a wild stab at any early meaning of *fet*. Some think that it may have been a dialectical form of "foot," but others do not agree with this notion.

catchpenny

Descriptive of any novelty, whether true or flimflam, that might literally "catch a penny." Its first use, two hundred years back, was of any printed matter that might conceivably inveigle a purchaser to the investment of a penny.

katydid

The name of this American insect is customarily said to be due to the repetitious sound produced by it—as if, over and over again,

it were saying *Katie did!* It does my heart good to be able to record that others also have not detected this flat statement in the creature's stridulous tones. To the naturalist John Bartram in 1751 the sound was *Catedidist*. To Meriwether Lewis, of the Lewis and Clark expedition in 1804, it was *Chittediddle*. To a writer in *Western Monthly Review* in 1827 it was *Cataded*. And I have the notion that many would agree in saying that the sound is *Kaykihet*.

pea jacket

Frederick Marryat, in *Poor Jack* (1840), thought the spelling should be *P-jacket:* "A short P-jacket (so called from the abbreviation of *pilot's jacket*)," he wrote, "reached down to just above his knees." But Marryat was wrong. The original first element was *pee,* back in the fifteenth century, taken from Dutch *pij,* and that was the name of a kind of coat made of a coarse cloth and worn by men. Coat and name died out in England, but were revived in America in the early eighteenth century, first as *pee-jacket* and later in the present form, both apparently from Dutch *pij-jakker* of the same meaning—a short, double-breasted coat of thick woolen material, worn by sailors in severe weather.

tambourine

Etymologically speaking, there seems to be little doubt that *tambourine,* which comes to us from the French, is the diminutive of *tambour,* "a drum." The actual instrument, as we know it, though, is that which was known in France as *tambour de Basque,* because of its popularity in Biscay. *Tambour* is apparently a variant spelling of *tabor,* which is a much older name for a drum, and seems to have come from either of two Persian words, both of which mean "drum," *tabirah* or *taburak.* Both *tabor* and *tambour* have, in English, become practically obsolete since the introduction of the word "drum" into the language in the mid-sixteenth century, except in some specialized uses.

hamstring

We are so accustomed to the thought of a *ham* as consisting of that part of the upper leg which includes thigh and buttock as to forget entirely that this is, literally, an extended meaning. Originally the *ham* of a man or beast was only that part of the leg directly back of the knee. The *ham strings* were (and still are, though now united into *hamstrings*) the tendons at the back of the knee, or in an animal, the great tendon at the back of the hock. To be *hamstrung* is to be disabled or crippled through the severing of a *hamstring.*

balm of Gilead

Jeremiah, in the King James Version of the Bible, says: "Is there no balm in Gilead; is there no physician there?" But, so says the *Oxford English Dictionary,* "The term 'balm of Gilead' is modern, and . . . originated in the assumption that this is the substance mentioned in the Bible as found in Gilead." The Hebrew term, it adds, was *tsori,* "resin," which Miles Coverdale (1488–1569) mistakenly rendered "balm" in his translation of the Bible. However, the term is now applied to several Oriental trees and to various other aromatic plants, as well as to the resinous exudations which they yield.

mortarboard

Inasmuch as, nowadays, even American kindergartners appear in "cap and gown" upon the eve of stepping into the first grade, to say nothing of youngsters about to take the great step of entering high school, it may be well to know what the *mortarboard* they wear as a cap originally indicated and why it was so named. In its early form, back in the sixteenth century, the crown of this cap, though square, was unstiffened and was little more than a rim extending about the upper part of the cap proper, topped with a round knob. It was then worn only by high dignitaries of the church. Though continued as a churchly vestment, the squared crown was gradually extended in the seventeenth century and eventually required a stiff support to keep it in shape. And in the eighteenth century the crown was frankly a cloth-covered board, surmounted by a round knob and held to the head of the wearer by a skullcap. By this time the cap was worn not only by high officers of the church, but also by deans and rectors of universities. By the early nineteenth century a cap of the same style, but with a tassel replacing the round knob, both cap and tassel of black, was a required head covering of university students. With a black robe, also required, no distinction of rank was then in evidence.

Thanks to the squared shape, these flat caps reminded some wag in the mid-nineteenth century of the square boards used by masons for holding the mortar used by them. He then dubbed them *mortarboards.* As usual, no one knows who this wit may have been, but, though at first classed as college slang, the name is now definite. Alas, however, in America neither cap nor gown is limited to academic wear, nor is its color limited to black. Nor is it a required garb upon a college campus. In fact, it is more frequently seen as the vestment of a choir, the cap worn only by the feminine members. And, though black remains the customary color for male students in a college or university, female students sometimes appear in white. In lesser halls of learning, fabrics in any hue of the rainbow may appear.

By curious coincidence, the cap worn by certain French judges has also the name *mortier*, "mortar." The object from which this name is derived, however, is the vessel used with accompanying pestle by pharmacists or cooks, and in which ingredients are pounded or ground.

fer-de-lance

The name of this extremely poisonous snake, whose bite is most likely to be fatal, actually indicates the shape of the head—*fer*, "head" or "iron," *de lance*, "of the lance"; i.e., lance head. But it might also indicate the speed with which the serpent strikes or the fact that it springs at its victim like a charge with a lance. This lance-headed or yellow viper is found chiefly in tropical America, infesting especially the sugar plantations of the West Indies.

catboat

Entered merely not to skip a curious word, though little can be said about it. Two hundred years ago the name was applied to vessels of four to six hundred tons, built according to Norwegian design and used in the British coal trade, but no reason has been found for the designation and none for the transfer of the name to the small single-masted sailboat, with mast stepped well forward, used for pleasure.

vinaigrette

Taken directly from the French *vinaigrette*, "vinegar sauce," a condiment prepared with vinegar, from *vinaigre*, "vinegar." The name, though, became transferred to the container rather than to the sauce, and to similar containers, finally being settled on a container of smelling salts.

ladyfinger

The poet Keats, who knew these delicate pastries back in 1820,

called them *lady's-fingers*. Both of these were fanciful names, however, merely indicative of size. As applied to the modern bakery-made American product the name is distinctly inappropriate. The name *finger biscuit,* also in early use, would be more fitting: the finger could be that of a heavyweight prizefighter.

ember days

Three days (Wednesday, Friday, and Saturday) of fasting observed quarterly in the Roman Catholic and Anglican churches. Though the first is but a week after Ash Wednesday, the term *ember* has no relationship to the ashes of a fire. It is, in fact, only a corruption of the Old English word *ymbrene,* meaning "quarterly," or "seasonal," for the periods of fasting celebrate the four seasons—spring, summer, autumn, and winter.

talisman

Completely unrelated to **talesman** (which see), despite all similarities of spelling, this word comes to us through the Romance languages from the Arabic *tilsam,* "a magic charm." The earlier derivation is from the Greek *telesma* of the same meaning, but having had the former meaning of "a religious rite," and coming from *telein,* to "fulfill," from *telos,* "end."

sadiron

In its original sense in English, *sad* had the meaning "fully satisfied, sated." From this sense it underwent alteration, as so many

English words do, and came to have the meaning of "solid, heavy, dense." It is in this sense that it is used in the *sadiron,* which is a heavy, solid flatiron used for pressing and smoothing clothes. Regardless of how sorrowful the housewife may be that she is compelled to use this weighty tool, her sadness has no part in its name.

villain

Originally, apparently, one of the retinue attached to an estate, for the word stems from the Latin *villanus,* from *villa,* "a country house," and this meaning was largely retained in an alternate spelling of the English word, *villein.* But, progressing from the general sense of "a peasant," in which sense the word dates back to the early fourteenth century, the use of the term was broadened to include anyone of low birth, then to one of ignoble instincts, and finally to its present sense where it applies to a scoundrel or criminal. Related terms are known in most of the Romance languages, and the immediate source of the English form was the Anglo-French of the same or slightly different spelling.

catawampus

No one now knows the source. It showed up in print shortly after 1840 and, most likely, had already been American slang for ten or fifteen years before that. With humorous reference to General Zachary Taylor at the Battle of Buena Vista in the Mexican War, the New York *Herald* carried the squib (June 17, 1846):

> *On Taylor came and met the foe*
> *All marshall'd forth so pompously,*
> *And there he's slain two thousand men,*
> *All chaw'd up catawampously.*

That is, to translate the meaning, as if they had been met by a fierce or savage bogy.

umpire

Although this word has been in the language since the late fourteenth or early fifteenth century, it is a variant of a still older word, *noumpere,* which entered the language in the mid-fourteenth century but lasted less than a hundred years. For *a noumpere* became altered to *an oumpere,* which then underwent many changes of spelling until the one we know was adopted in the seventeenth century. The original English form was adopted from the Old French *nonper, nomper,* "not equal," from *non,* "not," plus *per,* "peer." It has reference to the third man who was called in to settle a dispute when the two arbitrators first appointed could not agree, that man thus making the total number of referees unequal so that there would necessarily be a majority opinion.

fearnought

You may run across this in your reading of tales of the sea especially. That is, it is the name of a heavy woolen cloth, or the outer clothing made from it, that is specially adapted for use by sailors aboard ship in inclement weather. Those wearing it "fear nought" from the elements. Sometimes the cloth is known as *fearnought* and the garments made from it are *dreadnoughts,* but the terms are often used interchangeably.

peacock

Six hundred, even four hundred years ago, this bird was just called a *po,* though by the latter time *pokok* and *pocock* had begun to come into favor. (The female was the *pohenne* or *pohen.*) But the *o,* sounded as in "cost," gave rise also to the spelling *paa.* Carelessness turned this into the sound *pay,* which, by the pronunciation of the English alphabet of that period, caused it in turn to be spelled *pe* and thence to *pea,* for "ea" then represented the sound we still have in "break," "great," "steak." Change to the present pronunciation began in the eighteenth century. (See also **Argus-eyed.**)

rambunctious (rambustious)

This Americanism (possibly brought to us by Irish immigrants) seems to be a variant of the British term of equivalent meaning, *rambustious.* The latter, it is suggested, may have been coined from *ram* plus *bust*. To *ram,* of course, is "to butt, strike," and generally to behave in the manner of a frolicsome male sheep. And *bust?* The earliest recorded use of the verb, which has been traced to the early thirteenth century, is in the sense, "to beat, thrash." (This sense still exists, as in the colloquial, "I'll bust him in the nose!") So if we have a man, or especially a small boy, in boisterous mood, *ramming* around and *busting* people, he may certainly best be described as *rambustious!*

leapfrog

It is the boy beneath who is the *frog,* his bent back, chin on chest, somewhat resembling a ranine attitude. The sport is not recent. Shakespeare speaks of it when, writing *Henry V,* in 1599, he has the king say to Katherine of France that he would marry, "If I could winne a Lady at Leape-frogge, or by vawlting into my Saddle, with my Armour on my backe."

eggnog

There is nothing particularly tricky about this term; it, like the concoction it designates, is a combination of *egg,* the product of the hen, and *nog,* "strong ale," the product of the brewer. Originally, that is, strong ale was the spirituous ingredient, but it is often replaced by wine, rum, cider, or other spirits. Incidentally, the beverage is of American origin, known by this name in Revolutionary times.

amateur

Though this was derived from Latin *amator,* "a lover," the French gave it a slight alteration in sense, which we have adopted, "a lover or devotee of an art, pastime, sport, or the like." And, nowadays, we have even extended the sense to include one who is a dabbler or tyro, one without training in an art, sport, or skill, but who enjoys its activity.

124

catamount

In North America, a name applied to the cougar or the lynx. Although the *Hazlitt Diary,* describing the appearance of one on Cape Cod, says: "It was said to be five feet long; besides, the tail was as much more; and it could mount trees, whence its name," the name is actually formed by contraction from "cat of the mountain," because the critters are usually to be found in hilly country —or, at least, the critters of the cat family known to the English by this name, the leopard or the panther, frequent such regions.

kingfish, kingpin, etc.

Long years before radio gave Amos and Andy, and their pal, the Kingfish, to the American audience *kingfish* was a name bestowed upon any of several fish notable for size or importance. It is for similar cause that *king* became the first element in such terms as *kingbolt, kingpin, kingpost, king snake, kingwood,* etc.

landlubber

Though we might honestly say that a *landlubber* is one who "lubs de land," we would rightly be called a punster, rather than a tracer of origins. The fact is that a *lubber,* even six hundred years ago, was a clumsy lout, one who didn't know B from a bull's foot. And so he was to sailors who, through later centuries, had to put up with him on shipboard. First it was new green seamen who, in contempt, were called *lubbers,* then, as *landlubbers,* it was applied with equal contempt to passengers or others who knew not one rope from another.

talesman

It was formerly the practice (and may still be in some places) to make up a trial jury in whole or in part of men selected from among the bystanders in the court. Men of law, like doctors, like to express things in Latin when possible, and people drawn on to fill a jury in this manner were called *tales de circumstantibus,* "such

125

persons as those standing around." This was soon shortened to *tales*, which is the plural of *talis*, "of such a kind." So it follows that a *talesman* was one of such persons impaneled to complete a jury, from which it has become, simply, any juror.

jalousie

In our own Southern states this is now a misnomer. In Spain, back in the sixteenth century, spelled *gelosia*, and later in France as *jalousie*, both indicating "jealousy," the term denoted a kind of slatted blind somewhat similar to the modern Venetian blind. It was then made of wood, however, and the immovable slats excluded not only rain and sun, but also the prying eyes of possible suitors of señoritas within. But, less than a score of years ago, Florida genius found that rain could still be excluded and sunshine admitted by replacing the wooden slats with slats of glass, and that the admission of air could be controlled by having these slats movable. They are still called *jalousies*, but no longer safeguard a jealous husband or father.

litterbug

A term coined by an unknown person, probably about 1945, and now designating one who strews litter wherever he goes. The term

 was descried in 1950 on the back of a truck by Mrs. Henry W. Land, a member of the Mount Dora, Florida, Lakes and Hills Garden Club, and it was suggested that *litterbug* be adopted by the club in connection with a roadside clean-up campaign planned by that organization. Announcement of the plan, in the June 22, 1950, issue of the weekly *Mount Dora Topic,* closed with the statement, "The cleanup campaign . . . will carry the theme: 'Don't be a litter-bug!' " The slogan and litter campaign were subsequently adopted, in order, by the Florida Federation of Garden Clubs, Inc., The South Atlantic Region, and the National Council of Garden Clubs.

126

catacomb

The name was, originally, merely applied to a low-lying plot—Greek *kata,* "down," *kumbe,* "hollow"—on the outskirts of Rome along the Appian Way. The church of San Sebastiano was erected on this plot, and, by tradition, the bodies of St. Peter and St. Paul were briefly interred beneath it. In consequence, however, the ground here was considered peculiarly blessed among early Christians and, in time, thousands, after death, were interred in niches carved along innumerable galleries leading in all directions in the soft tufa beneath the church. Other similar subterranean cemeteries, some in tiers of galleries, were developed in other parts of Rome, all known as *catacombs,* but all were closed and forgotten in the ninth century until chance rediscovery in 1578.

talbotype

One of the words describing a process or product that was named after the inventor (like *daguerreotype* and *pasteurize*), the *talbotype* is named after W. H. F. Talbot, an English inventor, who, in 1841, patented his discovery of making photographic images directly upon sensitized paper. Talbot himself called his process *calotype* (from the Greek *kalos,* "beautiful," plus *typos,* "type"), but his friends renamed it after the discoverer.

castanet

Identical in sound though it may be with the words "cast a net," this comes through Spanish *castañeta* from Latin *castanea,* "a chestnut," probably from resemblance in form, faint though it may be. The instrument, used as an accompaniment to dancing, was introduced to Spain by the Moors, but is actually a variation of the *crotalum* used by Roman dancers and the corresponding *krotalon* of the Greeks.

eavesdropper

The eighteenth-century jurist, Sir William Blackstone, really told the whole story: "*Eaves-droppers,* or such as listen under walls or windows or the eaves of a house to hearken after discourse, and thereupon to frame slanderous and mischievous tales, are a common nuisance, and presentable," he adds, "at the court leet." Regrettably, however, the old "court leet" having jurisdiction over such offenses has gone out of existence; eavesdroppers frame their "slanderous and mischievous tales" with impunity nowadays.

jackstone

The name of this children's game comes from its similarity to the older name, *chackstone,* which in its turn came from *chuckstone,* in Scotland called *chuckiestone.* Nowadays, in America at least, the game is played with five or six six-pointed (or knobbed) small iron pieces which are tossed or *chucked* into the air by the player and caught in the hand. Formerly, however, the pieces so chucked were pebbles or small *stones.* In still earlier times, dating back to ancient Rome and Greece, the objects so tossed and caught were the ankle bones of sheep, the *tali* and *astragaloi.*

Paris green

This term, which dates at least to the 1870's, seems to be of American origin, but has spread to Europe by this time. Today, it refers to the compound copper aceto-arsenite, which has had extensive use both as an insecticide and as a pigment, and which is better known in Europe as *Schweinfurt green.* When the name *Paris green* was first coined, it was more often used to designate the related compound, copper arsenite, of similar use and color, more commonly known as *Scheele's green. Paris green* has also been used as a name for the color obtained on using these pigments. The origin of the term is obscure—it may have indicated that the material was manufactured in or exported from Paris, but it seems equally plausible to suggest that the name was coined by some shrewd Yankee merchant who reasoned that "Paris green" would be a much more attractive shade of paint or wallpaper to the American housewife than would one of "Schweinfurt green" or "Scheele's green."

taffeta

Although this name has been applied and misapplied to many different fabrics during the span of the nearly six centuries during which it has been in the language, its original sense, "a plainly woven, glossy silk," reflects its origin closely. The word has been through just about all the Romance languages on its way toward English (Old French *taffetas* or *taphetas,* Medieval Latin *taffata,* Italian *taffeta,* Portuguese *tafeta,* Spanish *tafetan*), but it came originally from the Persian *taftah,* "silken cloth," a substituted use of the past particle of *taftan,* "to shine."

lotus-eater

According to ancient Greek myth, the people dwelling in a certain region in northern Africa derived particular enjoyment from  the fruit of a tree which the Greeks called *lotos.* The fruit itself was pleasant to the palate, but a wine made from it was especially enjoyable. Those who partook of it forgot all cares and worries. Thus, to the Greeks, these people, and also any others who allowed themselves to become similarly lulled into a state of indifference or a sense of luxurious ease, were *lotophagi,* "lotus-eaters." It was said by Homer that the companions of Odysseus lost all desire to return to their native land when, in their wanderings, their vessel reached these shores and they tasted the fruit and wine of this tree. Botanists have identified the tree with the jujube; today's lozenge so named is flavored with the juice of its fruit or an imitation thereof.

jackknife

Certainty is lacking of the source of this American name, known since the early eighteenth century. Obviously *jack* was not employed in the sense of smallness, for the true jackknife is always large. This has given rise to the surmise that the American name is a corruption and contraction of the Scottish (later also English)

129

clasp knife, the *jockteleg*. If so, there is a possibility that the Scottish historian, Lord David Hailes, gave the true source of both names in 1776 by attributing the latter to a corruption of the French name *Jacques de Liége,* the original maker of the knife. However, though admitting the plausibility of this account, Sir James A. H. Murray, editor of the *Oxford English Dictionary* and a Scot himself, was unable to find confirmation of the statement.

moonstruck

"The sun shall not smite thee by day, nor the moon by night," said the Hebrew psalmist. And from early Greek and Roman times, Selene of the Greeks and Luna of the Romans, goddesses of the moon, were also believed to be capable of affecting the brains of mortals. Those, especially, who slept with head exposed to the light of the moon would become *selenobletos* or *lunatikos,* maddened by Selene or, in Rome, by Luna. No one knows the age of the superstition; it was held also by the ancient Egyptians.

fata morgana

Nothing to do with "fate"; the expression is Italian for "the fairy Morgana," and you'll see it in French as *Morgan le Fay.* By English legend she was the fairy who reported to King Arthur, her brother, the love affair between his wife, Guinevere and the knight Lancelot. But the fairy appears in many medieval romances, especially Italian. And, because she was anciently supposed to have been the cause, her name, *fata morgana,* has long been applied to the kind of mirage most frequently seen in the Strait of Messina, in which the spectator may see images of men, houses, ships, sometimes in the water, sometimes in the air, or doubled, with one image inverted above the other.

ball peen

This is recorded merely for the benefit of those who don't know one kind of hammer from another. But this one is used chiefly by metalworkers. It is one in which the side opposite the face or flat surface of the hammer or sledge is rounded or ball-shaped. *Peen,* that is—also sometimes spelled *pane, pean,* or *pein*—designates that end of the head of a hammer, and it may be pointed, sharp, thin, or ball-shaped.

yardarm

There is some uncertainty about the origin of *yard.* It is known to be descended from the Anglo-Saxon *gierd* of which there are related forms in the Teutonic languages generally, and it has been suggested that the ultimate origin may be either the Latin *hasta,* "spear," or the Russian *zherd',* "a thin pole." Either, though, is relatively long and slender and could as easily have led to the nautical *yard,* the relatively long and slender spar that is hung upon and crosswise to the mast of a ship to support a square sail. As is so for other such crossed configurations, either part of the cross-member is one of its *arms*—hence, *yardarm,* "one of the arms of a yard."

viking

The word is found in Anglo-Saxon, with the spelling *wicing,* as early as the eighth century, but, curiously, it is not found in modern English until the early nineteenth century, having been introduced then from the Norwegian *vikingr.* However, the evidence indicates that it was the Anglo-Saxon term that was the earliest ancestor, having been formed from *wic,* "camp." The name was apparently formed because of the practice of the vikings to set up temporary encampments while carrying out a raiding expedition. The word was adopted into the various Scandinavian languages and, in Old Norse and Icelandic, acquired the meaning of "the practice of piracy."

gagman

Apparently on the theory, "If an audience will swallow this joke or yarn it won't *gag* on anything," *gag* developed, some hundred and fifty years ago, as an improbable story, some tale or yarn taxing the credulity of the listener, or, eventually, a joke that would bring forth hearty laughs from the hearers. In the theatrical world the *gag* was likely to be a line or so of his own inserted into his part, usually to evoke a laugh. He was the original *gagman*. But, especially when radio began to make heavy demands upon the wit of professional humorists, the capacities of others were needed in the promotion of laugh-producing mirth. Then the writers of humorous lines, rather than the speakers, became the *gagmen*.

Queen Anne's lace

I am indebted to Dr. Nellie Payne for this tale of the origin of the common name of the wild carrot, *Daucus carota*. She recalls having read it in a child's primer published perhaps some fifty years ago. It seems that a ward of the Queen, learning to tat, had chosen the delicate flower of this weed to use as a pattern. Having been found innocent of a suspected childish prank, the little girl came to the attention of the Queen, who observed and praised the child's handiwork, and gave her her royal permission to name the pattern for Her Majesty. It soon followed that the name of the pattern was transferred to the flower itself, and to the plant. As for the Queen, Dr. Payne believes it was Anne of Bohemia, who married Richard II of England in 1382.

ultimatum

Diplomatic negotiations between countries are traditionally carried on with the utmost of politeness and in courteous language. When, however, an impasse is reached, the "mailed fist in a velvet glove" is extended, by one side or the other, in the form of an *ultimatum*. The word itself is the neuter singular of the past participle of the Late Latin verb *ultimare*, "to be at the end," from *ultimus*, "last, final." Although *ultimatum* is Latin in form, it is probable that it came into English through the French, which is, historically, the language of diplomacy. The word is known in the same form in many of the European languages, both Romance and Teutonic.

monkey wrench

Though this useful device is little more than a hundred years old we can't even be sure whether it was of English or American origin,  let alone how it came by its name. Stimpson, in *A Book about a Thousand Things* (1946), believed that it was devised by a London blacksmith named Charles Moncke, and that *monkey wrench* was a corruption of *Moncke wrench*. But Mencken, in *The American Language* (1936), points to the fact that our cousins-across-the-sea call this wrench a "spanner wrench." In an effort to establish a case for an American origin, Dr. M. M. Mathews, in *American Speech,* February, 1953, reporting on a number of newspaper clippings about words that had been collected over a period of years by Dr. John W. Cummins of Boston, largely undated, had this to say about *monkey wrench:* "There is in the Cummins material a digest that appeared in the Boston *Transcript* sometime during the winter of 1932–33. According to this note, about 1856 a Yankee named Monk employed by Bemis & Call of Springfield, Mass., invented a movable jaw for a wrench. It was given a special name there in the shop, but it soon came to be called *Monk's wrench* and then *monkey-wrench*. This explanation is suspiciously easy and 'pat,' but it is somewhat odd that the date given, 1856, tallies pretty well with that of the first occurrence of the term in the *Oxford English Dictionary* [a listing of the name in Simmonds 1858 *Dictionary of Trade Products*]. I am hoping that Mr. Monk may stand up under investigation, but he may have been disposed of long ago in some article not seen by me."

hamlet

Yes, it does mean "a little ham," but the *ham* therein has nothing to do with any member of the *Sus,* or hog, family. It had originally, that is, to do with members of *Homo sapiens,* those who, in the times of Alfred the Great, lived in a small collection of cottages, a small village, then called a *ham*. The term survives in such place names as Shoreham, East Ham, Oakham, and others.

farthingale

Heaven grant that this garment doesn't come into style again, but it may, of course, though it can have nothing to recommend it. It was a kind of hooped skirt, extending from hips to feet, and as nearly a perfect cylinder as skill could make it, the top covered by flounces. It was the height of fashion in England just three hundred years ago. But the name had to do with neither farthings nor gales; it was a curious corruption, through French, of Spanish *verdugo,* meaning "rod," for the garment owed its shape to a framework of rods.

alyssum

The Greeks had the notion that if one were bitten by a rabid dog, hydrophobia or madness could be averted by promptly chewing the leaves of this plant. Accordingly they gave it the name *alyssos,* from the negative prefix *a* and *lyssa,* "madness," hence, "preventive of madness." The meaning was preserved in the Roman alteration, *alyssum.* None of our modern physicians, however, recommends it as a cure for hydrophobia.

carpetbagger

Shortly after the War Between the States—in the North, the Civil War—hordes of gentry, mostly poor whites, piled their paltry belongings into the traveling bag of the period, its sides made of carpet, and moved South. Their intent was to pick up what they could, financially, socially, and politically, with the aid of the newly enfranchised Negro, from the impoverished former slave owners. The selfish "carpetbagger," operating through unworthy motives, became "a hissing and a byword" among Southerners and a disgrace to the North.

134

jack-in-the-pulpit

This American wildflower, growing only in marshy woodlands, is unknown in some parts of the country. To anyone who has seen it in springtime, the cause of the name is obvious. The upright sturdy spadix or flower spike stands under a protecting canopy or spathe, vividly resembling a priest at his pulpit with sounding board curved above him. The plant is also called *Indian turnip,* but woe betide the unfortunate lad whose mates beguile him into being misled by the name! The tuber, edible when properly cooked, is burningly pungent when eaten raw, the effect lingering for hours.

moonshine

Perhaps a good covering definition would be an operation or a product achieved in the light of the moon. In England, the operation is that of smuggling spirits into the country without the payment of excise. In America, the end objective is the same and the product is also spirits, but the spirits are produced within the country by stealth and in violation of law. Neither usage is old. That of England dates back barely more than a century and a half, and that of America has perhaps half that age.

carboy

It's the genius of any language, I suppose, to alter an adoption from another language into familiar syllables. It was the famous grapes of Shiraz in Iran—or rather, the wine from those grapes—to which we owe this word. The wine was put up in large bottles of green or blue glass, which, for protection, were encased in basket-work. The native name for such a globular bottle was, by transliteration, *qaraba,* a term difficult to English tongues. But merchants and traders speedily surmounted that difficulty by resolving it into the convenient syllables, *carboy.*

rakish

Many years ago some enterprising naval architect, perhaps tired of the squared-off look of the vessels of his day, or perhaps to increase the deck area of his ship, designed a craft with bow and stern at sharp angles fore and aft of the keel—literally *reaching* out over the water. To our forefathers, a craft so designed was described as *rakish,* and the slope of the bow or stern as the *rake* thereof. The word is said by some authorities to have been derived from the Anglo-Saxon *ræcan* or *reccan,* "to reach, stretch," and probably to be cognate to the German *ragen,* of similar meaning. Regardless of origin, our word has been extended in use so that it now applies to various things, including ships, that "reach out" from their bases at a sharp angle.

Mother Hubbard

Greatly remembered, not so much by what she lovingly tried to do, but by what she wore while trying. She was unable, you remem-

ber, "to get her poor dog a bone," because the cupboard was bare. But she was not. At least, according to the crude illustrations adorning the pages of *Mother Goose's Melodies* of the early nineteenth century, she was robed in a cloaklike coverall, unconfined from shoulder to hem. And it was upon that shapeless garment her name was imposed.

allspice

This aromatic spice was not known in Europe before the discovery of the West Indies. The Spanish name was *pimienta,* "pepper," and because of that and the place of origin the dried seeds of the berry were known to English traders as "Jamaica pepper." However, because the housewives of England thought the seeds conveyed the combined flavor of cinnamon, cloves, and nutmeg, they began, in the seventeenth century, to demand *all spice* of their tradesmen. Nowadays, incidentally, the name is also given to other aromatic shrubs of North America and Japan.

136

tadpole

If this name of the early stage of frog or toad had gone along with other changes in our language through the centuries, no explanation of its source would be needed. *Tad* is merely a survival of the way *toad* was spelled and pronounced four hundred years ago, and *pole* was a seventeenth-century substitution for *poll,* "head." The name *toadhead* for the larva in the stage when it consists of little more than a round head with a tail is simple.

panhandle

Undoubtedly, in the sense of "to beg," this originated among the hoboes or vagrant tramps of the United States in the late nineteenth century. The significance is by no means evident, but I see no likelihood that it had any direct reference to any of the geographical regions known as "Panhandles," such as northern Texas, western Oklahoma, or northern West Virginia. But possibly, taking the idea of "to pan out," meaning to yield good returns, from the placer-miner's lexicon, some hobo evolved a *panhandler* as one who handles the pan hopeful of good returns.

ventriloquist

The first record of a related word is found in a book, *The discouerie of witchcraft,* by Reginald Scot, printed in 1584, where the author speaks of a *ventriloqua* (feminine of *ventriloquus,* "a ventriloquist"), and of her "practising hir diabolicall witchcraft and ventriloquie." It is not surprising that men of that time thought of witchcraft in this connection, for a *ventriloquist* is, both literally and in the original meaning of the word, "one who speaks in his belly," from the Latin *ventri-, venter,* "belly," plus *loqui,* "to speak." It was only later that the practitioner's art improved to the point that he could seem to cast his voice to distant places, and the word was transferred to mean "a voice-caster."

hamfatter

Theatrical slang, of course, now often abridged to *ham* or altered to *ham actor.* Whatever you wish to use, it is applied somewhat contemptuously to an actor or actress who may wish ardently to succeed on the stage, but who just can't act. A writer in *Century Magazine* in 1882 said the term came from an old Negro song, "The Hamfat Man," but H. L. Mencken, in *Supplement II* of his *The American Language,* says that among theatrical people the preferred belief is that the term first denoted those actors who, probably from the cost of cold cream, used ham fat instead to remove grease paint.

balderdash

A dash more bald than others of its kind? No, the fact is that no one knows for a certainty how this word originated. When, in the late sixteenth century, it first appeared in print it referred apparently to a light frothy or bubbly liquid—"barber's balderdash" was the term used. Not long after, in 1637, John Taylor, the "Water Poet," said that beer mixed with wine was called *balderdash.* Beer and buttermilk, said Ben Jonson, is "balderdash." Thus anything frothy, bubbly, or impossibly mixed, whether liquid or language, became so termed. As to origin, it may have been formed from the slang *balductum,* a hundred years the elder but itself of unknown ancestry, which also met Jonson's definition.

neat's-foot oil

When I was very young and my dad, of a Sunday morning, would apply this dressing to my rather scuffed shoes, by natural logic the inference was that the oil gave one a neat foot, hence the name. But not so. Though now so rare as to be called obsolete, *neat* was formerly a general term for cattle, more especially for oxen. *Neat's-foot oil,* accordingly, was and still is an oil extracted from the hoofs, now also the shin bones, of oxen or cattle. Now used as a lubricant and for dressing leather, it was at one time also used medicinally.

taciturn

It has nothing to do with any other kind of a turn, but comes to us almost unchanged from the Latin *taciturnus,* "silent," through *tacitus,* the past participle of *tacere,* "to be silent." Although *taciturn,* today, rarely implies the absolute silence suggested by its ancestor (meaning, rather, "disinclined to conversation, uncommunicative"), the expression of this quality has been retained in *tacit,* which is also derived from *tacitus, tacere.*

nightmare

A relic of ancient superstition dating in England at least from the eighth century, but, under the name *incubus,* known to the  Romans of Caesar's time. People thought this kind of *mare,* said to appear only at night, to be a female monster, spirit, or goblin. She sat upon the bosom of a sleeper, causing a feeling of suffocation, from which, in later times, the sleeper sought to free himself. The male counterpart was termed a *succubus.* We moderns attribute our nightmares to overindulgence in food or drink.

cantilever

In college speech this becomes, "Can't I leave her?" Though most certainly this interpretation has no bearing whatsoever on this type of "flying-lever bridge," no satisfactory source of the *canti-* element has been determined. As a term in architecture, the name appeared in the seventeenth century, pertaining to a masonry bracket of much greater length than depth. Two such brackets united at the tips became a *cantilever bridge* early in the nineteenth century.

ultima Thule

Thule (pronounced *thew'-lee* or *thoo'-lee,* with *th* as in *thank*) is the ancient Greek and Latin name for the most northerly habitable place in the world, said to be six days' sail north of Britain. Although it was presumably named for a real place, there is considerable uncertainty as to just what place was that designated as Thule, and guesses range from Norway to Iceland. The Thule in Greenland at which the United States has recently established an Air Force base is named in remembrance of this unknown land of the ancients and is pronounced *too'-lee*. But *Thule* has also acquired a figurative meaning, which is "the extreme limit of travel," and this has led to the phrase *ultima Thule* ("farthest Thule"), with the meaning of "the utmost attainable, the limit, 'the most.' "

backgammon

A game of considerable antiquity, believed to have been invented in the tenth century, but possibly related to the game *Ludus duodecim scriptorum,* "twelve-line game," played in ancient Rome. In England the game was always called *tables* prior to the seventeenth century, when the new name was introduced. Apparently the name was made up of *back* and *gammon,* a variant form of *gamen,* "game," because the rules provide that a player's pieces must be taken up, under certain circumstances, and go back to the starting point.

sundowner

Sundown itself is presumed to be a contraction of "sun-go-down" or perhaps the archaic "sun-gate-down," and a *sundowner* is either a person who times a certain action relative to sundown, or a deed performed at sundown. There are at least three quite distinct applications of the term. The oldest is an Australian usage found as early as 1875, and applies to a nomad who times his arrival at a dwelling with sundown, so that he will be invited to spend the night. The second is an Americanism, found near the turn of the century, denoting a person now known as a "moon-lighter"—a hustler who holds down a secondary job, usually in the evening, in addition to his regular employment. The third, dating to the 1920's, is a South African term applied to a drink of conviviality taken at sundown.

zodiac

The Greeks reckoned their calendar from the twelve principal constellations as they took their turns in the sky overhead, but the calendar was represented graphically by a circle in which figures representing the constellations were entered. This representation was called *zodiakos kyklos,* "the circle of the figures," from *zodion,* "a figurine" (diminutive of *zoön,* "animal"), and *kyklos,* "a circle" (which led to our *cycle*). The term became abbreviated to *zodiakos,* which was taken into Latin as *zodiacus* and hence through the Romance languages and into English with appropriate spelling changes along the way.

fantan

Neither portion of this is an English word; the whole merely approximates the Chinese name of a simple game of chance. In the native form a small heap of coins is covered by a bowl and the players then place bets, not on the number of coins so concealed, but on the remainder—one, two, or three—when the total is divided by four. The Chinese name means "remainder." Variations have, of course, been introduced.

hackamore

Easterners and Englishmen may rarely hear this word, but it is common among horsemen and cattlemen of the West. No one ever accused the forty-niners in early contact with California Mexicans of a close ear for the Spanish words they adopted, but it is now generally accepted that *hackamore* was intended to represent the sound of the Spanish *jáquima,* a term in that language for the part of the harness of a horse that we call "halter" or, more exactly, "headstall."

hallmark

Whatever the present application, the original term has designated the official stamp or mark of the Goldsmith's Company of

London or other assay office applied to gold and silver articles to indicate their purity. Such stamping was introduced by order of Edward I in the year 1300, and there have been but few changes in the designs so employed since that date.

nuthatch

This small bird, of several varieties, got its name from certain of its feeding habits. Although it eats a profusion of insects, it is

 especially notable as an eater of acorns and the nuts found in pine cones, the shells of which it breaks with its sharp beak. Our ancient forebears therefore gave it a descriptive name, combining *nut* with *hatch,* a term borrowed from French *hacher,* "to chop, hack"; hence, a bird that hacks nuts for its food. Our words *hatchet,* "that which chops," and *hash,* "that which is chopped," came from the same French source.

alewife

Although the early settlers on our New England shores knew this plentiful fish by this name (*New Plymouth Laws,* 1633), so many other pronunciations were also used in the early years that to this day there is no certainty of its source. Some think that an Indian name was adopted which sounded something like "alewife." Nevertheless, the traveler John Josselyn in his *An Account of Two Voyages to New England,* 1674, wrote: "The alewife is like a herrin, but has a bigger bellie, therefore called an alewife."

nightingale

Bits of our language have been picked up from almost every people with whom our English forebears came in contact. Thus, in remote times, when Norse vikings made settlements along the coasts of England, the Norse *gala,* "to sing," entered the native speech. Thus *nahtigala,* the early name of the bird, merely meant

142

"night singer." At some time down through the years, as spelling altered, an *n* was inserted without rhyme or reason. In fact, by all rules and precepts, our name for the bird should be *nightgale*.

pallbearer

In England, to this day, a *pallbearer* is one who does about what the name indicates—one who, at a funeral, is assigned the duty of holding up the corners or edges of the pall draping the coffin. But in America, unless serving in an honorary capacity only, he is one of those delegated to the bearing of the coffin itself.

sackbut

This musical instrument, a precursor of the trombone in that it contained a hairpin-shaped bent tube which was slid in and out to vary the tone, may have derived its name from the Old Norman French *saqueboute,* a lance with a curved hook at the end, which was used to pull riders from their horses. The further etymology of *sackbut* may remind my contemporaries of the *pushmi-pullyu,* that mythical animal found in Hugh Lofting's tales of Doctor Dolittle which had a head at either end, for it is based on the fusion of *saquier,* "to pull," and *bouter,* "to push."

akimbo

One can't be certain about this, but the prevailing opinion among the word-delvers is that this arose from a corrupted pronunciation of the medieval phrase *in kene bowe,* meaning "in a sharp bend," just as is the shape of one's arm when the hand rests on the hip, the present usual sense of the word. But there was an Old Norse word, *kengboginn,* "bent double; crooked," which may have been the source of our word. Our language has undergone some mighty strange transformations, yet I mention this only because it has been given serious consideration.

fakir

Through the fact that some of the practices of certain religious devotees, especially of India, appear to be quite fictitious, clever

143

trickery, the word *fakir* is sometimes considered to be merely another spelling of *faker*. It isn't; it's an Arabic term and, strictly speaking, it should be applied only to those followers of Mohammed who, with him, can truly say, "Poverty is my pride," *el fakr fakhri*. However in India the Hindu *fakir* is likely to be an expert juggler, adept in sleight of hand, in hypnotism, in ventriloquism, and in producing illusions.

bachelor's button

Almost any kind of small round flower the petals of which present a jagged appearance goes by this name. Why? Because garments anciently worn were held by buttons of cloth which, in the case of helpless bachelors, became frayed around the edges.

sabotage

The etymology of *sabotage* is clear—it is derived from the French *sabot,* "a wooden shoe," which, in turn, has been traced to the Spanish *zapato,* "a shoe," probably from the Biscayan *zapatu,* "to tread." The origin of the present-day meaning of *sabotage,* though, is less clear. It has been suggested that it may have been derived from the clatter of children in their noisy sabots, driving their parents or teachers to distraction; or that it may have arisen as an allusion to shoddiness, as by the comparison of crude wooden shoes with those of leather; or that it may have been applied to the practice attributed to French millworkers who, averse to the introduction of mechanization, cast their sabots into the looms; or, because it is also applied to the cutting of shoes or sockets used in attaching the rails of a railroad to the ties, that this sense of the word became warped to the deliberate destruction of these same rail attachments with the concomitant disabling of the railroad. In any event, *sabotage,* as an instrument of industrial warfare, had become firmly established by the French General Confederation of Labor in 1887, and was adopted into English by 1910, being accepted as a labor weapon by the I.W.W., though Weekley, writing in 1911 (*The Romance of Words*), said that it was not even then known to the great French dictionaries in that sense.

O.K.

Although these initials are now known and used around the world and have been in common American usage for a hundred  years, the source was a matter of great disputation through most of that period. Some attributed it to illiteracy displayed by Andrew Jackson, who, they said, wrote *O.K.* as the initials of *"Oll Korrect."* Others thought the source was a misreading of the initials *O.R.,* "Order Recorded," indicating official approval of a document. And some believed that the initials were an erroneous rendering of the Choctaw *okeh,* "it is so." All dispute ceased in 1941. In that year, in the July 19 issue of the *Saturday Review of Literature,* in an eight-page article, "The Evidence on *O.K.,"* Allen Walker Read laid the ghost for all time. By dint of much research he traced the initials back to 1840, finding the first appearance in print in the New York *New Era* of March 23. The reference was to a political organization supporting the candidacy of Martin Van Buren for a second term in the White House. The members called themselves the Democratic *O.K.* Club, taking the initials from *Old Kinderhook,* a title bestowed upon Van Buren from the name of the village, *Kinderhook,* in the valley of the Hudson where he was born. The mystifying initials, as a sort of rallying cry, caught the fancy of other supporters immediately, and were used, according to the New York *Herald* of March 28, by these supporters in a raid upon a meeting of the Whigs the previous evening. "About 500 stout, strapping men," the paper reported, "marched three and three, noiselessly and orderly. The word *O.K.* was passed from mouth to mouth, a cheer was given, and they rushed into the hall upstairs, like a torrent."

kickshaw

And of all the ways in which we who speak English have altered words of other languages this is literally something. Yes, that is what it meant—"something." It began as the French plural, *quelque choses,* which, especially when used in cookery, and, generally, with a shrug of the shoulders, indicated, "just something dainty; mere trifles." By the elite, the pronunciation was *que'que choses,* which became in English speech, of the seventeenth century, *keck shaws.* Our forebears then turned this back into a singular and the permanent pronunciation, *kickshaw.*

numskull

If the first syllable were spelled *numb,* as it once was, the sense and source would be clearly recognized. *Numb* in the *skull,* with the brain benumbed, dulled. Actually, however, if we were to follow *numb* back through the centuries we would find that it should be spelled *num* after all. Anciently, our language had a verb *nim,* meaning "to deprive, to take away." A past participle was *num,* "deprived, taken away." But *nim* has been *num* from our speech these five centuries.

humbug

My, but how the learned scholars of the 1750's did rave and rant against this neologism. After its coinage—out of whole cloth, presumably—it must have sprung into immediate popular favor. But here is what was said of it by one writer, probably Thomas Warton, in *The Student:* "I will venture to affirm that this *Humbug* is neither an English word, nor a derivative from any other language. It is indeed a blackguard sound, made use of by most people of distinction! It is a fine make-weight in conversation, and some great men deceive themselves so egregiously as to think they mean something by it." Nevertheless, despite all railings, *humbug* assumed a place of utmost respectability in the language as a synonym for "Nonsense!"

quarter-

The casual student of etymology may well be intrigued by various compound words starting in *quarter-,* as there seems a good likelihood that certain of these may have odd and unusual beginnings. But *quarterback,* for instance, is found to be, in football, the back whose position is one-quarter of the way between the line and the fullback; *quarterdeck* is, on a ship, a deck for the use of officers which covers approximately one-quarter of the area over the main deck; and *quartermaster* was originally a petty officer who was responsible for the troops' living quarters, but whose duties have now been enlarged to include responsibility for supplies in general as well as for quarters.

falderal, folderol

It had no basic meaning; originally used just as a refrain in songs, probably first in Scotland about three hundred years ago. But just because it was so often employed as a meaningless termination to silly little songs it did eventually come to be employed for a flimsy trifle, an empty bit of nothingness.

hunky-dory

Some of the dictionaries say, "Source unknown." I'll agree with that as to the *dory* element, but, considering that the common meaning of the American term is "Quite satisfactory; all safe and secure," the *hunky* element is logically explainable. Though not recorded until a hundred years ago, to be "all hunk" was probably as familiar to New York City schoolchildren from the time of Peter Stuyvesant as to be "O.K." is today, and had a similar meaning—to reach goal; to be home. It was from the Dutch *honk,* "goal." Change from *hunk,* "home," to *hunky,* "safe at home; hence, safe," was as natural as the modern change in slang *corn* to slang *corny.* Printed use goes back to 1861.

The full *hunky-dory* seems to have arisen during or soon after the Civil War. Definite record occurs in 1868. Credit for its introduction is thus stated by Carl Wittke, in *Tambo and Bones* (1930): " 'Josiphus Orange Blossom,' a popular song with many disconnected and futile stanzas, in a reference to Civil War days, contained the phrase, a 'red hot hunky dory contraband.' The Christy's [well-known blackface minstrels of that period] made the song so popular, that the American public adopted 'hunky-dory' as part of their vocabulary."

vampire

Neither of the living nor yet of the dead, a vampire is a reactivated corpse doomed, not to peaceful rest in its tomb, but to spend each night in search of a living victim of whose blood to drink. Belief in vampires is virtually world-wide, but the Slavic countries and their neighbors are the center of this belief. Thus, although the word comes to us from the French of the same form, its origin is the Hungarian *vampir,* in which form it is also known, together with variations, in Russian, Polish, Bulgarian, and other languages of the area. It has been suggested that the ultimate source may have been the North Turkish *uber,* "witch."

cantankerous

We must thank Oliver Goldsmith for developing this word from an older source. In *She Stoops to Conquer,* he proclaims, "There's not a more bitter cantanckerous road in all christendom," meaning that the road would try one's soul, is perverse, contrary, ill natured. Apparently Goldsmith dug up a word of similar meaning, long since obsolete or surviving only in country speech, *contecker,* a person who "contecks," quarrels, disputes, is contentious. But whatever his source, he gave us a mighty useful word.

pantywaist

This American appellation for an effeminate young man is not much more than thirty years old. The idea, however, takes us

 back to about 1890. Small American children, then, and some perhaps not so small, were encased in a sleeveless undervest, bedecked with buttons at the waistline, to which their panties were severally attached. The garments were for children and, especially, for girls; ergo, feminine and nonheroic.

Fahrenheit

He was only fifty when he died, in 1736, and only twenty-eight when he introduced the mercury-filled thermometer and devised the scale for measuring temperature still called by his name, Gabriel Daniel *Fahrenheit,* a German citizen, born in Danzig. His father was a merchant, and the son had been trained to follow that pursuit, but, interested more in the science of physics than in commerce, he removed to Holland.

ladybug

The usual American name; *ladybird,* the usual name in England. So named, not, as childish fancy may have assumed, because these beneficial insects are all female, but in honor of "Our Lady," the Virgin Mary.

table d'hôte

Lifted directly from the French over three hundred years ago, this literally means "the host's table." The original sense was that of a common table set for the guests at a hotel or other eating place, but from this has come the more usual meaning today, which is the complete meal served at a hotel or restaurant.

camelopard

No, no one ever thought this beast was a cross between the camel and the leopard, but the Greeks of old gave it the name—*kamelopardalis*—simply because its body somewhat resembled that of the camel and its spots were like those of the *pard* or leopard. We call the animal by the shorter name, *giraffe.*

strawberry

Although derived from the Anglo-Saxon *streawberige,* this word is curious in that its parallel is not found in other Teutonic languages. A synonymous Anglo-Saxon word was *eorthberge*

149

(earthberry), which failed to live in English, but is related to the German *Erdbeere* of the same meaning. Both *straw* and *berry*, though, have living relatives in the other Teutonic languages. *Strawberry* is of great age in its English ancestry, the early forms having been found to date from about the tenth century. The age of the word leaves us in considerable doubt as to the reason for its origin, but the best accepted derivation is that the small seed-like growths on the berry (called "achenes") were taken to resemble bits of straw, giving the fruit its name.

nincompoop

Sorry, but there's not much we can do with this word. It was coined sometime in the last half of the seventeenth century, though variously spelled *nicompoop, nickumpoop, nincumpoop,* but no source has been established. Dr. Samuel Johnson, in his dictionary of 1755, believed it to have been a corruption of the Latin phrase, *non compos,* "without ability," but the earliest forms of the word do not support that theory. It looks to me as though someone had merely elaborated upon the older *ninny* of almost identical meaning.

yesterday

Related forms of the word are to be found throughout the entire group of the Teutonic languages, and, indeed, more distant relatives are known in many of the languages of the large Indo-European family of which the Teutonic and Romance are two important branches. In English, the word goes back to the Anglo-Saxon *geostrandæg* or *gestordæg* (sometimes as two words, *geostran dæg*). It is uniquely in English, though, that the two elements always go together (some writers have experimentally written *yester* or *yestern* alone, but the practice has never won wide acceptance). In German, for example, "yesterday" is expressed by the simple word *gestern*. Interestingly, in some languages the related term has also had the sense of "tomorrow," so it is presumed that the original sense was "a day either before or after today."

haberdasher

The term is so old and so beguiling in appearance that there really should be a good story behind it. We have record of its continuous use through more than six hundred years, back to the early fourteenth century. John Minsheu, a dictionary compiler of around 1617, derives it from the German, *Hab' Ihr das?* "Have you that?" as a shopkeeper might say in showing his wares to a customer. But, though our word probably crept into English usage as a corrupt version of some alien term, the most likely being the Old French *hapertas,* "a dealer in furs," there is no clear account of its source. However, the original *haberdasher* sold hats and caps, as well as the notions he now deals in.

petticoat

In the fifteenth and sixteenth centuries this garment was actually, as the name indicates, a "little coat." At first it was a

man's coat, worn under his armor as a protection against chafing. Later he wore it as an undergarment beneath his doublet, as a waistcoat or sort of vest. And it was thus, then, that women first wore it, as a sort of chemise. But in the seventeenth century women began to extend the name to the underskirt appended from the chemise, or, as at present, to any underskirt.

jack-in-the-box

Nowadays the name is usually applied to a toy, a box from which a frightening figure, such as a dragon, serpent, clown, or the like, springs out when the fastening of the lid is released. The toy, however, is a very modest proxy for the original box of the sixteenth century, which was also designed to delude or deceive the person who opened it. That is, it was a box, empty or containing worthless trash (the *jack*), which a clever cheat or sharper substituted for the box or small chest of money that a tradesman expected to receive for his merchandise. Hence, the sharper himself became a *jack-in-the-box*. One of the *Satirical Poems of the Time of the Reformation,* in 1570, has the lines, in modern spelling:

> *Jack in the box,*
> *For all thy mocks*
> *A vengeance might [on] thee fall!*
> *Thy subtlety*
> *And palliardy [knavery]*
> *Our freedom brings in thrall.*

gaffer, gammer

The terms did not break into print before the latter end of the sixteenth century, but both must have been in common dialectal speech many long years earlier. And, of course, dispute reigns as to what were the original words. As now used, almost wholly only in rural England, they are usually terms of address, respectively, to an elderly man and an elderly woman. The present consensus is that they have gradually evolved as contractions of *godfather* and *godmother,* but there is also a strong belief that the original forms were *grandfather* and *grandmother.*

humdrum

Hum, yes, because that which is *humdrum* has the monotony of the humming of a bee or other insect. But *drum*—well, did this added syllable, back in the sixteenth century, also convey the monotone of a drumbeat? It is doubtful, though such could have been the case. But it is more likely that *drum* was added merely because it rhymed with *hum* and just happened to be a word itself.

stripling

The etymology of this word is uncertain. Most authorities suggest that it is derived from the noun *strip,* "a narrow piece of substantially even width," plus the suffix *-ling,* "one having some speci-

152

fied attribute." This derivation is based on the use of *stripling* as "a youth, not yet having filled out in manhood, hence, one slender as a strip." However, the best authorities then immediately point out that *strip*, as a noun, was not recorded in the language until more than a half-century after the first recorded use of *stripling*. The verb to *strip*, to divest someone of something, though, is much older, and it seems remotely possible that *stripling* may have originated with the sense of beardless, i.e., one *stripped* of his beard. This is not too likely, since presumably such a person never had had a beard of which to have been stripped.

ait

If it were not for the needs of crossword puzzlers, this rarely used word might peacefully fade away from American dictionaries. In England, where it is still applied occasionally as a term of ancient lineage for a small island, especially in the Thames river, the spelling may be *ait, eyot,* or *eyet,* according to one's whim, each having the same pronunciation as "eight."

rabble

Every generation has them—people who lose their tempers quickly, people who make more noise than they do sense—and the Romans had a name for them. (The Greeks did, too, but right now it's the Romans who concern us.) The Latin term meaning "to rave, to rage" is *rabo,* and the petty advocate who pleaded his cause with more temper than temperateness was a *rabula.* Although the derivation is not clear, it seems probable that this term became applied to any noisy person and finally to a noisy collection of people—a mob—which is the sense of our modern word, *rabble.*

callithump

Back in 1856, B. H. Hall, in *College Words and Customs,* attributed this name to a noisemaking band composed of Yale College students. Maybe he was right, but if so, the *callithumpians,* as members of any similar band were known, had also spread out by 1830 from New Haven to New York. At least the term sounds as if it had a college source—made up from Greek *kalos,* "beautiful," and *thump;* "a beautiful thump." What did these beautiful thumpers do? Strummed on pans, kettles, coal buckets, and any other discordant noisemaker to make the night hideous. The name, sometimes degenerated to "cowthump," was also applied to the "shivaree" or *charivari.*

tabernacle

This word first entered our language in the mid-thirteenth century as applied to the curtained tent that, in the Old Testament, contained the Ark of the Covenant and other sacred items. Its use in the broader sense of "a portable, temporary dwelling, such as a tent" began about a century later, as so used in the Wyclif translation of the Old Testament, although there exist some records of its use in differing senses in the interim. The word comes to us through the French (of the same spelling) from the Latin *tabernaculum,* "a tent, booth, shed," this being the diminutive of *taberna,* "a hut, booth" (from which we also get *tavern*).

polecat

A *cat,* sometimes called "pussy," that is fond of *poles*—not, however, the kind stuck in the ground. This *pole,* back in the four-  teenth century, was a French word which, in modern French, is spelled *poule.* It means a chicken. For the *polecat* is a chicken thief, just as is its American cousin, the skunk. Incidentally, the European polecat does not have the broad stripe down the back, so characteristic of the American skunk.

oakum

You might not think it to be so, but in its original form *oakum* was "off-combing." It referred to the hard, coarse strands of retted

154

flax which were combed out before spinning, the tow. The Old English word was *acumba,* considerably modified in spelling down through the years. This tow, or "hards" as also called, was found to be useful in the calking of boats, and later the name was transferred to the strands of old rope, untwisted into its fibers and used for the same purpose.

keelhauling

By comparison, this, in the modern navy, constitutes a mild punishment. It actually amounts to nothing more castigating than a severe tongue-lashing. Not so in former days. The literal procedure was so severe a punishment that many a sailor failed to survive. It is said that the device was first copied by the Dutch in the sixteenth century from earlier practices among Mediterranean pirates, and it was then speedily adopted by the British. The malefactor to be punished was dropped from the end of a yard and hauled under the vessel from side to side, a weight being attached to his feet to keep him clear of the ship's bottom. Or if his misdeed were adjudged worthy of more severe treatment, he was hauled lengthwise under the vessel, from stem to stern. This latter, called *keelraking,* was more likely to be fatal.

gadabout

One *gads* who merely roams here and there idly or as if in meditation, but without special destination. But the *gadabout,* though he may have no special objective, does have a definite purpose in mind, and his roaming is rarely meditative. He seeks news. And the news he wants is that which will satisfy curiosity or some choice bit of gossip about a neighbor. Perhaps the pronouns should be changed from "he" and "his" to "she" and "hers," for the typical *gadabout* is more likely to be feminine than masculine. The term is little more than a hundred years old; a short-lived predecessor was *gad-abroad.*

Babbitt

No relation whatsoever to the chief character in Sinclair Lewis's satire of that title. This is the name of a soft, whitish alloy used to

155

reduce friction in machine bearings and was that of its American inventor, Isaac Babbitt (1799–1862), who first produced it at Taunton, Massachusetts, in 1834. The invention contributed so greatly to the development of the "Machine Age" that Babbitt later received a Congressional award of $20,000.

mooncalf

In Shakespeare's youth this was a figment of the imagination, a monster of some horrendous sort conjured up by moonlight in the eye of a frightened person too scared to see straight. But by the time Shakespeare wrote *The Tempest* (1613), he or others took it to be an actual being, a congenital monstrosity such as a malformed calf. The term was then applied to a person who was a congenital idiot or, as though moonstruck, acted as if deranged.

eaglestone

Actually these small, hollow, globular, stony balls, varying in size from a golf ball to a man's head, were so named by the Greeks —*aetites,* which, translated, is "eaglestone." According to Pliny, that is, this early name arose from a belief that unless the eagle were able to transport one of these stones into its nest the eggs would not hatch. How that belief came about is, of course, unknown, but as the nests are just about inaccessible, it is possible that an ancient climber, finding such a stone near a nest, embellished the tale of his daring ascent with the story, and the stone itself as proof of his discovery. The Greeks had their "tall stories" too.

stereotype

One of the greatest advances in the art of printing was the invention of movable type, for this permitted the printer to be free of the time-consuming process of having his plates individually engraved by hand. Yet movable type, too, had disadvantages, for it had to be carefully adjusted for even depth of impression and, once set up, had to be firmly locked in place to avoid becoming "pied" (i.e., scrambled). Then there came another great advance, said to be the invention of Firmin Didot, a French printer, in about 1798. This was *stereotype,* from the Greek *stereos,* "solid," plus *typos,* "type" (from *typtos,* "to strike"); hence, "solid type." In this process, movable type is set, as before, but it is then used to form a mold which, in turn, is used to cast a solid plate of type, releasing the original type for reuse and avoiding pieing. But one of the greatest advantages to the printer was that the invention of stereotype permitted the running of much larger editions, at lower cost, than had theretofore been possible, and each copy assuredly being exactly like all its mates. This absolute duplication of copies led to the figurative use of the word to describe people who behave in uniform patterns, also to characterize hackneyed phrases or those who use them, hence any formalized or uniform pattern of behavior.

Milquetoast

This fictitious character—in full, *Caspar Milquetoast*—was created by the cartoonist H. T. Webster. The series, continued at intervals through the 1930's and 1940's, depicted episodes in the life of "The Timid Soul," episodes of harrowing nature to a nonassertive, timorous man.

ragtime

As all cool cats know, this precursor of jazz is heavily syncopated, but with a strong beat. To its listeners in the late nineteenth century, the timing was most certainly ragged, compared to the tunes with which they were more familiar. What more logical than that this music of "ragged time" should become popularly known as *ragtime?*

leatherneck

Doughboy, gob, and *leatherneck,* as familiar designations of members of the Army, Navy, and Marine corps, respectively, of the

United States, have long been subject to speculation—and still are. No one knows; the origins remain inscrutable. As to *leatherneck*, H. L. Mencken said at one time, "It obviously refers to the sunburn suffered by marines in the tropics," overlooking the fact that sailors, with their low-cut collars, were even more exposed to sunburn. Among the theories advanced is the Navy version as it appears in George Stimpson's *Book about a Thousand Things* (1946): "Many sailors maintain that *leatherneck* originally referred to the dark and leathery appearance of a dirty and long-unwashed neck. It may be a myth, but according to Navy tradition marines in the early days were dirty of person. In sailor slang, washing without removing the undershirt and jumper is called a 'leatherneck' or 'marine wash.' When a sailor washes, according to the sailors, he usually strips to the waist and washes his face, neck and arms; but when a marine washes he does so after the fashion of civilians, that is, he merely takes off his coat and rolls up the sleeves of his shirt to the elbows and washes his hands to the wrist and his face to the neck. That, at any rate, was the version formerly given by sailors."

ignis fatuus (jack-o'-lantern, will-o'-the-wisp)

All names apply to the same natural phenomenon, which was apparently of quite frequent occurrence at one time, but is now infrequent. From printed records it would seem that the Latin term, appearing in the sixteenth century, was the earliest in English use, but it is more likely that *ignis fatuus,* "foolish fire," was some unknown scholar's translation into Latin of the French *feu follet,* of the same meaning, accepted by other writers as more learned, more highbrow, than the colloquial *jack-o'-lantern* and *will-o'-the-wisp*—sprites or hobgoblins locally termed Jack or Will and supposedly misleading unwary foot-travelers with lighted lantern or blazing wisp of hay into treacherous bogs. German *das Irrlicht* and Spanish *fuego fatuo* are respective translations of the Latin.

blue-sky law

Any law enacted for the protection of suckers who, without some such safeguard, might part with cash for the purchase of hot air, scenery, or even the blue sky from unscrupulous promoters. The first of the laws that acquired the term was enacted in Kansas in 1912. Our "blue sky" in such connection is the equivalent of the German *blauer Dunst,* literally "blue haze," but in colloquial speech, "humbug."

Airedale

Literally, "valley, or dale, of the Aire," a river in the southern part of Yorkshire, England, joining the Ouse and emptying into the Humber. The name is applied specifically to a breed of terrier originating in this valley, wire-haired, with crown, back, and sides black, and face, throat, and limbs tan. The dog, usually 40 to 50 pounds in weight, is noted for speed, sagacity, and scenting ability; hence, an excellent hunter. The Airedale is also said to be a pleasant companion and a good watchdog, though, never having owned one, I can't vouch for that.

dragoman

Even a woman may be a *dragoman,* for the terminal syllable is not an English word, even though we do, through long custom, make its plural *-men,* rather than *-mans,* as we should. We borrowed the term from the French, who had borrowed in turn from Spain, and there it had come, through the Moors, as a transliteration of Arabic *targuman.* When you hear some traveler use it, or meet it in the works of some author, be lenient; he wants to air his knowledge. He'd rather say *dragoman* than the English equivalent, "interpreter."

hocus-pocus

It is often stated as positive fact that this conjuror's formula, this indication of sham or trickery, owed its origin to a mocking corruption of the first three Latin words of the Consecration in the Catholic Mass, *Hoc est corpus meum* (This is my body). There is no proof of that. The conjecture was first advanced in 1694 in a sermon by the Protestant Archbishop, John Tillotson, seventy years after the term first appeared in print, though then in the form *Hocas Pocas.* Even at the early appearance there is repeated evidence that the term had been taken by various conjurors in imitation of an earlier and more famous one. At least Thomas Ady (c. 1656), though writing of witches and witchcraft, tells of a conjuror in the time of James I who called himself "Hocus Pocus, and so was called, because that at the playing of every Trick, he used to say, *Hocus pocus, tontus talontus, vade celeriter jubeo,*" which, as Ady goes on to say, was "a dark composure of words, to blinde the eyes of the beholders."

Frankly, that is to say, I do not know the source of *hocus-pocus,* and neither does anyone else. It may have had some such blasphemous Latin origin, and so may have had the Norwegian equivalent, *hokuspokus filiokus,* and the American expression current in my childhood, *hocus-pocus dominocus,* possibly corrupt Latin, respectively, for "This is the body of the Son," and "This is the body of the Lord."

But there is abundant evidence that "Hoky-poky," the cry of street vendors of ice cream in my childhood who so named the commodity they cried, was derived from the old juggler's term, and it is also probable, though not a certainty, that *hoax,* the art of the conjuror, is a shortened form of *hocus.*

firecracker

England knows this jubilant explosive as merely a *cracker,* though if part of a pyrotechnic display, such as a set piece, it is there, as here, a *firework.* Both terms have been in use from the sixteenth century. But with us, especially with a child, a *cracker* is first of all something to be eaten, harmlessly known as *biscuit* in England. Consequently the paper tube containing gunpowder which explodes with a bang when fire is applied became, naturally enough, a *firecracker* to American childhood from at least the early nineteenth century.

banshee

The Gaelic is *bean sidhe,* "female fairy," which, believe it or not, is transcribed phonetically as *banshee* in English. The *Standard*

Dictionary of Folklore (1949) describes her as, usually, a beautiful woman, though sometimes a hag, whose appearance, according to Irish folklore, foretells the death of someone close to one's family.

ramshackle

The Icelandic language has contributed relatively little to English, which has drawn so heavily on the various languages of the

world for its present make-up, but there seems good reason to believe that *ramshackle,* in its present sense of "tumble-down," or "on the verge of falling to pieces," is derived from the Icelandic *ramskakkr.* (Remember that in the Scandinavian languages, of which Icelandic is one, *sk* has a value very close to *sh* in English.) *Ramskakkr* is made up of the words *ramr,* "very," and *skakkr,* "wry, twisted"; hence is *very twisted,* and this is very close to what we mean when we call Sonny's old jalopy a "ramshackle automobile."

marchpane

Included merely to show that it wasn't overlooked, but there is little of a positive nature to explain its origin, despite much discussion. Similar forms appear in various of the languages of Europe, apparently all derived from Italian *marzipani.* Some say that that was derived from the name of a Venetian coin, the *matapanus,* and was transferred to the confection purchasable by that coin. Others say its source was the Latin *Martius panis,* "bread of Mars." The latter certainly bears greater plausibility.

sweepstakes

Used more or less interchangeably with the singular form. It is generally conceded that the original sense was "winner take all," that is, that the person winning the race or game "swept" all the "stakes" into his own pocket. Later the winnings did not accrue entirely to a single winner, but were divided in some set manner among the first several winners, and still later the term became applied to the event occasioning the wagering (for example, the famous Irish *Sweepstakes*) rather than to the disposition of the spoils. Curiously, though, *Sweepstake* (also spelled *Swepestake*) is recorded as used as a ship's name at least a hundred years earlier than its first recorded use in the gambling sense, but without any sound clue as to the reason for its choice as a nautical term.

martingale

Whether part of a harness, part of the rigging of a ship, or a gambling term, the name is supposed to be connected, in some peculiar manner, with a type of stinginess characteristic of the inhabitants of the town of Martigues in Provence, France. At least such is the deduction that one draws from the sixteenth-century writer Rabelais. *Chausses à la martingale,* according to him, were hose or breeches fastened at the back in the custom of Martigues. I should add, perhaps, that some authorities prefer to say, "Source uncertain."

aftermath

Consequences; especially, in current general use, ill consequences. Also, which indicates the origin of the term, a second crop of hay after one crop has already been cut. *Math,* a term no longer in use, meant "a mowing" in olden days, or the produce of a mowing; hay, that is. Thus an *aftermath* was a later or "after" mowing. Used figuratively it meant later results or effects; consequences.

periwig

False hair, called *phenake* by the Greeks and *galerus* in Rome, was worn by the ancients. But, though imitated in the Middle Ages, especially in the early sixteenth century, attendants at the courts of Louis XIV of France and of Charles II of England brought the wearing of false hair into fashion. Men went so far as to have their own natural hair cut off and converted into wigs. But they were not then called "wigs." That word had not yet been coined. The term was the French word *perruque*—a word which, of course, few Englishmen could correctly pronounce, though which was eventually turned into the pronounceable *peruke*. But *perruque* was first corrupted to *perwyke,* to *perewig,* and ultimately to *periwig.* We still have both *peruke* and *periwig* in the language, but the latter, perhaps because there was long such diversity of its forms, became abbreviated to the much more convenient *wig* before 1675, while Charles II still reigned over England.

synagogue

Literally, a congregation or assembly, it has also come to mean the place of assembly, specifically the meeting place for Jewish worship. The word comes to us through the Late Latin *synagoga* from the Greek *synagoge,* "assembly," from *synagein,* "to bring together," a compound of *syn,* "together," with *agein,* "to lead, bring." The Greek, in turn, is a direct translation of the Hebrew *keneseth,* "assembly," from *kanas,* "to collect, assemble."

draggletail

Just what it appears to be—a tail, especially a skirt tail, that drags, and particularly the person thus dragging her skirt in wet and mud. And inasmuch as one so careless of appearance is likely to be careless in morals as well, the term has frequently denoted a woman of loose character. Not always, though, and not always applied to women. A group of woebegone soldiers, for instance, defeated in battle, anxious for nothing but to save their skins, too tired to maintain any semblance of order, just dragging themselves along, may also be *draggletails.*

aide-de-camp

Without by-your-leave or even the courtesy of an attempt to observe the original pronunciation, we "borrowed" this from the French. Literally it means "an assistant of the field"; hence, one upon whom a general officer relies, on the field of battle, to receive and transmit orders. However, the duties of such a confidential assistant nowadays are not limited to attendance upon a field officer.

roorback

Political campaigns have rarely been entirely free of invective and diatribe regarding the candidates for office, and the presidential  campaign of 1844 was no exception. Widespread publicity was given by those opposing the election of James Polk to a purported book by a mythical Baron von Roorback (sometimes Roorbach), in which certain unsavory practices involving Polk were said to have been described. The falsity of these allegations was soon exposed, and a lie, particularly a lie told for political advantage, is still sometimes referred to as a *roorback*.

milksop

Perhaps it's too obvious; just an infant, or one of infantlike caliber, who sops up milk; hence, one unfit by temperament for conflict. But of interest is the fact that this term for one lacking in spirit is very old in our language. It was used, not only by Chaucer, but a hundred years before his time.

tycoon

Commodore Perry's expedition of 1852–54, which played so great a part in bringing Japan into the fellowship of the world's nations, brought back with it the Japanese word *taikun,* "great prince," the descriptive title of the army's commander-in-chief, whose military title was *shogun.* Upon being taken into American English, the word was respelled phonetically, becoming *tycoon,* and wholly losing all resemblance to its actual Chinese origin. For much of the Japanese language is borrowed from the Chinese, and *taikun* is made up of the Chinese *ta,* "great," plus *kiun,* "prince." Once in English, of course, the word quickly lost its strict meaning, and became applied to anyone who displayed real or imagined power, particularly in the business world.

stucco

Taken into English directly from the Italian, without change of spelling or meaning, this word seems originally to have come from a Teutonic rather than a Romance background. Specifically, the Italians apparently adopted the Old High German *stucchi* or *stukki,* one of the meanings of which was "crust," although the more common meaning was "piece, fragment." *Stucco* has been taken back into modern German with the spelling changed to *Stuck,* whereas the original German *stucchi* has also lived with the spelling modified to *Stück,* but with the meaning "piece" retained.

Jack

As a familiar form of *John,* one of the most common of English masculine names, *Jack* was early applied to any male representative of the common people, especially to a serving man, a laborer, sailor, odd-jobs man, etc. Thus came such names as *steeplejack, jack-tar,* etc. Through association of the name with common labor it became attached also to mechanisms or devices that might be substituted for common labor. Hence such terms as *jackscrew* (now usually contracted to *jack* and operated often by means other than a screw), *bootjack, jackhammer,* etc. Or again, the name was applied to animals, birds, and plants, either because of their common occurrence, their usefulness, or their smallness. Hence such names as *jackass, jackrabbit, jackdaw, jack oak, jack pine, jack plane,* and so on. The list of applications is by no means exhausted though most of them fall within the categories mentioned.

surly

Although, today, *sir* is commonly used as a title of respect for any man, when it first entered the language in the late thirteenth century (as a shortened form of *sire,* which preceded it by a scant hundred years) it was employed solely as the title of a knight or baronet. With the growth of the language, it followed shortly that a man, not necessarily knighted but who comported himself in knightly fashion, came to be described as *sirly*—that is, he was "like a sir." But, as has been remarked so many times, spelling in those days was much more of an art than a science, and individual authors followed their own whims. Thus *sir* was sometimes spelled *sur,* and *sirly* became *surly,* the latter becoming fixed. And the meaning changed from "knightly" to "haughty" to "arrogant" to "rude," which is its present sense.

firedog

No fireplace has less than two, one on either side for supporting logs or grate. But today, possibly because the name sounds more highfalutin, we speak of them as andirons. Formerly, however, the dogs, as they were then called, were of utilitarian iron, serving as supports, and the andirons, in households that afforded them, were state affairs of highly polished brass. Why *dog?* Because they were low, serviceable, and stood (usually) on four legs.

agate

A gem or semiprecious stone of quartz, waxy in texture and marked by bands of color. The name was formerly and should still be *achate* (pronounced *ak'ate*), after the Sicilian river Achates, near which, according to Pliny, the stone was first found.

hellbender

This peculiarly repulsive amphibian looks not unlike an uncouth young crocodile, and I can well imagine that the first white men to run across it in the valley of the Allegheny thought it a salamander direct from hell. Why the *bender* part of the name is not certain, but it may be that the man who named it thought it to be "bent for hell," rather than to have come direct from hell. Another common name for the hideous, though harmless, creature is *mud puppy,* for, though it is able to live several hours out of water, its natural habitat is in the muddy bottom of a stream.

rubberneck

As Mencken has so amply documented, Americans are well known for their adroitness in coining a catchy and appropriate  phrase, yet they seem to have been a little slow in connecting the elasticity of caoutchouc with the craning of the over-curious. *Rubber,* as a contraction of *India rubber,* first appeared in print at least as early as 1788, but it was over a century later, in 1896, before *rubberneck* did so. To be sure, it was probably known in the spoken language a little sooner, but Americans also have the practice of publishing their catchy phrases soon after they are coined, so very little additional age can be assigned this colorful term for a snooper.

finnan haddie

Either of two fishing villages in Scotland is credited with the first source and naming of this delicacy, but no report has been circulated that either has claimed first honors. The delicacy, if your taste runs that way, is merely smoked haddock—*haddie* to the Scots—haddock usually smoked with green wood. Sir Walter Scott attributed the source and name to *Findhorn,* a village on Moray Firth, but a few years earlier, Walter Thoms, in his *History of Aberdeen* (1811), gave the credit to the village of *Findon,* to the south of Aberdeen.

coxcomb

The spelling, though common from Shakespeare's time, conceals the source. The original was *cock's comb,* the comb or crest of a cock, and, back in the time of Queen Elizabeth I and later, it denoted the cap worn by the professional fool or jester, having the cut and color of such a crest, sometimes with small bells sewn to the tips. The jester himself became the *coxcomb,* and, because of his foolish pretensions and conceits, it was not long before any man of like characteristics, any pretender, became a *coxcomb* in the eyes of his fellows.

kaleyard, kailyard

It is likely that few of the so-styled literati who speak with authority are aware of the fact that a *kaleyard* (also spelled *kailyard*) is nothing more nor less than a cabbage patch or kitchen garden. The Scottish authors—Barrie, "Ian Maclaren" (John Watson), S. R. Crockett, and others—who wrote, a half century ago, of common Scottish life in ordinary Scottish villages were said in sarcasm by their critics to have introduced their readers to a "kaleyard school of writing." Despite these sneers, nevertheless, the books of these authors became immensely popular—another proof of Lincoln's "God must love the common people; He made so many of them."

isinglass

One seeing this for the first time could not be blamed if he thought it to be "is in glass." Nor did I, as a boy, comprehend that the thin, transparent, noncombustible material through which fire could be seen in the pot-bellied parlor stove, and which we called *isinglass,* was not *isinglass* at all, but sheets of mica. Our English name is again the result of mispronunciation and perhaps faulty hearing. Merchants who introduced the product from Holland in the early sixteenth century did not correctly give it the Dutch name, *huysenblas.* They dropped initial *h* and substituted *g* for *b.* The name meant "sturgeon's bladder," and the product was then used in cookery in the making of jellies, or for other purposes in which gelatin is now employed. When this gelatinous substance dried out into thin sheets, such as one can now observe with, say, glue allowed to harden on a pane of glass, the resemblance to mica was striking, thus giving rise to the erroneous substitution—carried from the mid-eighteenth century to the present—of the name *isinglass* for *mica.*

streetwalker

Literally, of course, a *streetwalker* is merely a pedestrian—anyone who is out for a walk either in or along a street. Even though this sense of the word is known and has been used for many years, a still older use is the one applied to a woman of easy virtue, and again the origin has been lost in the mists of antiquity. This sense dates to the sixteenth century, and was probably known to Shakespeare. It seems probable that the term was coined as being descriptive of the practice of prostitutes in pursuing their trade openly on the streets rather than awaiting a customer's chancing to seek them out at home.

quarterstaff

Those who have read *Robin Hood* and other adventure tales of the same period will certainly recall this ubiquitous weapon of the period. One theory is that it got its name from its having been constructed by quartering the bole of a young tree lengthwise, yielding a *quartered staff*. It seems more generally accepted, though, that it is named from the manner in which it is held in combat—one hand at the center, the other at the quarter point, midway between the center and the untipped end (the striking end was tipped with metal). The staff itself was between six and eight feet long.

merry-andrew

If there ever was an Andrew whose jokes and antics were so remarkable that all other men of like disposition would subsequently be known by his name, it's a doggone shame that the history books overlooked him. An attempt was made by Thomas Hearne in 1735 to tie the first *Merry Andrew* down, but it was quickly proved that Hearne had insufficient knowledge of the man he designated. In his work, *Benedictus Abbas Petroburgensis,* he pointed to Dr. Andrew Boorde, a man who, two centuries earlier, had been physician to Henry VIII of England. Some color was given to the statement, because Boorde did have the reputation for attending country fairs and for enjoying salacious jokes. But he was not a buffoon nor a mountebank, however, nor, as sometimes said, the author of a joke book. The fact is that *Andrew,* in the seventeenth century, was a name carelessly bestowed upon any manservant, just as today we call a Pullman porter George.

whortleberry

A general name for the fruit (or the plant) of a number of the members of the genus *Vaccinium,* in particular *V. myrtillus.* An earlier name for the fruit was *hurtleberry,* from which the present form was derived, and the shortened forms *whort* and *hurt* are also known. There have been several suggestions attempting to explain the formation of the first part of the word, one of the more interesting of which is that, since the berry has some resemblance to a small black-and-blue mark as might be obtained by a smart blow upon the person, it was named a *hurt,* even as the mark has been so called. The other forms are then presumed to have followed as extensions of this, although in fact the first recorded form is the longer *hurtleberry* (as *hurtilberyes*). The American word *huckleberry* is presumably derived from one of these.

sack coat

A *sack coat* is not (or at least, is hardly ever) made of sack-

cloth, but, because it is a loosely fitting garment, hanging straight from the shoulders, is so-called simply because it gives the impression of having been fashioned from a sack. *Sackcloth* is just that—a coarsely woven cloth from which sacks are made.

two-by-four

Although *two-by-threes* and even *two-by-twos* are known and employed for certain purposes, the *two-by-four* is the smallest size of standard dimension lumber used today in the construction of frame buildings. The name refers to the nominal size, in inches, of the thickness and width, respectively, of the piece, although the actual size of the standard, dressed two-by-four is, at the present time, one and five-eighths by three and five-eighths inches for a net cross-sectional area of just under six square inches rather than the eight square inches the name would imply. The smallness of the size has led to the figurative use of the term as a derogatory appellation for anything of small or insignificant area, such as, "He lives on that little two-by-four farm on the edge of town," or, "His shop is that two-by-four hole-in-the-wall in the middle of the block."

syllabus

A word created by a printer's error, but which is now firmly fixed in the language. Cicero had written, in his *Epistles to the Atticans,* "indices . . . quos vos Graeci . . . *sittubas* appellatis" (indexes, which were called *sittubas* by the Greeks). The key word was misprinted *syllabos* in a fifteenth-century edition of Cicero, and the misprint was adopted as a learned synonym for "index" (with our present spelling). From its use as "index" or "table of contents," the meaning has spread to its modern sense —"the subjects of a series of lectures."

quahog, quahaug

Early settlers in New England found that the Indians prized this bivalve for a twofold reason. First, the succulent meat provided many a welcome feast; finally, the dark spot on the inside of the shell was cut out and used for money—black wampum. Our word is a contraction of the Narraganset *poquauhock,* or the Pequot *p'quaughhaug,* meaning "hard clam." The ever-romantic biologists, however, seized upon the monetary use of the clam in assigning it its Latin name, *Venus mercenaria. Quogue,* another variant spelling, is also the name of a small community on Long Island, New York.

Adam's apple

"In Adam's fall We sinned all," ran the first stanza of the seventeenth-century *New England Primer.* His "fall" has since been marked on all mortals, by superstitious belief, by a projection on the fore part of the neck representing, 'tis said, a piece of the forbidden fruit of the Garden of Eden that stuck in Adam's throat as he ate it. Eve did the tempting and ate first, but the projection is much larger in men than in women, often quite con-

171

spicuous in the adolescent male. Physicians call it *pomum Adami,* just to say "Adam's apple" in Latin.

hodgepodge

Although originally a corruption of *hotch-potch,* taking over most of the sense of the older term, this became the more common form from the seventeenth century onward, probably because *hotch* was assumed to be an altered form of the proper name *Hodge,* nickname for Roger. But *hotch-potch* was itself a rhyming corruption of a still earlier (thirteenth century) *hotch-pot,* from French *hoche,* "a shaking," and *pot;* hence, "a shaking together in a pot." At that early period it was a law term, relating to the commixture of property in order to secure an even distribution, and it is still so used. But probably suggested by *pot,* the *hotch-pot* became a culinary potpourri, especially a stew of mutton broth and vegetables. By the late sixteenth century, *hotch-potch* had become the usual term in cookery and is still so used in England. Figurative usage, indicating a jumbled assembly of miscellany, persons or things, dates from the fifteenth century, and is the sense most familiar to us in America in the term *hodgepodge.*

firedamp

Damp in this word has nothing to do with moisture, as we ordinarily associate it, but rather with deadening, or choking, or stifling. In fact the earliest meaning of *damp* when it mysteriously appeared in the language in 1480 was as a kind of noxious gas exhaled by a goat. "After this dragon," wrote Caxton in *The Cronicals of Englond,* "shal come a goot and ther shal come oute of his nostrel a *domp* that shal betoken honger and grete deth of peple." So *firedamp,* then, is in itself a choking gas, often encountered in coal mines, that may become violently explosive upon contact with a flame.

lazy Susan

One is tempted to parody Shakespeare: "Who was Susan? what was she?" All that I have learned is that this "Susan" appeared on the American scene perhaps seventy-five years ago and probably in New England. She, or rather it, was the successor of the dining-room article which, in both England and America, had been called a "dumb waiter." This device, known since the mid-eighteenth century, usually stood alongside the host, its three shelves, laden with wine, rotating about a common spindle. Presumably—the presumption being entirely mine—in some American family this silent servitor replaced a living, energetic, and anything-but-dumb waitress. In ironic honor of her activity, let us say, they called it *lazy Susan*. We can readily assume that the name would remain when, as a matter of further convenience, the shelves were reduced to one and the shortened device was lifted to the center of the dining table.

madstone

The New Orleans *Times-Picayune Magazine* of June 19, 1949, as quoted by *Dictionary of Americanisms,* reported a statement to the effect that there had been an estimated "4000 actual cases in which the application of the Mad Stone brought about instant relief and final cure of snake bites, black widow spider stings, bee stings, and mad dog bites," etc. Obviously we should know what this miraculous stone is, especially as no less a person than Abraham Lincoln believed in its efficacy when he took his son Robert, bitten by a dog, to Terre Haute to have a madstone applied to the wound. Actually, various substances of stonelike nature have been given the name. Generally, however, it is a hard substance that may occur somewhere in the digestive system of an animal, such as a calculus within the gall bladder or a mass of hair or calciferously coated pebble within the stomach of, say, a deer. Where and how the popular belief arose in America is not known. Literary reference goes back only to the early nineteenth century, but it was undoubtedly much earlier.

hogshead

For six hundred years, at least, this measure of liquid capacity has been in our language (and taken into other Teutonic languages, with *hog* sometimes changed to *bull* or *ox*), but as yet the mystery of its source or a plausible reason for the name remains unsolved. One guess, quoted by the learned W. W. Skeat, is that the earliest cooper of these casks of two-barrel size branded his product with the outlines of the head of a hog or of an ox. But Skeat also says that most of the conjectural sources are "silly." And I have nothing to add to that.

Sam Browne belt

General Sir Samuel James Browne was a British army officer of the nineteenth century who was born, and later served, in

India. It may be presumed that some time during his career he became annoyed at the drag of his sword on his belt, which most certainly caused the belt to go askew, marring his smart military appearance. If the general had smallish hips, the weight of the sword may even have tended to pull his belt down over his posterior. In any event, it was General Browne who attached an auxiliary strap to his belt, passing it over his right shoulder (the sword being hung on the left side), thus supporting the sword and permitting the general to maintain his poise. The military belt with strap over the shoulder is still known by the name of its inventor, Sam Browne.

green soap

Anyone who has ever had occasion to use it, in the treatment of impetigo or other skin affection, knows that its color is brown, not green. Nevertheless the name is a reminder that the color was formerly green. Possibly to make the appearance less repulsive, indigo was added to the soft soap, imparting a green hue.

turncoat

In medieval times, the retainers and servants of any given nobleman were clothed in livery of distinctive color and design for easy recognition. If, as might happen under the stress of war or of sharp political differences, it became expedient that a man not be recognized as associated with another, it was a simple matter for him to slip his coat inside out, thus disguising his allegiance. One who so *turned* his *coat* was, literally, a *turncoat,* and the designation soon came to be applied in the figurative sense as well. Legend has it that one astute landholder, whose estate lay on the border between two warring factions, had a coat fashioned with the colors of one army on one side and those of the other on the reverse. According to the tides of battle, he wore first one side out, then the other.

pot cheese

Now we call it "cottage cheese," probably because the old-fashioned names, *pot cheese, bonnyclabber,* and *smearcase* (which comes to us from the German *Schmierkäse,* "spreading cheese"), are no longer sufficiently elite for the modern dining room. But in grandmother's time the curds were separated from the water by heating the coagulated milk in a pot. Hence the name, *pot cheese.*

cranberry

Most of the dictionaries agree that we Americans got this name from the Low German *kraanbere,* "crane berry," from the fact that the plant flourishes in marshy lands frequented by cranes. But Dr. Mathews, in *Dictionary of Americanisms,* questions this assumption. The name, he points out, was used by John Eliot in *Day-breaking,* written in 1647. He doubts that the Low German word would have penetrated to eastern Massachusetts at that early date, and thinks it more likely that our word was already in dialectal English use.

squash

Roger Williams (he who settled Rhode Island) called them "vine apples," and described them as being about the size of apples, and as quite tasty. From this it can be inferred that the

175

gourds which the Narragansett Indians called *asquutasquash* were a sort of melon, especially since the Indian word, literally translated, means "that which is eaten raw." But it is the abbreviation of that same Indian word that gives us *squash,* which, as we know it, is rarely eaten raw. An earlier, now obsolete form was *squantersquash.*

groundhog

We should properly call this largest member of the squirrel family a marmot, or even a woodchuck, for there is definitely nothing hoggish about him. (Or her, as the case may be. It is a "her" who rears her young annually under the pantry of my summer home.) Because there is American usage, a theory has been advanced that the name is a translation of the Dutch *aardvark,* earth pig or hog, an animal of South Africa which, though somewhat larger, has similar burrowing propensities. Dutch colonists in America may have supposed the two to be members of the same family. (See also **woodchuck.**)

sans-culotte

In the latter part of the eighteenth century, it was still fashionable for men to wear knee breeches, this fashion prevailing both

in this country and in Europe. The laboring class of France, largely responsible for the first French revolution of 1789, sought for some symbol of dress which would distinguish them from the aristocracy against whom they were pitted, and decided to abandon knee breeches in favor of trousers. Their aristocratic adversaries thereupon bestowed upon them the epithet *sans-culotte,* literally, "without breeches" (*sans,* "without," plus *culotte,* "breeches," from *cul,* "posterior"). Having been applied to the "rabble" of France, the word has now been transferred to apply to any ragamuffin.

176

quadroon

The descendants of mixed racial unions have been known by many names, most of them sufficiently distinctive to identify immediately the races of the parents. Many of these names can be traced to the Spanish, who were the great adventurers and explorers of the sixteenth and seventeenth centuries. We owe to them the terms *mestizo* and *mulatto,* the former the child of a European and an American Indian, the latter the child of a European and a Negro. The Spanish word *cuarteron* (from *cuarto,* "one fourth") identifies the child of a European and either a mestizo or a mulatto, and from this word we have our *quadroon* as a corruption of the French spelling, *quarteron.* In more recent times it has acquired the unequivocal meaning indicating an ancestry three-fourths white and one-fourth Negro.

cracker

A name now used with pride by native whites of Florida as a distinction from the influx of residents from other states, but also applied in other Southern states to ignorant, shiftless white people, commonly called "poor whites." Among various explanations, one often recurring is that the term originated from the "cracker" or snapping of long whips in the hands of expert freighters over early Southern roads. In fact, however, back even in 1509 a *cracker* was one given to boastful braggadocio, tall stories, or, to speak plainly, lying. In a letter written in 1766 to the Earl of Dartmouth, those known by the name in America were said to be "a lawless set of rascalls on the frontiers of Virginia, Maryland, the Carolinas, and Georgia, who often change their places of abode."

honeymoon

The definition in an old dictionary, Blount's *Glossographia* (1656), on my shelves delights me: *"Hony-moon,* applied to those married persons that love well at first, and decline in affections afterwards; it is hony now, but will change as the moon." Thomas Blount, however, merely paraphrased the definition in

Richard Huloet's *Abecedarium,* printed a hundred years earlier, reading: *"Hony moon,* a terme prouerbially applied to such as be newe maried, whiche wyll not fall out at the fyrste, but thone [the one] loueth the other at the beginnynge excedyngly, the likelyhode of theyr excedynge loue appearing to aswage, ye which time the vulgar people cal the hony mone, *Aphrodisia."*

turkey

It was apparently just about four hundred years ago that the bird, native to Africa, that we know today as guinea fowl was imported into England by way of Turkey, even though the bird itself had been known for its delectable qualities for long previously (it had been mentioned by Aristotle and Pliny). Because of coming from Turkey, and ignoring its African origin, the birds were named *Turkey-cocks* and *Turkey-hens*—later just *turkeys*. A few years later some of the same variety of bird were imported directly from Guinea in West Africa. Not, at first, being recognized as the same species, the latter were called *Guinea-fowl,* and, for a while, the two terms were used interchangeably. Then, with the exploration of America, the large, native game birds found there were at first thought to be the same, and they, too, were called *turkeys*. When it was realized that the two were distinct species, the American bird was given the older name of *turkey* and the African bird retained the name of *guinea fowl*. Unfortunately, though, the distinction was not recognized in time to avoid confusion in their scientific names, the genus of the former and the species of the latter both having been given the name *Meleagris,* which is the ancient name by which Aristotle and Pliny knew the African bird.

dovetail

In the mid-sixteenth century, when this term used in joinery and carpentry first appeared in print, the joint was also known as "swallowe tayle," to follow the spelling of the period. You can see an example of the joint on well-made bureau or desk drawers. It is composed of a series of wedge-shaped tenons and mortises which fit snugly into a corresponding series of mortises and tenons.

178

The name arises from the shape, that of the V-like or wedgelike shape of the tail of dove or swallow.

portmanteau

In France, back in the sixteenth century and earlier, a *porte-manteau* was an officer in the king's service who carried the mantle (*manteau*) of the king when traveling—the royal mantle bearer, we might call him. The mantle or cloak was precious, of course, and was accordingly carried in a case of soft leather. Eventually, in England, the case itself became the *portmanteau* and was used as a traveling bag for carrying articles of various nature. Lewis Carroll (Charles L. Dodgson) adopted the term, coining *portmanteau-word,* to designate his blendings of two words into one suggesting the meanings of each, a device that he employed in *Through the Looking Glass,* such as *chortle,* from *chuckle* and *snort; mimsy,* from *miserable* and *flimsy.*

coxswain

The spelling *cockswain,* sometimes used, better indicates the source. Five hundred years ago a *cock* was a small rowboat, often called a *cockboat.* Such a boat was usually carried on a larger vessel for the use of the captain, to take him ashore or the like. And the *swain* in charge of that small boat, assigned to row the captain where he listed, was the *cockswain.* With passing years the boat under his charge increased in size and, whether manned by many oarsmen or moved by sail, his prime duty was that of helmsman. The corrupted spelling, *coxswain,* has been general since the seventeenth century.

greenroom

That's what is was, originally—a room near the stage in a theater, the walls and, sometimes, the furniture of which were painted or covered with green cloth. Some say that color was selected for the relief of the eyes of the actors, who rested in that room between appearances on stage, from the glare of the footlights. But it is more likely that the first assemblyroom for artists when dressed just chanced to be painted green. Such is also the opinion of Sir St. Vincent Troubridge, for whom the theater has long been of special interest and study, and to whom I am indebted for the further statements. That first assembly room was in the Dorset Garden theater, mentioned in Thomas Shadwell's *A True Widow,* produced in that theater in 1678. Four years later, 1682, from economic causes, the Dorset Garden and Drury Lane companies were amalgamated at the latter theater. Then at some time within the next eighteen years a room similar to that at Dorset Garden and now called a *greenroom* made its appearance at Drury Lane. Definite reason for the choice of name is not known, but Sir St. Vincent surmises that "one half of the amalgamated company said so often and naggingly 'I wish we had a retiring-room here like the greenroom at Dorset Garden,' that the management had to provide one at Drury Lane, and it was in consequence called the *greenroom* generically for the first time."

But, as Sir St. Vincent adds, any notion that the actors were affected by eyestrain from footlights at that period can be dismissed. It was the spectators, especially those in the galleries, who suffered from the overhead chandeliers above both stage and auditorium. The diarist Samuel Pepys records in 1669, "the trouble of my eyes with the light of the candles did almost kill me." Not until the next century, about 1758, were footlights introduced.

sputnik

This word which, as I write, has so recently leaped into the headlines of just about every newspaper in the world is not, as may have been felt, a pet name coined by the Russians to describe their man-made moon, but is actually the Russian word for "satellite." In the nonastronomical sense, it means "a companion or associate." *Sputnik* is derived from the root *sput-,* implying entanglement or admixture, plus the suffix *-nik,* which is closely equivalent to the English suffix *-er,* that is, one who or that which is involved in the action of the verb root. *Sput-* is probably a compound of the preposition *s,* "with," plus *put,* "road." Thus a literal translation of *sputnik* would be "a traveling companion."

180

scaramouch

Like our stock companies today, traveling groups of actors in the Middle Ages had a limited repertory, which then was often  but one play. Such a group of strolling players, from Italy, visited London in the latter part of the seventeenth century, bringing with them a pantomime in which one of the chief characters was *Scaramuccia,* a representation of a Spanish don who was a coward and a braggart. His part in the play involved a series of *skirmishes* with the hero, and his name is, appropriately, the Italian word for "skirmish." This character made a great hit with the London audiences, and they took his name, later modified by the French spelling, *Scaramouche,* into the language, applying it to a person having the characteristics of the boastful coward who was the original *Scaramuccia.*

butterscotch

This candy—toffee, in England—does not concern Scotland nor the Scottish people, nor does it contain any of the liquid known as "Scotch." No, the chief ingredients are just butter and sugar. Where does the *scotch* come in? Well, all directions for the preparation of this candy after it is properly cooked close with some such statement as: Pour upon oiled paper or well-buttered pan and when slightly cool *score* with a knife into squares. And "to *scotch*" is merely an old-fashioned word for "to score, notch, mark with shallow cuts."

trousers

The more recent etymology is fairly certain; the earlier is somewhat cloudy. The turning point comes with the medieval Irish and Scottish Gaelic *triubhas,* pronounced *triwas.* This was taken into English in the sixteenth century, and became *trouse.* Although the term describes the entire garment, the word has the appearance of a singular and the garment that of a plural, so that the word was given the plural form *trouses* which, perhaps in analogy with such words as *tweezers, scissors* (plural forms describing singular objects), became altered to *trousers* soon afterward. Meanwhile, in a parallel development, *trouse* was adopted into Scottish English as *trews,* as the name of a particular form of trousers still worn by certain Lowland regiments. As for the earlier development, it may be that the Gaelic *triubhas* is derived from the French *trebus,* a sort of leg covering, from Latin *tubracos.* This, it has been suggested, is a word coined as a play on the words *tibia,* "shin," and *braca* (*bracca*), "buttocks," that is, "they are called *tubracos* because they reach from *tibia* to *bracas* (accusative plural of *braca*)." But "buttocks" is only a derived meaning of the term *braca,* the primary meaning of which (usually as the plural *bracae*) is "breeches." And *braca* has been identified as coming from the Old Celtic *bracca,* "covering for the legs." Which brings us around nearly full circle, for Old Celtic is one of the ancestors of Irish Gaelic, and *bracca* has, with fair certainty, been identified as the ancestor of the Irish *brog,* "a shoe," from which we get our English *brogue,* "a shoe." And just to make the whole thing slightly more confusing, an obsolete meaning of *brogue* is, you guessed it, "trousers."

cowslip

Sorry, but the name of the plant has nothing to do with the lip of the cow. The English wildflower, the primrose or *Primula veris,* to which the American plant is allied, commonly grows in cow pastures, and the name pertains to the *slip,* anciently *slyppe,* "dung," among which the plant flourishes.

doughboy

In her book, *Tenting on the Plains* (1887), Elizabeth Custer, wife of the General, says, "A *doughboy* is a small, round doughnut served to sailors on shipboard, generally with hash. Early in the Civil War the term was applied to the large globular brass buttons on the infantry uniform, from which it passed, by natural transition, to the infantrymen themselves." That is a reasonably logical explanation. It might be acceptable if it were not for the fact that twenty years earlier, just two years after the close of the Civil War, a writer in *Beadle's Monthly* said, "To us *doughboys* (the origin of the name is one of the inscrutable mysteries of slang) who wore light blue shoulder-straps and chevrons, and were our own pack-horses, . . . the constant . . . skirmishing into positions, only to abandon them, . . . became a wearisome iteration." Regretfully, then, we must continue to say, "Origin uncertain."

sponging house

A sponge is characterized as "readily absorbing fluids and yielding them on pressure." It is the latter part of this that led to one of the slang senses of sponge—the noun, "an object of extortion," and the verb, "to deprive one of something." It is this meaning of extortion that resulted in the coining of *sponging house,* sometime in the sixteenth or seventeenth cenury, as a slang name for the house (usually the bailiff's home) in which men arrested for debt were held overnight prior to being led off to debtors' prison. The reason is that the bailiffs made a good thing of this. They charged exorbitant prices for food and items of comfort given their prisoners, pocketing the profits, and also took advantage of their wards' temporary quarters to try to pry from the prisoners' friends either payment of the debt or further tribute intended to ensure the comfort of the "sponge."

holystone

This term for the soft sandstone formerly used by sailors for scouring the wooden deck of a vessel has led to all sorts of speculation. Why *holy?* One opinion was that *holy* was just a humorous corruption of *holey,* the stone being full of holes like a sponge. Admiral Smythe, in *The Sailor's Word Book* (1867), allowed us other choices: "So called," he said, "from being originally used for Sunday cleaning, or obtained by plundering church-yards of their tomb-stones, or because the seamen have to go on their knees to use it." In *Naval Customs* (1939), by Lt. Comdr. Leland P. Lovette, U.S. Navy (now Vice Admiral, ret.), is the statement that the name came from fragments of gravestones "from Saint Nicholas church, Great Yarmouth, England," first used by English sailors. One hesitates to doubt so positive a statement, but, unable to find other mention of a specific churchyard, I sent a letter of inquiry to Admiral Lovette. His reply, which I am privileged to quote, was, "I don't think we will ever get the full story. One British authority, Rear Admiral Gerard Wells, R.N., definitely states: 'So called because when using them an attitude of prayer is taken.' You know the larger ones in the British Navy were called 'hand bibles,' the smaller ones 'prayer books.' I think the fact that all were of tombstone material and many from old tombstones got the word launched."

porterhouse

Originally, about the beginning of the nineteenth century, a house at which *porter* was served. This *porter* was a kind of dark brown beer or ale favored by porters and ordinary laborers, often called *porter's beer* or *porter's ale*. The *porterhouse steak* is supposed to have been introduced about 1814, according to the *Dictionary of Americanisms,* in the porterhouse conducted by Martin Morrison in New York City.

trombone, trumpet, tuba

The common grandfather of all these seems to have been the straight bronze war trumpet of the ancient Romans, which they called a *tuba*. The word is undoubtedly related to the Latin *tubus,* "a tube." It has been suggested that, in passing into the modern Romance languages, there took place a threefold change in this word—insertion of an *r,* change of vowel, and insertion of an *m* —resulting in the Italian *tromba,* Provençal *trompa,* French *trompe,* "a trumpet." This came into English as the now archaic or poetic *trump*. But there came to be different sizes of the instrument, and in Italian, the larger was given the augmented form of *tromba,* which is *trombone,* whereas in French the smaller was given the diminished form of *trompe,* namely *trompette,* this then coming into English as *trumpet.* Finally, with the development of the extra-large size, the original name of *tuba* was revived and applied to it.

shuttlecock

Although this name has only been in the language since the sixteenth century, it is composed of two words, *shuttle* and *cock,* that are found in the earliest forms of the language. *Shuttle* is the modern spelling of the Anglo-Saxon *scytel,* "an arrow, missile," and is related to our verb *to shoot.* The name became applied to the weaver's shuttle, probably because it seemed to shoot back and forth across the web, but this has resulted in having the back-and-forth concept become more closely tied to the shuttle than the shooting concept (as a *shuttle train*). When, then, a cork was fitted with a crown of feathers, thus gaining some resemblance to a bird, or cock, and was batted back and forth, as in badminton or its predecessor, battledore and shuttlecock, the *shuttlecock* itself (shuttled cock) was born.

avoirdupois

The *Oxford English Dictionary* calls this "a recent corrupt spelling," and adds: "The best modern spelling is the 17th century *averdepois;* in any case *de* ought to be restored for *du,* introduced by some ignorant 'improver' *c* 1640–1650." The term was borrowed from France about the year 1300. Though its literal meaning was "goods of weight," the sense of its early use was merchandise sold by weight. "Avoirdupois weight" became legalized in England in 1303, but we have long discarded the longer name.

cousin-german

This matter of cousinship is sometimes made more complicated than it should be. *German* is now rarely used in such relationship, replaced by the more readily understood *first* or *full,* coming from Latin *germanus,* denoting such relationship. My brother's son is my son's *cousin german,* or first or full cousin. My brother's grandson is my son's first cousin once removed, and is my grandson's second cousin. If you wish to carry it further, my brother's great-grandson is my son's first cousin twice removed, my grandson's second cousin once removed, and my great-grandson's third cousin. But, even in the South, this degree of relationship scarcely constitutes a "kissing cousin," unless the third cousin is female and very pretty.

greenhorn

Yes, it did at first apply to horns that were green—green, that is, in the sense of young and tender, such as those of a young ox. Then the term was next applied in a more figurative sense to raw, untrained, and inexperienced soldiers, those who might be characterized as not yet dry behind the ears. And from that, still in the seventeenth century, the final extension was easy, and the *greenhorn* became what he is today—one who is a novice or an ignoramus in any given trade, line, or profession.

spindrift

Years ago, the verb *spoon* had a now obsolete meaning, "to run before the wind, to scud." The origin of this sense is not known, but the similarity in sound to *spume* (from the Latin *spuma,* "foam") led to an alternate spelling, *spoom.* Then, through some confused process of reasoning quite difficult to reconstruct, the two meanings, "foam" and "scud," were connected in *spoondrift,* the sea foam generated by high winds. As though this weren't sufficiently complicated, there now came the problem of dialectal pronunciation. In parts of England, *spoon* was pronounced *speen;* in other parts, *spin.* From the latter, *spoondrift* became *spindrift,* and this, some seventy-five years ago, became stabilized as the accepted spelling and pronunciation.

Dutch treat

We of Pennsylvania Dutch extraction have always been of an independent spirit, unwilling to be "beholden" to anyone—and, by the same token, taking it for granted that a neighbor or companion is of the same spirit. In consequence, though far from any justifiable accusation of ungenerosity, we expect that anyone fully able to pay his own way will do so. Thus, when, by design or chance, one of us is accompanied by an acquaintance into a place of entertainment or refreshment, we think it but natural that each pay his own scot. And that is Dutch treat—or Dutch lunch, Dutch supper, or Dutch party.

trespass

The original sense was "to pass beyond or across," and the word comes to us from the Old French *trespasser* from the Medieval Latin *transpassare,* "to pass beyond." This is made up of *trans,* "beyond" (which became *tres* in French), and *passare,* "to pass." Modern French has developed a derivative meaning, "to pass away, to die," which also existed briefly in English in the fifteenth and sixteenth centuries, but did not survive. The sense of passing beyond some limit became applied to passing beyond the limit of some law or regulation, which led to the meaning of "transgression, sin." This is the sense implied by the use of the word in the Lord's Prayer, as first appears in Wyclif's translation of 1382.

quatchgrass

A variant form, of minor importance, of the common name for various grasses, especially *Agropyron repens.* This is only one of several onomatopoetic names for the same thing. Others include *couchgrass, quitchgrass, quackgrass,* and *twitchgrass,* or just *couch* or *quitch.* This last is the oldest known form, and it seems to be related to older forms of *quick.* From this, we assume that the name was given to show that this weed grows and spreads *quickly* unless the farmer is on his toes and roots it out promptly.

stockade

One of those curious words which have entered English with both Romance and Teutonic backgrounds, *stockade* comes to us through the French *estacade* from the Spanish *estacada,* "a fortification consisting of a row of stakes." But *estacada* is from *estaca,* "a stake," which is derived from the Teutonic root *stak-,* a variant of the verb root *stek-,* "to pierce." In more normal fashion, this same Teutonic root has given us our own *stake* through the Anglo-Saxon *staca,* "a post stuck in the ground." *Palisade,* which is a quite similar fortification, is purely of Romance origin, coming from the French *palissade,* from *palis,* "a fence"; *pal,* "a stake"; and ultimately from the Latin *palus,* "a stake, especially one used for punishment of criminals."

sitz bath

This term, describing both the process of taking a bath while in the sitting position, with the legs and feet outside, as well as the  tub in which this uncomfortable process may be accomplished, is taken directly from the German word for the same. The curious feature of the term is that it is half the original, half the English translation. The German is *Sitzbad,* literally "a sitting bath," but the first element has been left in German, possibly to introduce an aura of mystery to the process and render attractive, psychologically, a process that most certainly has nothing to commend it from the standpoint of comfort.

buckwheat

This reminds one of the noted comment on *oats* in Johnson's *Dictionary of the English Language* (1755): "A grain which in England is commonly fed to horses, but in Scotland supports the people." Buckwheat in Europe has been grown for many centuries as a grain for cattle, horses, and poultry, but in the United States a meal is ground from it for making the breakfast delicacy, buckwheat cakes. Because the grain appears similar to the seed of the beech, the Dutch called it *boekweit,* "beech wheat," from which came the English *buckwheat.*

spindleshanks

A quick review of *The Legend of Sleepy Hollow* reveals that Irving seems not to have used the term, but it would most certainly have well described Ichabod Crane. "He was tall, but exceedingly lank, . . . long arms and legs, hands that dangled a mile out of his sleeves, . . . and his whole frame most loosely hung together." For this is the picture one gets of a person so unfortunate to be hailed as *"Spindleshanks." Spindle,* from *spin,* is the slender, tapered rod upon which fiber is twisted into thread, and *shank* is from the Anglo-Saxon *sceanca,* "leg." Specifically, then, a *spindleshank* is a long, thin leg, but in the plural it commonly refers to the possessor of such legs. German and Dutch, respectively, have *Spindlebein* and *spillebeen,* "spindle-leg," while French has *doigts fuselés,* "spindly fingers."

dornick

Had anyone, in my youth, told me that a *dornick* was a kind of fabric, I would certainly have thought either that he was trying to spoof me or he was an ignoramus. In Ohio, and later in Brooklyn, it was a brickbat or cobblestone that could be, and was, hurled by hoodlums through store windows. But this, I learned later, is an American usage, the name probably derived from Irish *dornog,* "a small stone." The fabric *dornick,* known since the fifteenth century, was so named from the Flemish town where first made, the town known to the French as Tournai.

graham bread, crackers, flour

We take our food fads very seriously in this country, and some continue for many years. Along about 1830, a young Presbyterian minister, Sylvester Graham (1794–1851), an ardent temperance advocate, got the notion that if one lived wholly on a vegetable diet

189

he would have no interest in any alcoholic beverage. *Graham boardinghouses* sprang up in many of the larger cities. Then within a year or two he extended his dietetic reform into encouraging the substitution of unbolted flour for all wheaten products. The latter advocacy still meets with much medical favor and it is due to the efforts of this preacher that we continue to have *graham flour, graham bread,* and *graham crackers.*

buckram

Despite the appearance of a compound word, this is wholly unrelated to either *buck* or *ram.* In fact, though it has counterparts in other European languages, its ultimate source is unknown. The fabric itself was originally of fine linen or cotton, costly and delicate. Such was its nature through the Middle Ages. But in the fifteenth century the name was transferred to linen of coarser weave and stiffened with paste, henceforth serving as a stiffener for clothing, as a backbone in bookbinding, and similar purposes.

span-new

This concept of absolute, perfect newness is very old in itself, dating back past medieval English to the Old Norse, in which its form was *span-nyr,* from *spann,* "a chip," plus *nyr,* "new." The allusion is to the newness of a chip freshly cut by the woodsman's ax. Variants such as *spang-new, spanking new,* etc., are merely inventive expansions giving additional emphasis, as is the longer term *spick-and-span-new.* In this last, *spick* is identical to *spike,* and the allusion is to a spike just off the blacksmith's forge. The later extension of *spick-and-span* to imply neatness or cleanliness, of course, is with reference to the appearance of newness. *Brandnew* (*bran-new*) refers to the newness of something, such as pottery, perhaps, fresh from the fire (*brands*), and this has led to the sometimes-heard *bran-span-new.*

hockshop

The term is included here simply because someone may look for it, but I can't retail much information. *Hock,* in the sense of "pawn," has been in American usage at least seventy-five years; hence, a *hockshop* is a pawnshop, but no one knows why. It is my supposition that our *hock* is related to the first element of the English *hock-day, hocktide, hock Monday* or *Tuesday,* which referred to an ancient custom: on the second Monday after Easter the women of a parish seized and bound men, holding them for redemption by a payment of money; on the second Tuesday, men had their turn. Men and women were thus, in effect, held in pawn. In modified form the custom persisted in some parts of England through the nineteenth century.

country-dance

Attempts have been made to give this a French background, insisting that it was first the *contre-danse* of French, Italian, or Spanish origin. Such is not so. It was the other way round. Those dances were eighteenth-century adaptations from the English country-dances. It is not known when nor in what part of England these folk dances originated, but they were certainly much older than the earliest printed record of late sixteenth century.

slipshod

A *slipshoe* was, at one time, the name used for a shoe or slipper that fitted loosely and was worn for comfort, within the home,  rather than for street wear. However, it happened that even back in the sixteenth century, when the term was in vogue, there were certain of the citizenry who valued comfort more than propriety, and who allowed themselves to be seen in public wearing slipshoes, hence, were *slipshod*. Proper people looked down their noses at such goings-on, of course, and thus it came to be that anyone careless of dress in general came to be described as "slipshod." From this it was an easy step to apply the adjective to any thing or action kept or performed in careless, slovenly fashion.

191

hobnob

We don't use it as Shakespeare did. With us it is a verb—to hold intimate conversation with (another); to be convivial with. But Shakespeare used it (*Twelfth Night,* III, iv) as an adverb: "He is [a] knight . . . ; but he is a diuell in a priuate brall; . . . and his incensement at this moment is so implacable, that satisfaction can be none, but by pangs of death and sepulcher. Hob, nob, is his word: giu't or take't." And the sense then was that of the earlier *hab nab,* "have it, have it not"; hence, "give or take," "hit or miss." The supposition is that our present sense developed from social drinking among two or more with clinking of glasses, giving or taking wine with one another alternately. So, at least, was the occurrence of the expression onward from the eighteenth century.

curtail

The "curtal friar," Friar Tuck, of the Robin Hood ballads, was merely so called because the frock worn by the friar was short, *curtal* being derived from the Latin *curtus,* "short." Other things were also "curtal" four hundred years ago, especially a horse whose tail had been bobbed—a "bobtailed horse," we would say now. And just through this association of *curtal* and *tail,* pronunciation and spelling were altered and remained altered to *curtail.*

poppycock

Now and then difficulties are presented in stating the sources and original meanings of some of our words, especially, as here, of words which through use in a different sense have become completely respectable in our language. Thus, in America, *poppycock* is merely an equivalent of "stuff and nonsense; bosh," but among the Dutch ancestors of some of us or by a present-day Netherlander the original form, *pappekak,* would never be used in polite society. In euphemistic terms: soft ordure.

soupçon

Coming to us directly from the French, in which it has the same meaning, "a trifle," this has gone through several spellings as the

French language itself was evolved. It stems from the Late Latin *suspectio,* which comes, in turn, from the Latin *suspicio,* "a suspicion." A *soupçon,* therefore, is a quantity so small that it may exist only in the imagination.

furbelow

One could make a poor pun by asking, "Was it fur below?" But the source of this stylish flounce of bygone years did not derive from a mispronounced "far below" nor from the pelt of an animal. The flounce was much more likely to have been made of silk than of fur. No, we owe the term only to the carelessness of the dressmakers or their customers of the early eighteenth century. The true name, used also in other languages though from an unknown origin, was *falbala,* accented on the first syllable. Through ignorance, perhaps, this became *falbeloe* and, eventually, *furbelow.*

Pollyanna

The "glad" girl. She was created by Eleanor Hodgman Porter in a novel of that name published in 1913, with a sequel, *Pollyanna Grows Up,* in 1915. She was an orphan, turned over, after the death of her missionary father, to live with a stern puritanical aunt. But Pollyanna steadfastly practiced a game taught to her by her father of always finding something to be glad about, no matter how grim the immediate circumstances. Through her continued unquenchable optimism, always seeing a bright side in every catastrophe, the entire community became infected and developed an air of friendliness. Thus anyone who appears unduly optimistic or cheerful in the face of discouragement is now a *Pollyanna.*

atlas

Greek mythology tells us of a terrific struggle between the gods and the rebellious Titans, a race of giants, led by the powerful Atlas. When defeated, Atlas was compelled in punishment to bear the heavens upon his shoulders through all eternity. Ancient artists pictured him as supporting an enormous globe, and a copy of such a picture was used in the sixteenth century by the Flemish geographer Mercator as a frontispiece to his collection of maps. Through his and the subsequent use of some such picture, any volume of maps came to be known by the name of the mythical Greek hero.

treble

The usual sense, of course, is "threefold," and in this sense the word is fully equivalent to *triple*. Whereas *treble* came to us from the Old French, of the same spelling and meaning, which, in turn, was derived from the Popular Latin *tripulus, triple* came directly from the latter source. The original Latin form was *triplex,* from the Greek *triplous,* "threefold." The musical sense of *treble* seems to be from the soprano part having been the third part to be added to harmonized musical composition, in about the fifteenth century.

solfeggio

In the eleventh century, there lived an Italian monk and musician, one Guido d'Arezzo, who proposed the group of syllables that is

now known as "Guido's scale," or the "Aretinian syllables." These were to be used, in lieu of words, in singing exercises, one for each note of the scale, now known to every school child as the familiar *do, re, mi, fa, sol,* etc. (Our *do* was *ut* to Guido, though.) These syllables were widely adopted, and the verb *to sol-fa* was coined to describe singing with them. The corresponding verb in Italian is *solfeggiare,* and the noun *solfeggio,* taken into English directly from the Italian, is a musical exercise sung with the Aretinian syllables.

asses' bridge

Sometimes called *pons asinorum,* which, perhaps more politely, says exactly the same thing in Latin. Germans translate the Latin into *Esels-brücke;* French use *pont aux ânes,* but they all refer to the fifth proposition of the first book of Euclid: If a triangle has

194

two of its sides equal, the angles opposite these sides are also equal. The proof of this simple bridge-shaped figure is so difficult for those beginning the study of geometry as to give rise to the name, whatever the native country of the student.

sophomore

An older spelling was *sophimore,* and it is believed that this resulted from *sophism* plus the suffix *-or,* "one who practiced sophism," which is the art of argumentation, especially on a fallacious premise. The present spelling stems from the theory that a second-year college student, having acquired some measure of erudition, tends to exploit this knowledge to a degree far beyond its actual worth. In so doing he is wise (Greek *sophos*) to the point of folly (Greek, *moros*), that is, he is a wise fool, *sophomoron,* or, in Anglicized form, a *sophomore.*

counterpane

Oddly enough, it started life as *counterpoint.* This was not the musical term of the same spelling derived from Latin *contra punctus* relating to combined harmonies, but a corruption of an Old French term which was itself corrupted from Latin *culcita puncta,* meaning "a quilt." As the early heavy quilt began to give way to a lighter and ornamental outer bedcover in the seventeenth century, the second element, *point,* was gradually replaced by *pane* (French *pan,* "cloth"), long previously in use for "coverlet."

funny bone

This name for that portion of the elbow over which the ulnar nerve is drawn has never seemed appropriate to me. To strike or be struck on that edge of bone distinctly gives rise to a tingling pain rather than to anything remotely amusing. The American synonym, *crazy bone,* is more fitting. But it has been *funny bone* since at least the early nineteenth century. Barham, in "Bloudie Jacke of Shrewsberrie," in *The Ingoldsby Legends* (1840), has these lines:

> *They have pull'd you down flat on your back,*
> *And they smack, and they thwack,*
> *Till your "funny bones" crack,*
> *As if you were stretched on the rack,*
> *At each thwack!*
> *Good lack! what a savage attack!*

soothsayer

As used today, a *soothsayer* is a person who can, or at least is alleged to be able to, forecast the future accurately. This is not a new meaning—it has been in use for about three hundred years —but it is not in agreement with the original sense. *Sooth* was, to start with, an exact synonym for *truth,* and a *soothsayer* was merely one who was truthful. But charlatan fortunetellers have been with us a long time, and they are most anxious that their gullible patrons should believe in the truth of their predictions. Hence it was quite to be expected that they should protest that they were *saying sooth,* i.e., "telling the truth." *Sooth,* today, lives only in this word and in *forsooth* ("in truth! certainly!"; chiefly ironically), except that it is sometimes used as a deliberate archaism.

doodlebug

The larva of the ant lion. But why this immature insect is held to ridicule by the contemptuous name *doodle,* "simpleton," is not easy to understand, for he's a wise little gazebo, well versed himself in the follies of ants, as you will see under the item **ant lion.** Because of the power, like that of a miniature rotary snow plow, with which he expels sand particles from his excavation, one would expect to connect *doodle* with *doodlesack,* the bagpipe, played by a current of air, but there is no such connection.

polliwog

If we called this immature amphibian a *polwygle* as our English forebears did five centuries ago, the source of the name might be more easily identified. That is, *poll,* "head," and *wygle,* which we now spell *wiggle*—a "wigglehead." *Tadpole* (which see) is the usual name in England; in America we use one or the other, whichever may first come to mind.

assassin

In today's underworld slang, he would be a gangster, a gunman, a gorilla, a trigger boy, or, from the murderous qualities ascribed to the tribe, an Apache. But the old term, dating to a band of Saracens in the eleventh and twelfth centuries, came from the practice by the members to dope themselves heavily with hashish, more powerful than marijuana, when ordered by the chieftain to commit a murder. A person thus doped to fanatical zeal was a *hashashin,* "eater of hashish." European Crusaders understood it to be *assassin.*

sombrero

Like the other head coverings *parasol* and *umbrella, sombrero* is named to describe its benefit when worn. Thus this wide-

brimmed hat from sunny Spain is so-called from the shade it affords its wearer, the Spanish for "shade" being *sombra. Umbrella* is similarly named, from the Latin *umbra,* "shade," with a diminutive ending, hence, "a little shade." *Parasol* is from the Italian *parasole,* from *para,* a form of the verb *parare,* "to ward off, parry," combined with *sole,* "sun," hence, "warding off the sun."

gooseberry

Sorry, but nothing has ever been found which would indicate that anyone anywhere ever thought geese were at all eager for these berries, or were even averse to them. They're just not interested. In fact, no reason for associating the bird with the plant or berry has been discovered.

197

sooner

In 1889 the Federal Government decided to throw open the Territory of Oklahoma for settlement, and those in charge took great pains to try to see that no potential settler received any unfair advantage over another with respect to the more choice land. The borders were closed, and policed to keep them closed until the starting gun was fired, whereafter the race was on, and the swiftest to reach a chosen site was the winner. But, despite all precautions, a few managed to cross the border *sooner* than the rest, and to nab some of the best spots. In so doing, they unwittingly caused the coining of a new noun, for not only were these cheats named "sooners," but the same appellation was applied to anyone thereafter who jumped a deadline. And, too, Oklahoma itself is now nicknamed "the Sooner State."

hobgoblin

Here again, as in *hobbyhorse,* we find *hob* as a nickname, this time as a variant form of *Rob,* the diminutive of *Robin.* And the allusion was to the tricksy sprite of ancient superstitious belief, Robin Goodfellow. But whereas *hob,* among our remote ancestors, was rarely more than mischievous, when they united his name with *goblin*—Robin the goblin, as it were—the mischief ascribed to him was usually ill humored, often malicious. And he himself was alleged to be a bogey, an ill-favored imp—to children, something bad "that'll git you, ef you don't watch out."

corn dodger

It's made of corn meal, all right, plus a little salt and water or milk, and then fried in a hot skillet, three or four at a time, and it's perfectly delicious, especially served hot at breakfast. Why it is virtually unknown north of the Mason-and-Dixon line is a mystery, as it is very filling and cheap. But what this comestible is or was supposed originally to "dodge" is beyond my comprehension, unless, possibly, its creator contrived it as a "dodge" to cover a shortage of another breadstuff. Earliest available record carries it only to the 1830's, but I have little doubt that Southern tables knew it long before that.

198

treadmill

The verb *to tread* is one of the oldest words known in the English language and its forebears, being found in that most ancient of Anglo-Saxon writings, *Beowulf,* which dates to the seventh century A.D. It, or rather, its close relatives, are also known in all the languages of the Teutonic group, with the general meaning of "to step upon, to walk on." The noun is less old, and that particular sense of the noun applying to the steps of a set of stairs is as recent as about the eighteenth century. Yet it is this sense that has entered into *treadmill,* for this machine, invented about 1820 as a means of employing prisoners, was a large cylinder, or wheel, arranged with a series of horizontal *treads* around its circumference. As the wheel was rotated by means of men "climbing" these steps, the resultant movement of the axle was used to operate a *mill,* thus giving us the compound term *treadmill.*

polka dot

Along about 1830 a lively dance originated in Bohemia which speedily took all of Europe and America by storm. It was named *Polka,* meaning a Polish woman, just as *Polak* means a Polish man. So popular did the dance become that tradesmen vied with one another to attach the name to jackets, hats, gauze, and even articles of food. About 1880 or a year or so later an American dress fabric was introduced, ornamented with round, evenly spaced dots of uniform size which, following the prevailing custom, the maker called *polka dots.* Actually, however, the textile bears no other connection whatsoever with the dance.

brimstone

Because this was formerly the common name for sulfur, one would suppose that it was so called because it could be stone taken from the brim, say, of a volcano. But, no; *brim* is just the surviving form, in this word, of a dozen ways in which *burn* was spelled four and five centuries ago. It was, that is, a "stone" which could "burn." "Brimstone and treacle" was a prime household remedy of Dickens' day, which, to the American grandmother, became "sulfur and molasses."

corduroy

The Draper's Dictionary (1882) blandly says, "The name is of French origin, where it was originally *corde du roi,* the king's cord." But, alas, no such name has ever been used in France. The French name for the material is *velours à côtes,* "ribbed velvet." First mention of the fabric was in the 1790's, but no hint accompanied that or later mention as to the reason for the name. It has the semblance of clever advertising. Material disguised as "the king's cord" would undoubtedly interest a prospective buyer.

sphinx

The name comes to us from the fabled monster of Thebes, which had a woman's head on the winged body of a lioness. This creature  would stop passers-by and propound to them the riddle, "What is it that in the morning travels on four feet, during the day on two feet, and in the evening on three feet?" All who could not give the answer were strangled and devoured. Finally, the Greek hero Œdipus gave the solution: "Man, who as a child creeps on all fours, in adulthood travels erect, and in old age needs the aid of a stick." Whereupon the monster destroyed herself. The tale was first recorded by the Greek poet Hesiod (circa eighth century B.C.), and the name itself is the Latin transliteration of the Greek *sphigx,* "the strangler," from the verb *sphiggein,* "to bind tightly, to strangle."

son of Belial

Belial is the Anglicized form of the Hebrew *b'li-ya'al,* from *b'li,* "not," and *ya'al,* "worth, profit." Thus the original sense of *belial* was merely "unprofitable." From this sense, though, the term came to have the meaning of "wickedness," and the many references in the Old Testament to a *"son of Belial," "daughter of Belial,"* etc., refer to someone who is very wicked. Later,

Belial, although never previously a proper name, became used as one of the names of the devil, the personification of all wickedness, so that now the phrase *"son of Belial"* is most often taken to be synonymous with "spawn of Satan."

dogwood

Sorry, there doesn't seem to be any valid explanation of the animal prefix. A botanist of the seventeenth century called the European plant the *dogberry* tree, because of its dark purple berries, but that throws no light on the "dog" element. One writer only gives this explanation: "It is called Dogwood, because a decoction of its leaves was used to wash dogs, to free them from vermin," but that was written in 1838 and no previous writer seems ever to have heard of such usage. In this I am inclined to agree with the statement in the *Century Dictionary:* "In this, as well as . . . in similar popular names of plants, it is not necessary to assume a definite intention in the use of the animal name."

somersault

Acrobats have been doing this for years, and the word has been in the language at least since the sixteenth century. It came to us from the Old French *sombresault,* which is from the Provençal *sobresaut.* An obsolete English spelling of equal age is *sobersault.* But to get back to the derivation. The Provençal word is equivalent to the Spanish *sobresalto,* and this, in turn, comes from the Latin word *supra,* "over," plus *saltus,* "jump." Thus *to somersault* is "to jump over," or, in practice, "to jump over oneself."

goldbrick

Of course the original *gold brick* was of the pure metal which, for convenience in handling, had been melted and molded into brick form. But skullduggery reared its ugly head among Western promoters of mining properties, and, especially after 1880, many of these gentlemen began to create bricks of identical form of lead, coated with gold. Gullible Easterners with money to invest were taken in by scores in mines from which these "gold bricks" were alleged to have been produced, until eventually the term became synonymous with a swindle, with faking. Later, first as military slang, to *goldbrick* became "to fake industrious toil, to shirk"; and *goldbricker,* "a shirker."

plus fours

Knickerbockers, such as we used to wear in the early years of the twentieth century, were gathered just below the knee. They were thus likely to be stretched pretty tight over the kneecap, especially on a growing boy or in certain sports, such as golfing. Some brave English tailor along about 1920 came to the rescue and, though still buckling the trousers just below the knee, he made the leg much fuller and added just four inches (*plus four*) to the length of the cloth. The garment was not becoming. Any man who wore it looked as if he had two bags suspended from the waist.

trainband

Nothing to do with any railroad, the *trainband* was a group of citizen soldiery organized to serve as reserves in depth for the regular militia. The term arose in the sixteenth century and lived in this sense as long as the practice of having such citizen reserves continued—that is, into the eighteenth century. It has continued to live in attributive senses with respect to especially trained groups of people or of animals. The word itself is merely a shortening of *trained band*.

bowie knife

The brothers Bowie—John J., Rezin P., and James—enjoyed better reputations after death than in life. The three, that is, were in the slave trade in Louisiana in the 1820's, smuggling Negroes into the country from Jean Lafitte's stronghold on Galveston Island. But James was among the defenders of the Alamo, butchered on his sickbed at its fall, and his name has henceforth been honored. The knife carrying the family name, though accredited to Colonel James Bowie, was actually the invention of his brother, Rezin P. It is a strong hunting knife, blade ten to fifteen inches in length, double-edged near the point, with hilt, crosspiece, and sheath.

stalking-horse

Hunters, almost since time immemorial, have made use of a variety of tricks and ruses devised to enable them to approach their quarry (or vice-versa) without being noticed. One of the oldest of these is the *stalking-horse*. At first, as the name indicates, it was an actual horse, behind or alongside of which the hunter walked in concealment. Later, the horse was draped with cloths or the like, and the hunter might be beneath rather than behind the covering. Either way, the game could see only the horse, and was duped into thinking there was no hazard. As time went on, the term became used as a general one to describe something used to conceal a secret project, usually a somewhat dishonorable one. In the political field, it has been employed to describe a third candidate deliberately entered into a race in order to draw votes from the more popular of the original entries with the hope that the less popular would become the winner.

touchstone

Ever since mankind began to practice chicanery upon his fellows, it has been found necessary to develop techniques for ascertaining the true value of those materials that are to be found in the marketplace—particularly gold and silver. Long ago it was discovered that if suspected gold were rubbed on the mineral known as basanite, and if the streak left on the stone was compared with the streaks deposited by gold of differing known purities, the quality of the unknown could be assayed with reasonably good accuracy. The Greeks called this stone *basanos,* which also

203

has the meaning of "inquiry, especially by torture." The Romans were less picturesque—the Latin term is *lapis Lydius,* "the stone of Lydia." But the French got right down to brass tacks and called it *touchepierre* (modern French, *pierre de touche*), literally, *touch-stone,* with that sense of *touche* that means "assay."

hobbledehoy

The dictionaries try to satisfy consultants by saying, "Origin unknown," or something of similar import. It might be more honest to confess, "I don't know." A lot of speculation by brainy men has been given, but no one knows yet whether the term came into England from some other language, or whether it was an English coinage. In fact, no one can be certain how it should be spelled, as there were some thirty different spellings used in the years following its introduction. It was first recorded back in 1540, under the spelling *hobledehoye,* with the definition, "the yeres that one is neyther a man nor a boye." Thirty-three years later, Thomas Tusser, though recognizing the term to mean an adolescent strip-ling, assumed it to have a French source in the lines, from his *Fiue Hundreth Pointes of Husbandrie:*

> *The first seuen yeeres bring vp as a childe,*
> *The next to learning, for waxing too wilde,*
> *The next keepe vnder sir hobbard de hoy,*
> *The next a man, no longer a boy.*

four-in-hand

Today most of us think of this only as a necktie, to be tied in its own special loop. But the horsemen among us may have another notion. To them it means four horses harnessed to a single vehicle and driven by one person. And it is to these sportsmen of the nineteenth century we are indebted for the necktie and its name. They formed themselves into "Four-in-Hand Clubs," and vied with one another for distinctive garb, especially as to neck scarfs. Just as some unknown sportsman evolved the knot which, com-memorating the racecourse, is still called an *ascot,* so another anonymous individual along about 1890 produced for his fellow members, and the rest of us, the *four-in-hand*.

soliloquy

St. Augustine, one of the most renowned fathers of the Christian Church, was, in his youth, rather a dissolute profligate. After embracing Christianity in his early thirties, though, he became a most devout member of the faith, eventually being awarded a bishopric. He was always a prolific writer, and many of the books of his later life were strongly introspective and devoted to criticism of his wanton youth. One of his books was entitled *Liber Soliloquiorum* (freely translated, "Book in which I talk to myself"), whereby he coined a word compounded from *solus,* "alone," and *loqui,* "to speak." As Augustine was not the first, nor yet the last, to talk to himself, his new word was found to be quite useful, and it lives today in our *soliloquy,* "a talk to oneself."

dogwatch

A two-hour vigil on shipboard, so arranged as to alternate from day to day the regular four-hour watches of the divisions of a crew. That is, instead of dividing the twenty-four hours of the day into six periods of four hours each, they are divided into five such periods and two of two hours each, one from four to six and the other from six to eight. The name derives from the fact that each of such crew has only a short period of rest before being aroused into alertness, comparable to the alertness expected of a watchdog.

sojourner

The verb *sojourn* comes to us from the French *sojorner,* which, with the related Italian *soggiornare,* has been traced to the Popular Latin *subdiurnare,* compounded from *sub,* "under," and *diurnus,* "day-long" (from *dies,* "day"). Thus the original sense was applied to some event lasting for less than a day, especially a short visit. The sense has become expanded with time, until now *to sojourn* is to visit for any length of time, but not permanently, and a *sojourner* is one who is temporarily staying somewhere other than at home.

quicklime

Here, *quick* has its original sense of *living,* and our popular term for this substance is a direct translation of the Latin *calx viva,* "living lime," as taken through the French *chaux vive.* To the chemist, quicklime is calcium oxide, and it was called "living" by virtue of its intensely vigorous reaction when brought into contact with water, seeming to be possessed of a living spirit. *Lime,* in its older sense of *"mortar,"* or *"glue,"* is closely related to the German *Leim,* "glue," and both have been traced to the Latin *limus,* "mud." *Calx* has come down to modern English as *chalk,* the great chalk deposits in England being the principal sources of lime to that country.

touchhole, touch-powder, touchwood

Touch-, in each of these compound terms, has the special sense of "to set fire to" or "readily ignited"—a sense not found in other uses of "touch" either alone or in combination except those derived from the above. There are two distinct theories to explain the origin of this special meaning, but it is uncertain which is correct—possibly both have contributed in some degree. The first is based on a passage in *Piers Plowman,* a tale written in the late fourteenth century, where the following quotation is found:

Bote thou haue tache to take hit with tunder and broches, Al thy labour is lost. [Unless you have touchwood to take it (i.e., the spark) with tinder and tapers, all your labor is lost.]

Skeat, in his *Etymological Dictionary of the English Language,* suggests that *tache,* in the above, is derived from the Low German *takk,* one of the meanings of which is "twig," and that the subsequent development of the word *touchwood* represents a tautological development giving the equivalent of "stick-wood." Skeat also

206

considers that this development represents a change in spelling from *tache* to *touch*. Militating against this theory is the absence of the use of *tache* in this sense by any other author, as well as the fact that *touchwood* is first found only two hundred years later (as *touchewoode,* but very soon afterward in its present spelling) with no intermediate forms representing what should have been expected in a change of this magnitude. The second theory is that presented in the *Oxford English Dictionary,* where it is suggested that *touch-* in the present sense is apparently from the Old French *tochier* (*le feu*), *touchier,* "to set fire." Thus *touch-powder,* which is found as early as 1497, probably represents a translation of an Old French *poudre-à-toucher* (*le feu*).

bonnyclabber

The Earl of Strafford, in the seventeenth century, wrote of this dish, "it is the bravest, freshest drink you ever tasted," a verdict with which I agree. But my sons agree with Ben Jonson, who, at about the same period, called it "balderdash." What is it? Just milk that has coagulated in souring. I always sprinkle it with a little sugar before eating. The name is anglicized from Irish *bainne,* "milk," and *clabair,* "thick."

stark-naked

Stark, in many of its senses in English, is closely—sometimes very closely—related in meaning to the German word of the same

spelling and with the meaning "strong." But this is not the case with *stark-naked,* for here *stark* is a corruption for the original term in the phrase, which was *start. Start-naked* dates to the thirteenth century, when *start* had the Anglo-Saxon form *steort,* with the meaning of "tail, rump," such as in *redstart.* Thus the meaning of *stark-naked* in its original form was not "strongly naked," but rather "naked even to the tail."

cofferdam

Though in my impious youth one was considered as very clever who could work this in as, "Let her cofferdam head off," it really has no connection with an oath. A coffer is merely a tight chest, as for the storing of valuables. By extension, it denotes a watertight box or caisson. And a *cofferdam* is nothing more than a series of such caissons so constructed as to become a dam for holding out water.

go-devil

I think our American male ancestors of a hundred-odd years ago took keen delight in playing with the word *devil*. It sounded just short of a swear word—and probably annoyed their wives. At least it is certain that farmers especially took to calling various mechanical implements which, in early stages of development, acted erratically or mysteriously, *go-devils*. Or perhaps, through comparative speed, because they went "like the devil." How many of such were so called is now uncertain, but the name was early applied to corn cultivators, hay rakes, road scrapers, snow plows, logging sleds, and later in other fields to instruments for clearing pipes of obstructions, to explosive devices in oil-well drilling, to handcars, etc., etc.

torpedo

In the slang of the submarine arm of the navy, a *torpedo* is called a "fish," and in applying this nickname our sailors are more nearly correct than they are probably aware with respect to the origin of the name. For the object which was the first torpedo was indeed a fish — in particular, that fish that is also called the electric ray, because of its ability to emit electric discharges that benumb the person who may unsuspectingly come into contact with it. And it is that ability that gave the fish its name. *Torpedo* has the meaning of "stiffness, numbness" in Latin, from *torpere,* "to be stiff or numb," and it is exactly this quality that led the word to be applied to military mines of both land and sea. In the evolution of military parlance, the term is now used almost exclusively for

the self-propelled marine mines that so closely resemble the action
of the fish from which they took their name.

glamour, gramarye

If those who seek to entice us into a movie theater with repeti-
tions of the word *glamour* knew its source, perhaps they would
use it less freely. Or more freely. Who knows? But originally it
was just a Scottish mispronunciation of *grammar*. The reference
was then to Latin grammar, the only grammar that anyone knew
anything about before the seventeenth century. And, among the
ignorant, anyone so learned as to be able to speak and write
Latin was believed also to possess occult powers, to be able to
work magic. In England he was said to have *gramarye;* the Scots,
who had difficulty with the word, said he had *glamour.* Both
meant that such a wonderfully knowing person must have the
ability to effect charms. Perhaps today's ad man would have us
believe he can read and speak Latin. Both *gramarye* and *glamour*
are still associated with the sense of magic, ability to charm or
allure, but *grammar* has not moved from its rut.

coconut

Though regarded as slang, it is fitting, nevertheless, to use this
in reference to one's head, for it was from that that the nut had
its name. Portuguese explorers of the fifteenth century, sailing
around Africa, found this fruit growing upon islands of the Indian
Ocean. Not only was the nut about the size and shape of a small
head, but the addition of the three dark hollows at its base conveyed so strongly the resemblance to a grinning face as to impel
the explorers to call it "a grinning face," which is what *coco* means
in Portuguese.

bock bier (or beer)

One couldn't do better than quote from an item in an issue of
the 1856 *Illinois State Register:* "There is a Bavarian lager beer
which is called 'bock'—in English buck or goat—and is so called

because of its great strength making its consumers prance and tumble about like these animals." This beer, incidentally, requires about two months for brewing, being brewed usually in midwinter, and is usually drunk in early spring.

sofa

The most curious feature of this word is its ubiquity, for it is to be found in all the Romance languages—French, Italian, Spanish, Portuguese—and has even been adopted into German, with the same spelling and meaning. It is thus far from clear as to the immediate source of the word into English; it could as well have been from any of these sources. What is clear is its origin, which is the Arabic *soffah,* "a raised and richly carpeted bench or platform upon which to recline."

cocktail

H. L. Mencken, in *The American Language: Supplement One* (1945), relates that he had accumulated "numerous etymologies" purporting to account for the name of this American beverage, but only seven of them could be regarded as plausible. His list, with dates, highly condensed, is: (1) from French *coquetier,* "egg cup," New Orleans, about 1800; (2) from *coquetel,* a mixed drink, introduced from France "during the Revolution"; (3) from English *cock-ale,* a concoction from the seventeenth century; (4) from a later *cock-ale* fed to fighting cocks; (5) from *cock-tailed,* "having the tail cocked up"; (6) from *cock-tailings,* tailings from various liquors dumped together; (7) as a toast to the cock, after a fight, which had the most feathers left in its tail. But, reduced to the last analysis, all that is so far definitely known is that Washington Irving, in *Knickerbocker's History of New York* (1809), called it a Dutch invention, and that in *The Balance,* Hudson, New York, of May 13, 1806, occurs this description: *"Cock tail,* then, is a stimulating liquor, composed of *spirits* of any kind, *sugar, water,* and *bitters* . . . It is said, also, to be of great use to a democratic candidate: because, a person having swallowed a glass of it, is ready to swallow anything."

stiff-necked

The use of "a stiff neck" to denote obstinacy can be found in Deuteronomy 31:27, where Moses uses the term to describe the

Levites to whom he entrusted his book of laws. The adjective *stiff-necked* is used in the same sense in Acts 7:51, where Stephen is pleading his defense against blasphemy. The German *hartnäckig* and the Vulgate Latin *dura cervice* have the same significance, and both have the literal meaning "hard neck." All are derived from the Greek, from which much of the Bible has been translated, where the term is *sklerotrhachelos,* a compound from *skleros,* "hard," and *rhachis,* "spine," and the Greek is a direct translation of the Hebrew *keshay oref.*

ascot

This was a popular tie affected by us young males in the late 1890's, narrow around the neck and broad and slightly padded where it was loosely tied at the throat, the broad sections then crossing diagonally. Popularity and name sprang from sporting circles attending the fashionable races held annually at Ascot Heath in Berkshire, England.

tornado

It is from the Spanish, who were the principal explorers and masters of the Atlantic in the sixteenth century, that we get this word. It originated from *tronada,* "a thunderstorm," from *tronar,* "to thunder." Somehow, very likely through a spelling error, the word was taken into English as *ternado.* Later, when it became noted that these strong tropical storms were characterized by whirling winds, it was theorized that the spelling should more aptly reflect this trait, and it was revised to *tornado,* as if the derivation had been from the Spanish *tornar,* "to turn, return," of which the participle is *tornado,* "returned." With the change in spelling, there was an accompanying generally accepted change in use of the word away from thunderstorms and more particularly to those storms chiefly characterized by whirlwinds.

horehound, hoarhound

The name of this herb is really contained in the second element, which, though considerably altered through the centuries, seems to have been earliest in use. That is, in England of about a thousand years ago, the name of the plant seems to have been *hune,* and, to distinguish the one covered with white cottony hairs and small white flowers from others similar, but less attractive, it was described as the *hare hune,* from *har,* "hoary, white." Both elements underwent change, *hune* becoming *houne* in the fourteenth century, *hounde* in the fifteenth, and *hound* in the sixteenth—and there's no association whatsoever between the plant and any member of the canine family.

plum duff

This delicacy originated in the north of England, probably early in the last century. It was a kind of plum pudding, boiled in a bag, but the "plums" in the dough, raisins or currants, lacked the variety expected in a pudding. Why *duff?* Well, in the north of England, *dough* then rhymed with *rough* and *tough.* In fact, though still so pronounced, the pudding was sometimes spelled *plum dough.*

dog's letter

The surest proof that the letter R was not formerly sounded as "ah," the approximate current pronunciation in parts of England, New England, and some of our Southern states, lies in the fact that, as Ben Jonson put it (1636): "R is the dog's letter, and hurreth in the sound, the tongue striking the inner palate, with a trembling about the teeth." That is, as still heard in the speech of Scotland, Ireland, and our Midwestern states, it resembled the snarl of a dog.

gewgaw

Probably this term for a gaudy ornament of little value was originally nothing more than a contemptuous duplication of nonsensical sounds, such as *shilly-shally, fiddle-faddle,* and many others. No definite source has yet been found for the term, but it is very old. Though then spelled *giuegoue,* it appears in the text of *Ancren Riwle* (Rule of Anchoresses) written in the first quarter of the thirteenth century.

soda jerker

The average drugstore soda fountain clerk would be quite upset to be called a drunkard, but this is what was meant by a *jerker* some hundred and fifty years ago. A habitual drunkard, in time, loses his ability to move smoothly; his actions become quite jerky, and this led to the coining of the slang term to describe such a person, then to *beer jerker* for the sot who was principally a drinker of beer. By 1873, the term *beer jerker* had been transferred to the bartender who dispensed the beer. With the widespread growth and popularity of soft drinks early in the present century, the many resulting soda fountains required the services of clerks who dispensed these more innocuous beverages, and it was quite natural that they should be called by the trade name of their predecessors, becoming *soda jerkers.*

sulky (carriage)

A sulky person is one who, at least for the moment, wants nothing but to be let alone, and it is directly from this meaning

that the vehicle *sulky* gets its name. For this vehicle is designed to seat a single person, and one choosing to ride therein presumably feels that degree of aloofness best described by the adjective giving it its name. The same line of reasoning has led to the application of the same name to such things as a bathing machine designed for one, a horse-drawn plow having a seat for a single rider, etc.

hors d'oeuvres

Your French dictionary will define the expression, "in composition, art, or the like, that which is not an essential part of the work." Then it may go on to say, "In cuisine, something such as radishes, olives, etc., served before the main dish." From this you may see that the literal idea of the phrase is, "Aside from the work; not essential."

stool pigeon

Today, a *stool pigeon* is usually someone engaged in illegal or shady activities who, to save his own neck, voluntarily turns informer against his confederates. Earlier, he was someone deliberately planted by the authorities to serve as a decoy to gather evidence against those among whom he was sent to spy upon, or to influence them in some way, such as at the polls. The modern usage dates to about the first of this century, and the former has been found as early as 1830. Authorities are in substantially unanimous agreement that both senses are derived from a still earlier literal meaning of *stool pigeon*—a pigeon fastened to a stool or perch (some say with its eyes stitched closed), thereby serving as a live decoy to entice others into the snare set for them by the hunter. To the dismay of students of word origins, though, no recorded use of the term in this literal sense has been found earlier than 1836, and even this is only suggestive rather than being a certain instance. Their belief, however, is supported by the recorded use of *stool-crow* in the sense of "decoy" in 1811, and of the use of *stool* alone in the same sense in 1825, this latter being presumably a shortened form of the supposedly earlier but yet unfound *stool pigeon*. All these terms are generally accepted as being Americanisms.

forget-me-not

In Germany they call the flower *Vergissmeinnicht;* in France it's *ne m'oubliez pas;* in Sweden, *förgäta mig ej;* in Italy, *non ti scordar di me;* in Spain, *nomeolvides,* all meaning "forget me not," and in these, as in other countries, the flower is used as a token of friendship or, by lovers, in token of undying love. How old may be these sentiments attached to the flower is anyone's guess, but the widespread symbolism leads to the inference of considerable antiquity.

boatswain

He was, back in Old English days, merely the lad—*swain*—with the duty of attending to the small open boats of that period. His duty involved the care of the boat, of its oars and steering paddle, of its sails and rigging, if so equipped, and the summoning of its crew. In very early days it is probable that the latter duty was performed by whistling through his own lips, but, by the fifteenth century or earlier, we may read that he "blewe his whystell full shryll." Corruption of the pronunciation to *bosun* was in colloquial use before the middle of the seventeenth century.

swashbuckler

Quite a number of words that have existed in the English language (and in other languages, as well) were coined in imitation of some sound. One of these is  *swash,* little used now, but apparently originally created as descriptive of the sound of a blow. A *buckler,* back when knighthood was in flower, was a particular kind of small shield, chiefly used to catch the blows of an adversary. So a *swashbuckler* was one who, when fencing, put on a show by making a great noise, striking his opponent's buckler with his sword. From this, the term was broadened to describe any swaggering show-off.

plaster of Paris

Gypsum would be a much simpler name. But English artisans of the fourteenth and fifteenth century thought the best quality of gypsum for conversion into plaster and mortar came from the large deposits in the region of Montmartre on the outskirts of Paris, and thus insisted upon *plaster of Paris*. The name remains, but has long been applied to any calcined gypsum, regardless of place of origin.

sobriquet, soubriquet

Depending upon the circumstances prevailing at the time, any act of familiarity may be interpreted in either of two ways. On the one hand, it may be an expression of friendly companionship— on the other, it may be a deliberate puncturing of pomposity. One such act of familiarity, very common today, is the bestowal of a nickname. Another, not so common today as at times in the past, is a chuck under the chin. In Old French, the latter was *sous bruchet* (modern French would have it *sous-brechet;* the synonymous term in Italian is *sottobecco*), "under the throat (beak)." This came to be applied also to the giving of a nickname, and the two-word phrase became telescoped to the single word *sobriquet,* in which form it was taken directly into English over three hundred years ago.

topsy-turvy

To have the world seem to turn upside-down is a feeling that must have been common to mankind for many years, and for at least almost that number of years people have needed to express this feeling. *Topsy-turvy* was coined for this purpose over four hundred years ago, and has the literal meaning of "top turned over." The first element is just *top,* to which the suffix *-sy* was apparently added for euphony. The second element is based on the now obsolete *tirve* (*terve*), "to turn," especially, "to turn over." Thus it is seen that *topsy-turvy* is, just as you probably thought all along, "top turned over."

sockdologer

It is characteristic of the American "man in the street" that he displays very little reverence for the purity or tradition of his language. If he can coin a new, catchy phrase, or twist an old one into a new meaning, he delights in so doing. Thus, early in the nineteenth century someone, just who is not known, observed that the singing of the doxology always meant that his church service was finished. Mental play with "doxology" revealed that reversal of the consonant sounds of the first and second syllables gave him "sock-dology." The similarity to *sock,* "a blow," was obvious, and forthwith was born the *sockdologer,* the mighty blow that was to the battle as the doxology was to the service, the finish.

tandem

The Latin word *tandem* means "at length (with respect to time)," that is, "for a long time." Back in the eighteenth century,

when the study of Latin was a normal part of English university curricula, some student noticed a carriage harnessed to two horses, one before the other, and, being somewhat of a wag, he coined a pun on the word by applying it, in the sense of "at length (with respect to distance)," to a team so harnessed. The pun caught popular fancy, so that it has lived long after most people realize that it is a pun, and the sense has become broadened to include any of many things or events which may be arranged in consecutive order, one after another.

cocksure

The great *Oxford English Dictionary* waxes facetious about this. It says, in effect, this should mean "as sure as a cock," that is, "as secure, safe, certain, trustworthy, reliable, etc.," as a cock. But what kind of cock? Certainly not a rooster. So, the dictionary suggests, possibly the reference, four and a half centuries ago, "may have been to the security or certainty of the action of a cock or tap in preventing the escape of liquor, or perhaps of a cock with a removable turning-key in leaving the contents of a tun secure from interference."

217

footpad

That brave hero Robin Hood was one—that is, a highwayman who, having no horse, *pads* along on *foot* to hold up and rob people in carriages or on horseback. Or, let us say, Robin might have been called one, had he lived in the seventeenth century, for it was then that the term came into use, during a long period of great destitution throughout Europe and when governmental authority was ineffective. (See also **slyboots.**)

thank-ye-ma'am

This, gratefully appreciated in rural American courtship in grandfather's day, is now rapidly disappearing, replaced by hum-drum metal or concrete culverts on hilly roads everywhere. On early roads in such country, an earthen diagonal ridge served to carry rain water or melting snow from high side to low side, thus preventing excessive wash. But, passing over it in carriage or wagon, the passenger on the side first hitting this ridge would sway involuntarily toward the other. The rural swain, needless to say, chose roads accordingly. With the head of the fair one thus within kissing distance, the grateful murmur, "Thank ye, ma'am," was of course passed along to the humble cause.

tomato

The explorers who invaded Mexico in the sixteenth century found, in addition to treasure of silver and gold, a vegetable treasure in the form of a new fruit, unknown in Europe, which the Mexican Indians called *tomatl.* They thought sufficiently well of this fruit to take samples back to the Old World, and the name they took into the Spanish and Portuguese languages was *tomate* (three syllables). On moving north to France the spelling was retained, but the pronunciation was shortened to two syllables, and this was also the spelling and pronunciation first taken into

English. It wasn't until the mid-eighteenth century that the present spelling first appeared, apparently having been coined in the belief that the word was of Spanish origin, the *-o* ending being common in Spanish. At an early date, the tomato was believed to have aphrodisiac qualities, because of the one-time name of *love apple,* (which see) for the fruit.

cockshy

It is to the credit of humanity that the original practice of this eighteenth-century "sport" was suppressed, in England and America, before the close of the same century. As practiced, by men and boys, a broomstick was cast from a distance of twenty yards at a cock tied by a cord attached to its leg. A small fee for the privilege was demanded by the owner, and he who succeeded in killing the bird might carry it off. But if the bird were merely lamed, it was propped up so that the sport might continue. It is the opinion of Professor Hans Sperber of Ohio State University (*Language,* vol. 31, 1955) that the verb "to shy," in the sense "to throw," descended from this sport, for it was the custom of the owner of such a bird to teach it in advance to become wary of objects thrown at it. That is, to quote, "in order to make the throwing competition a lucrative venture, it is necessary to make the bird shy, or, as it certainly would be expressed—*to shy him.* Since this 'shying' was accomplished by throwing at him, *shy* became a restricted synonym of *throw.*"

snood

The oldest words in the language sometimes seem to be among the most difficult to trace to their origins, perchance because these origins have become lost in the mists of age. *Snood* is such a word. It has been found to have been in English, in much its present meaning ("a fillet or ribbon for binding the hair"), since the eighth century. For quite some time it was to be found particularly in Scotland, where this type of hair covering was reserved to maidens alone, as a sign of virginity, being replaced by other forms of headdress after marriage. Skeat (*Etymological Dictionary of the English*

Language) suggests that the origin is to be found in the Teutonic root *snu-*, implying turning or twisting, from which come the Danish *snoe*, Swedish *sno*, "to twist, twine"; also the Swedish noun *sno*, "twine, string." The modern German *Schnur*, "string, cord, lace," is easily seen to be related. The etymological implication is that the first Anglo-Saxon snood may have been but a bit of string, or perhaps a fillet of string lace, about the hair, more likely to keep it from being blown into the wearer's eyes rather than for its decorative effect.

artichoke

Beyond the spelling, the name of this plant has no connection either with art or with choking, although the latter was at one time seriously suggested. Actually the name has been highly corrupted through various European versions of the original Arabic name, *al-kharshuf*. Italians eventually made that into *articiocco*, and through some four centuries of struggling with a score or more of various spellings we have, at least temporarily, settled upon *artichoke*.

trousseau

Taken into English directly from the French, in which it is the diminutive of *trousse* (from which we get *truss*), "a bundle, a pack." If taken literally, then, it would seem that a bride's trousseau would be "a little bundle," presumably consisting only of a few of her most needed personal effects and household linens.

hitchhike

The date of coinage is not definite but was probably during the period of training of American boys in military camps in the First World War. Making their way home on a brief furlough, that is, the boys would *hike* until a car or truck approached going their way, then *hitch* a ride. The term shortly passed into the general language—and into a recognized form of travel.

foolscap

Now it is a size of paper, usually folded, and running in size from 12 to 12½ inches in width and 15 to 16 inches in length. Rarely, if at all, does the paper now carry as a watermark the design in outline of a fool's cap, but that is what gave it the name. A specimen of paper with such a design, dating to 1540, is said to have been found. But why any papermaker ever marked his product in this manner is no longer to be determined. An often repeated story is that the Long Parliament, finally dissolved by Cromwell in 1653, ordered that paper with this design should replace that carrying the royal crown, but, though interesting, the account lacks foundation.

ultramundane

With all the current interest in space travel, rocketry, and so on, this is a word that should become ever more important, although,  being polysyllabic, it may never become part of the argot of the "man in the street." For, with the literal meaning of "out of this world," it can well apply to the various aspects of the exploration of outer space. As the appearance of the word would indicate, it is of Latin origin, coming from the Late Latin *ultramundanus,* from *ultra,* "beyond," and *mundus,* "the world."

slyboots

Although slyboots has the meaning of "a crafty or cunning person," it is closely related to *footpad,* "a thief"; *gumshoe,* "a detective"; *pussyfoot,* "a prying, nosy person"; also to the German *Leisetreter* (light treader), "a sneak, spy"; and the French *pied plat* (flat foot), "a sneak, knave." All of these carry the common connotation of a person who moves with quiet or stealth, and always these movements are contrary to the well-being or comfort of the one applying the term (even the *gumshoe* is so-called only by the one who is attempting some clandestine act). The American *flatfoot,* of course, is quite different from the French, being a policeman—specifically, one who has walked on patrol for so long that his arches are presumed to have fallen and, in fact, he has acquired flat feet.

hijack

It came into American speech shortly after the First World War, during the "silk shirt" era of prosperity when the prohibition amendment was still in force and people with money to spend wanted to spend it on liquor. Some say it originated in the Middle West, in reference to the activities of hoboes who preyed upon harvesters, even to murder, but the general consensus is that it originally indicated a holdup, at night, especially of a load or cargo of illicit liquor. The holdup might be with or without murder, and might include the transference of the load or cargo to another truck or vessel. Though the source of the term cannot be definitely traced, I think it probable that it came from the friendly hail, "Hi, Jack!" intended to disarm the suspicions of a truck driver by another who was apparently in trouble by the side of the road.

German silver

It was named in honor of the country where discovered, for the original alloy was found in nature in ore found in Hildburghausen, Germany. Actually, it contains no silver at all, but is about one-half copper and one-quarter each nickel and zinc. Being silvery in appearance, the alloy has been used for inexpensive decorative effects, and it also has useful electrical properties. During the First World War, when any name suggestive of Germany was anathema, it was given such euphemistic titles as *silveroid* and *nickeline,* but these have not lived.

slubberdegullion

It is said, and I believe it to be true, that there are far more English words having insulting or derogatory meaning than there are those carrying a complimentary connotation. Certainly *slubberdegullion* would rank among the most degrading of epithets short of foul speech. For *slubber* is an older form of *slobber,* "to befoul as with saliva, to slaver." The *de* may be a meaningless connective, or may be in imitation of the French *de,* "of." *Gullion* seems to be a variant of *cullion,* "a vile or despicable fellow," from the French *couillon* (*coion*), "a dastard, coward." Hence both the etymological and actual meanings of *slubberdegullion:* "a slobbering, worthless sloven."

velocipede

Early in the nineteenth century, a German, Baron von Drais, invented a machine that had a remarkable likeness to a modern bi-cycle, except that it lacked pedals, chain, and sprockets. The rider sat upon a saddle and propelled himself by pushing with the feet, and is said to have been able to achieve a speed of up to five miles per hour. The device was introduced into England and manufactured by one Denis Johnson in 1818, by whom it was patented under the name of *velocipede.* Although this name is now applied chiefly to a tricycle fitted with pedals, it was used extensively throughout most of the nineteenth century for nearly all the descendants of the original machine, whether of two or more wheels, with or without pedals. The name seems to have come from the French of the same form, but is of Latin ancestry, being made up of the combining forms of *velox,* "swift," and *pes,* "foot"; hence, "swift-footed."

highroad, high seas, etc.

It was not that the road, sea, way, or the like was elevated above others of its kind that it was labeled *high,* tracing back to Old English times, but that it possessed some quality that made it outstanding, especially notable. The *highroad* and *highway* were main or principal roads; the *high seas* were oceans; *high Mass* was celebrated in full ceremonial. And in a later day, *high tea* was an evening meal at which meat was served.

woodchuck

"How much wood would a woodchuck chuck if a woodchuck could chuck wood?" "He'd chuck as much wood as a woodchuck could, if a woodchuck could chuck wood!" Confirming this old tonguetwister, a wood-chuck can't and doesn't chuck wood, nor does *wood* as such have anything to do with his having been so named. The name comes from a Cree Indian word that has been rendered as *wuchak* or *otchock* (Chippewa *otchig*). Early settlers gave the word various spellings reminiscent of familiar English words, such as *wejack, woodshock,* and *woodchuck* (also *-chuk*), but all these names applied originally to the animal known as the fisher or pekan. Later, either through error or guile, the name of *woodchuck* was transferred by traders to the groundhog, and the two terms are now synonymous. (See also **groundhog.**)

INDEX

INDEX

drift, see under spindrift, 186
drum, see under tambourine, tympany
Drury Lane Theater, see under greenroom, 179
Dubrovnik, Yugoslavia, see under argosy, 70
ducking stool, 9
ducking tumbrel, see under ducking stool, 9
duff, see under plum duff, 212
dumb waiter, see under lazy Susan, 173
Duncombe, Sir Sanders, see under sedan, 64
Dutch treat, 187

eaglestone, 156
earthberry, see under strawberry, 149
earth-nut, see under peanut, 98
earwig, 48
eavesdropper, 127
ecphonesis, see under exclamation point, 113
Edward VII, King of England, see under Prince Albert, 10
eggnog, 124
electric, electricity, see under ambergris, 116
ember days, 121
epiphonema, see under exclamation point, 113
Erasmus, Saint, see under St. Elmo's fire, 105
erysipelas, see under St. Anthony's fire, 110
evil, see under king's evil, 116
exclamation point (mark), 113
eyet, eyot, see under ait, 153

fadoodle, see under flapdoodle, 22
Fahrenheit, Gabriel Daniel, 149
fakir, 143
falderal, folderol, 147
fanfare, 51
fantan, 141
farthingale, 134. See also roundabout
fat, see under hamfatter, 137
fata morgana, 130
fearnought, 123
feather-few, feferfuge, see under feverfew, 108

fer-de-lance, 120
Ferris, George W. G., see under Ferris wheel, 55
Ferris wheel, 55
fetlock, 117
fetter-foe, see under feverfew, 108
feverfew, 108
fiddle-faddle, 98
fiddler crab, 58
fife rail, 96
fifth wheel, 92
fifty-fifty, 76
figurehead, 61
Findhorn, Findon, Scotland, see under finnan haddie, 167
finger biscuit, see under ladyfinger, 121
finnan haddie, 167
firecracker, 160
firedamp, 172
firedog, 166
firework, see under firecracker, 160
fisher, see under woodchuck, 224
fizgig, 58
flabbergast, 53
flabby, see under flabbergast, 53
flagstone, 56
flam, see under flimflam, 32
flapdoodle, 22
flatfoot, see under slyboots, 221
flea-bitten, 42
Fledermaus, see under flittermouse, 29
flibbergib, see under flibbertigibbet, 26
flibbertigibbet, 26
flimflam, 32
flittermouse, 29
flophouse, 21
fly, see under dragonfly, 12
flybbergybe, see under flibbertigibbet, 26
folderol, see under falderal, 147
fool, see under April fool, 95
foolscap, 221
foot, see under neat's-foot oil, slyboots, tenderfoot
footpad, 218
forecastle, 65
forget-me-not, 214
forsooth, see under soothsayer, 196
four-in-hand, 204

Frankenstein, 69
French measles, see under German measles, 18
frog, see under leapfrog, 124
funny bone, 195
furbelow, 193

gadabout, 155
gad-abroad, see under gadabout, 155
gaffer, gammer, 152
gagman, 131
galligaskin, 72
galosh, 50
gammer, see under gaffer, 152
gangboard, see under gangplank, 43
gangplank, 43
gangway, see under gangplank, 43
gantry, 41
gap, see under stopgap, 54
gargoyle, 75
garrote, 38
gauntree, gauntry, see under gantry, 41
gazebo, 33
gee string, see under G string, 82
germane, 24
German measles, 18
German silver, 222
gestern, see under yesterday, 150
gewgaw, 213
gig, see under fizgig, 58
Gilead, see under balm of Gilead, 118
giraffe, see under camelopard, 149
glamour, 209
glove, see under hand-in-glove, 113
goblin, see under hobgoblin, 198
go-devil, 208
godfather, godmother, see under gaffer, 152
goldbrick, 201
goober, see under peanut, 98
gooseberry, 197
graham bread, crackers, flour, 189
Graham, Sylvester, see under graham bread, 189
gramarye, grammar, see under glamour, 209
grampus, see under hellgrammite, 65
grandfather, grandmother, see under gaffer, 152
grass, see under quatchgrass, 187

Great Bear, see under Charles's Wain, 76
green, see under Paris green, 128
greenhorn, 186
greenroom, 179
green soap, 174
gremlin, 78
grotesque, 16
groundhog, 176
ground-nut, ground-pea, see under peanut, 98
grubstreet, 5
G string, 82
Guido's scale, see under solfeggio, 194
guinea-fowl, see under turkey, 178
gullion, see under slubberdegullion, 222
gumshoe, see under slyboots, 221
guttersnipe, 27
gypsum, see under plaster of Paris, 215

haberdasher, 151
hab nab, see under hobnob, 192
hackamore, 141
haddock, see under finnan haddie, 167
halibut, 85
Hall, Sir Benjamin, see under Big Ben, 42
hallmark, 141
hamfatter, 137
hamlet, 133
hamstring, 118
hand-in-glove, 113
handkerchief, 110
handle, see under panhandle, 137
handsome, 105
hangdog, 88
hardtack, 94
harebell, 83
harlot, 79
harp, see under jew's-harp, 80
hash, see under nuthatch, 142
hatch, hatchet, see under nuthatch, 142
haul, see under keelhauling, 155
haversack, 71
hawk, see under jayhawk, 108
hedgehog, 74
heirloom, 73

Helena, see under St. Elmo's fire, 105
hellbender, 166. See also mud puppy
hellgrammite, 65
hiccough, see under hiccup, 56
hiccup, 56
hidebound, 55
highball, 44
highbinder, 29
highfalutin, 25
high Mass, see under highroad, 225
high-muck-a-muck, 30
highroad, 223
high seas, high tea, see under high-road, 225
highty-tighty, see under hoity-toity, 1
highway, see under highroad, 223
hijack, 222
hike, see under hitchhike, 220
hillbilly, 90
hitchhike, 220
hoarhound, see under horehound, 212
hoax, see under hocus-pocus, 159
Hobbard de Hoy, see under hobbledehoy, 204
hobbledehoy, 204
hobbyhorse, 93
hobgoblin, 198
hobnob, 192
hock-day, -tide, etc., see under hockshop, 190
hocker-mocker, see under huggermugger, 115
hockshop, 190
hocus-pocus, 159
hodgepodge, 172
Hoffmann, Friedrich, see under German measles, 18
hog, see under groundhog, hedgehog
hog Latin, see under dog Latin, 19
hogshead, 173
hogwash, 11
hoiting, see under hoity-toity, 1
hoity-toity, 1
hoker-moker, see under huggermugger, 115
holystone, 183
honeymoon, 177
hoodlum, 15
hoodwink, 96
hoosegow, 12
hop-score, see under hopscotch, 7

hopscotch, 7
Horace, see under sesquipedalian, 57
horehound, hoarhound, 212
hornswoggle, 4
hors d'oeuvres, 214
horse, see under cockhorse, dead horse, hobbyhorse, stalking-horse, sumpter horse
horse (large) (compound terms), see under horse chestnut, 33
horse chestnut, 33
horsefeathers, ix-x, xiii-xiv
hotch-pot, hotch-potch, see under hodgepodge, 172
hotspur, 95
house, see under flophouse, porterhouse, sponging house
hoyden, see under hoity-toity, 1
Hubbard, see under Mother Hubbard, 136
hubbub, 28
hucker-mucker, see under huggermugger, 115
huckleberry, see under whortleberry, 170
hudder-mudder, see under huggermugger, 115
huggermugger, 115
humbug, 146
humdrum, 152
hunky-dory, 147
hurling, see under hurly-burly, 35
hurly, see under hurry-scurry, 46
hurly-burly, 35
hurry-scurry, 46
hurtleberry, see under whortleberry, 170
hushpuppy, 99

ignis fatuus, 158
include, x
Indian summer, see under St. Martin's summer, 102
Indian turnip, see under jack-in-the-pulpit, 135
ineffables, inexplicables, inexpressibles, see under unmentionables, 75
Irving, Washington, see under knickerbockers, 35
isinglass, 168

Jack, 165. See also applejack, hijack

love apple, 40. See also tomato
lubber, see under landlubber, 125
Luke, Saint, see under St. Martin's
summer, 102

madcap, 28
madstone, 173
magpie, see under piebald, 36
marchpane, 161
mark, see under hallmark, 141
marshal, see under seneschal, 62
Martigues, France, see under martingale, 162
Martin, Saint, see under St. Martin's
summer, 102
martingale, 162
marzipani, see under marchpane, 161
measles, German, French, see under
German measles, 18
melancholy, see under choler, 34
merry-andrew, 169
merrythought, see under wishbone,
63
mica, see under isinglass, 168
milksop, 164
mill, see under treadmill, 199
Milquetoast, Caspar, 157
mimsy, see under portmanteau, 179
mire, see under quagmire, 8
Missouri meerschaum, see under
rarebit, 111
Moncke, Charles, see under monkey
wrench, 133
Monk (toolmaker), see under monkey wrench, 133
monkey-nut, see under peanut, 98
monkey wrench, 133
mooncalf, 156
moonlighter, see under sundowner,
140
moonshine, 135
moonstruck, 130
Morgan le Fay, see under fata morgana, 130
morning star, see under daystar, 44
mortarboard, 119
Mother Hubbard, 136
mouse, see under dormouse, flittermouse
Mozee, Annie Oakley, see under
Annie Oakley, 8
mud devil, see under mud puppy, 101

mud puppy, 101. See also hellbender
mugwump, 96
mulatto, see under quadroon, 177
mumble-peg, 92
mundane, see under ultramundane,
221
mushroom, 2

naked, see under stark-naked, 207
neat's-foot oil, 138
neck, see under leatherneck, rubberneck, stiff-necked
needle, see under devil's-darningneedle, 66
nickeline, see under German silver,
222
nickumpoop, nicompoop, see under
nincompoop, 150
nightingale, 142
nightmare, 139
nill, see under willy-nilly, 77
nincompoop, 150
ninny, see under nincompoop, 150
nog, see under eggnog, 124
non compos, see under nincompoop,
150
nought, see under fearnought, 123
numb, see under numskull, 146
numbskull, 146
nut, see under coconut, peanut
nuthatch, 142

Oakley, Annie, see under Annie
Oakley, 8
oakum, 154
O.K., 145
oxhead, see under hogshead, 173
oyez, 13

pad, see under footpad, 218
paddywhack, 112
padlock, 102
pallbearer, 143
pane, see under counterpane, ball
peen
panhandle, 137
pantywaist, 148
Paris green, 128
pasha, see under three-tailed bashaw,
36
peacock, 123
pea jacket, 117

236

237

238